STUDIES OF
CALIFORNIA INDIANS

A Publication of the E. H. Harriman Fund

C. Hart Merriam and blind Sam Osborn, Wuksache Yokut, near Badger, California, July 12, 1935.

STUDIES OF
CALIFORNIA INDIANS

C. HART MERRIAM

Edited by the Staff of the Department of Anthropology
of the University of California

UNIVERSITY OF CALIFORNIA PRESS

Berkeley and Los Angeles • 1955

UNIVERSITY OF CALIFORNIA PRESS

BERKELEY AND LOS ANGELES

CAMBRIDGE UNIVERSITY PRESS

LONDON, ENGLAND

Preface

The Department of Anthropology of the University of California, Berkeley, became the custodian, in March, 1950, of the original ethnological materials gathered by Dr. C. Hart Merriam and also of his working library, mainly devoted to the ethnology of California. When Dr. Merriam died in 1942, provision had been made that these materials be placed in the care of the Smithsonian Institution so that the large body of first-hand information which he had amassed be not lost. The program of the Smithsonian Institution and the existing scientific commitments of the ethnologists on its staff were such that after some years Dr. Merriam's daughters, Mrs. M. W. Talbot and Mrs. Henry D. Abbott, concluded that the usefulness of the material might be enhanced by having it in California, where active ethnological work on the aboriginal cultures of the area was being carried on. The Department of Anthropology made evident its interest and the Smithsonian Institution, in the persons of the chief of the Bureau of Ethnology, Dr. Matthew Sterling, and the then secretary of the Institution, Dr. Alexander Wetmore, readily and generously agreed with the wisdom of this idea.

The papers here presented were selected because of their value and because they were in final or near-final form. They represent a substantial addition to Dr. Merriam's previously published work. In the account in this volume of Dr. Merriam as an anthropologist the high intrinsic scientific merit of his work and records has been described more fully.

To R. F. Heizer should go the major credit in the initial selection of the materials here published, in carrying through the project as a whole, and in arranging several of the papers for publication. One or more of the studies were prepared for publication by J. A. Bennyhoff, E. W. Gifford, A. L. Kroeber, and T. D. McCown.

Mrs. M. A. Whipple's services were of consummate value in the preparation of the manuscript as a whole and in the handling of the proofs.

The publication of these essays has been financed by funds available from the E. H. Harriman Fund, as part of the provision to ensure the further preparation and publication of Dr. Merriam's field materials. The cooperation of the Smithsonian Institution as administrator of these moneys is gratefully acknowledged.

C. Hart Merriam as Anthropologist

By A. L. KROEBER

C. Hart Merriam was one of the great naturalists of his generation. It is because of his intense drive as a naturalist that he undertook the geographic, ethnological, and linguistic studies of the surviving California Indians of which a part constitutes this book.

For the first half of his adult life, from 1876 to 1910, Dr. Merriam would have been unhesitatingly classified by all who knew him as a biologist. From 1910 to 1942 the greater part of his time was spent in the study of historic and living Indians of California, and he was thus *de facto* an anthropologist. In fact, during at least the latter part of this second period he changed his nominal adherence from the section of biology to the subsection of anthropology in the National Academy of Sciences.

Nevertheless, the same points of view and similar motivations and methods characterized his work in the two halves of his life.

Dr. Merriam was born in northern New York state in 1855. At the age of seventeen he went with a government exploring expedition to the Yellowstone region and at the age of eighteen published a fifty-page report on the mammals and birds encountered there. Subsequently he studied medicine and practiced actively for several years but never laid aside his preoccupation with living animals. He was only twenty-two when he reviewed the birds of Connecticut and their habits in a publication of the Academy of Arts and Sciences of that state. He was twenty-seven when the first volume of his great *Mammals of the Adirondack Region* began to appear. A year later he helped found the American Ornithologists' Union and became its secretary and probably most active member.

vii

At the age of thirty Merriam gave up the practice of medicine to join a section of the government's Department of Agriculture. This section was gradually expanded and became famous as the Biological Survey, of which he was Director.

From the beginning the Biological Survey specialized in mapping the geographical distribution of animals with a view to ascertaining the natural faunal areas or life zones of North America. In 1892, Merriam for the first time formally outlined the life zones of the continent, with increasing emphasis on the mammals.

In 1899 E. H. Harriman, the railroad financier, asked Merriam to organize and direct an Alaskan expedition to accompany him on a vacation during the summer of that year. Merriam also edited the series of volumes that resulted from this many-membered expedition. More important, a personal friendship resulted which led in 1910 to Mrs. Harriman's establishing a trust to be administered by the Smithsonian Institution to provide Merriam with lifetime living and support for research of his own choosing. At the age of fifty-five, accordingly, he resigned his government position, wholly relieved of economic cares, and free to follow his own interests in the work he was henceforth to do.

It was then that he formally switched from subhuman mammals to California Indians. Not that the change was abrupt. In following the intricacies of the life zones of birds, mammals, and plants in California, he had increasingly come across remnants of the aborigines, mostly tucked away in remote spots off from highways. In 1903 he had published his first ethnological paper, one dealing with basket materials, and in the years that followed until 1910, he had issued eight more such publications, including a book of tales called *The Dawn of the World*. Nor did he ever abandon biology. As late as 1918 he published his monumental review of the bears of North America. And his very last two papers dealt with Roosevelt as a naturalist and with ocean-dwelling seals. But, as time passed, more and more of Merriam's working time as an explorer and field student was devoted to his Indian friends. He took to living half the year in the wooded country at the rear foot of Mount Tamalpais whose front looks from across the bay down on San Francisco. From there he sallied forth, first on horseback and with wagon, later by automobile, hunting up and interviewing and pumping Indians who were still lingering on in the most out-of-the-way spots of the length and breadth of California.

While the subject matter of Merriam's studies shifted from animals to men in the second half of his career, he brought the same interests, attitudes, and approaches to bear. In each case the distribution of the phenomena dealt with was in the forefront of his attention. His attack merely swung from questions of the precise ranges occupied by species and subspecies to the problems of the exact location of aboriginal human languages, tribes, villages, beliefs, and customs. Merriam's definitions of distributions were precise and particularistic, never sketchy. The finest detail of fact seemed worth recording in the interest of accuracy. What he valued was the primary and original data as he secured them in the field: classification and generalization would come later.

As a biologist, the main classification he made was into the life zones already mentioned. Positing of causes was something he scarcely attempted—except for asserting cumulative temperature as the principal determining factor of life zones. Similarly in his ethnology Merriam went as far as to accept and validate the classification of villages into tribes, of tribes into speech families. He did not try to push beyond the family into superstocks or orders, but aimed rather at precision of geographic occurrence of tribes, subtribes, and on down to villages and settlements. This was entirely parallel to his being what used to be called a "splitter" and not a "lumper" in regard to recognition of animal species—as evident in his famous discussion in *Science* with President Theodore Roosevelt about coyotes and bears. So with his Indians: he cut his data probably finer than did almost any of the anthropologists; but he declined to deal with the principles and general factors that lay beyond the primary organization of the data. As in his biology he wanted to know everything about the mammals and birds of America, but was not concerned with those of other continents, let alone the world as a whole—so in ethnology he restricted himself to the Indians of California and the nearer parts of Nevada and other adjacent states.

In regard to both bodies of material, then, it is evident that Merriam practiced "natural history" rather than "natural science." In some respects his work was comparable to that of a philologist studying a particular language, or a group of related languages, rather than to that of the theoretical linguist. He had the same value for factual accuracy even in minutiae. His work was empirical, basic, and oriented toward attainment of precision and completeness.

Yet in some respects his ethnological work did differ from his biological. He was now working alone, instead of with a corps of associates and assistants as in the days of the Biological Survey. This may have been due to his having become an unhampered free lance; and again it may have had something to do with the restriction of his ethnology to California, whereas his biology ranged over North America. Perhaps the continent was too large for him to cope with singlehanded. Another reason may also have been of some influence. Over most of the United States and Canada the Indians tend to live on reservations that represent only shrunken fragments of their aboriginal habitat. Sometimes they have even been moved far from their original centers. In California, however, the Indians, where they survive at all, mostly dwell today where their great-grandfathers did; or if they have retreated, it is usually only a few miles. They have therefore kept contact and familiarity with their old sod. Their distribution is essentially the "native" or wild one—as in the case of nondomesticated animals. California thus lent itself much more advantageously to precise distribution studies of its Indians than any other part of our country. This fact may have tended to influence Merriam in concentrating his human studies in California.

For decades he spent five to six months each year actually traversing the countryside, interviewing aged Indians and writing down voluminous records of what they were still able to tell him. For while the Indians might live where their ancestors had, they were no longer following the old customs, but were living as best they might as modern Americans—mostly very poverty-stricken Americans at that. The task thus was one in the main of searching their memories. This Merriam did with a patience, tact, and sympathy which elicited coöperation from his informants. To this I can testify from having spoken to many of them with whom Merriam had worked, who always remembered him with affection and approval.

In the course of his many years of this field work, Merriam also read all that had been written on the California Indians and copied and extracted from it voluminously—even to assembling newspaper clippings and personal letters. All this material survives in the vast collection which he left. The core of it, however, consists of his own recordings from the lips of Indians; and what he published during his lifetime is based almost wholly thereon.

Much the same proportion of source holds for the essays which constitute this volume. True, the "synonymies" of tribal and place names are of course from previously published work. Also based on the literature are discussions of the appropriateness or correctness of certain names like Piute, Beñeme, Mono. And again based on records are the Tcholovone vocabulary and the baptismal records from the California missions—the last doubly valuable because the originals from which Merriam's copies were made have since in part been lost.

Yet the great majority of papers printed here rest flatly and completely on Merriam's own recordings and observations. Perhaps because in his ethnology he worked singlehanded; perhaps for other reasons, such as that an adequate vocabulary is necessarily longer than the description of a species; or that a list of all place names known to a tribe in their territory is more voluminous than a delineation of their geographical range—at any rate Merriam published during his own lifetime only a small fraction of all the Indian material he had gathered. Indeed, though nearly half of his professional career was primarily devoted to Indians, he published only twenty-nine papers, articles, and books on them, as against five hundred biological ones. Even during the years when his interest in Indians was most active, 1911–1930, his bibliography shows only twenty titles in ethnology as against sixty in biology. His biological work in the period was evidently still traveling on momentum from the past; whereas the time-consuming preparation of ethnological manuscript was slow in getting under way.

By far the greater mass of Merriam's data on Indians thus has actually never seen the light of publicity. Even the present volume does not too seriously diminish the bulk of what remains unpublished. In fact, what this volume represents is a sort of skimming of the cream, a putting together of those scattered portions of his data which Merriam left most nearly in finished form ready for publication. The much larger but less organized remainder of his original data will no doubt continue to be drawn on for generations as a rich mine of information on the California Indians.

Merriam stipulated that, whoever it might be that published any of his collected Indian data posthumously, should reproduce him exactly, without alteration, either of his statements or of the form in which he wrote native names.

Both stipulations have been observed in this volume and will be maintained in any future ones.

As regards substance, the proviso obviously is only one of fairness. One does not use another man's laboriously accumulated but unpublished information as grist for one's own mill, as material for one's own views. Scientific as well as moral responsibility are at one in this matter. What Merriam wrote, we, the selectors and editors, have left exactly as he wrote it. Anything added to clarify statements or supply relevance or context has been put into square brackets or otherwise indicated to be clearly distinguishable.

As regards orthography, Merriam held all his life that the "scientific spelling" of anthropologists was a technical mannerism and an unnecessary one. He employed the "common" usage of Webster's Dictionary. It is hard not to have sympathy with this or any view slanted away from pedantic technicalities. It can be said fairly enough that an artificial orthography is in a sense a necessary evil even though it be more accurate —more unambigious. Anthropologists did not come to write native words with the special characters which they have successively employed merely in order to parade arcana of learning before the world. They used them because they felt they had to use them, if they wished to be as clear as possible to other scientists. As a matter of fact, the way they were writing

Indian words when Merriam entered the field was in a system different from that used when the Bureau of Ethnology was first established in Washington in 1879; and it has in turn been considerably modified since then under the influence of the pure linguists.

Merriam's position corresponded somewhat to that of a hypothetical anthropologist entering the biological field and insisting on never calling a coyote *Canis latrans*, even in professional journals. If such a hypothetical newcomer to biology brought new information on coyotes, his papers would no doubt be printed, though his insistence would be considered a mannerism. After all, the Latinified binomial nomenclature with its rigid and often embarrassing rules of strict priority, its perpetual preservation of typographical errors, its decapitalization of proper names like Washington or Virginia, and other literary barbarisms, has been gradually and in the main reluctantly accepted as a needed instrument by biologists—not as an ornament, flourish, luxury of ostentation, or trademark. And their verdict has been accepted by nonbiological scientists. Similarly as regards the recording of the sounds of words in new or exotic languages: the tendency of general science is to let professional linguists decide how these sounds are best represented in international and scientific writing. So Merriam stood proud and pretty much alone in his adherence to the "common English" ways of writing non-English words; but one can respect the courage and integrity of his aesthetic or temperamental resistance to the majority.

Also, it is to be remembered that Merriam did not set out to do linguistics, did not profess to, and obviously would not have known how. He remained a natural historian recording the *distribution* of words as a means to ascertaining the precise distribution of dialects, languages, tribes, families, and their beliefs and customs—as earlier he had recorded the distribution of song sparrows and grizzly bears and yellow pines, of species and subspecies of *Canis latrans*, in order to delimit life zones. What was at stake was not phonetic or phonemic accuracy as the basis for elucidating grammars—which Merriam never dreamed of doing—but an identification of words. Was the name for house, or for, say, jackrabbit, the same here and in the native village ten miles away, or was it similar, or drastically different? For this purpose, Merriam's nontechnical means definitely sufficed.

As a matter of fact, when simon-pure linguists come to utilize his data for comparative or historical purposes they will almost certainly prefer them in his "everyday English" orthography than if he had tried to write as an imitation linguist. As it is, they will know they have his own original forms. And if they are like the linguists of today, they will themselves transpose his spellings into whatever orthography they will then be using, rather than have to guess, from rewritings orthographically "normalized" or "standardized" by, say, Heizer or myself, what in such forms was likely to have been Merriam's and what Heizer's or Kroeber's idea of what Merriam heard. So we, his editors, approve of the rule of unalterability which he laid down, and approve it cheerfully.

While the twenty articles in this book represent not so much what Merriam considered most important in his own work, but what he had happened to have put together most completely, I should like to point out some of his contributions that seem likely to be valued and used most by anthropologists, historians, and those interested in Indians.

There are, for instance, detailed eyewitness accounts of native rituals attended by Merriam, such as the Wintun Big-head, the Pomo Sahte, the Mewuk Mourning Cry, the Autumn Ceremony in Yosemite; or, where the rite had long since been abandoned, like the Kotomut at Tejon, Merriam recorded its description by a surviving native witness and participant. This last account is a genuine treasure recovered, to rank with the accounts of southern California religion by Boscana and Reid. The Sahte record somewhat parallels Barrett's Patwin-Wintun Hesi in both being revivalist versions of parts of ancient aboriginal cult systems. The Big-head is touched on also by Cora Du Bois in her Ghost Dance volume. Mourning Cries were held over much of California; Merriam's is perhaps the fullest description extant.

Of unusual and permanent value are Merriam's photographs of native dwellings and dance houses. This is a uniquely full series, further supplemented by descriptions in other articles, as the one on the Yokiah Pomo.

Very typical are the tribal territory studies, as for the Tuleyome, Mono Paiute, Beñemé, and under "Distribution" in the notes on "Tribes of Wintoon Stock." These are little monographs of intimate landscape utilization and detailed ethnic local history. The pattern for these Merriam had set as early as 1904 with an article in *Science* on the distribution of tribes in the southern Sierra, and had followed up with detailed studies of the Mewan stock (1907), Yosemite Valley (1917), Pit River tribes (1926), New River Tlohomtahhoi (1930), and Emtimbitch (1930). All of these, like their successors herein, contribute precise information not to be found anywhere else.

From the great mass of vocabulary material which Merriam secured from subtribe after subtribe according to a standardized list, and some of which he also subsequently brought together comparatively, we have extracted for this volume only a slight sample: the native words for "tobacco" and "pipe" in 161 California and Nevada dialects.

From Merriam's copies of the Baptismal Records kept in the Franciscan Missions we reproduce five sets. These give the native name of the settlement, rancheria, or subtribe to which the converts belonged. They are thus a treasury of local geographical information for those missionized parts of California in which Merriam could not secure the data from the Indians themselves because these had died out before his time or become absorbed in the Mexican population. As these records are dated by years, they also possess direct historical value. They make possible the tracing out of the year-by-year spread of each mission's influence and tributary territory.

Finally, there is a wide array of most diverse themes treated either in short separate topical articles or in sections of tribal ones. Such are native hats; Indians as basket collectors; wild tobacco; native doctors; great Wintun chiefs; acorn cooking; battles and massacres. They illustrate the range of Merriam's interest and activity.

KEY TO DIACRITICAL MARKS*

THE ALPHABET

My vocabularies are written, so far as possible, in simple phonetic English. The words are divided into syllables separated by hyphens. The accented syllable is marked with the acute accent (').

1. Sounds that have a fixed and definite value in English, like our words pin, peg, hat, not, and so on, are pronounced exactly as in English. In such syllables diacritical marks are unnecessary and as a rule are omitted.

2. Sounds represented in English by a double consonant, or by a syllable the pronunciation of which is not phonetic, are always spelled phonetically. Thus the sounds represented by our words *all* and *who* are written *awl* and *hoo*.

3. Unmarked vowels, except in syllables having a fixed value like those mentioned in section 1, have the usual long or pure sound given them in the English alphabet.

4. An unmarked vowel standing alone (as a syllable or word) always takes its long or pure alphabetic sound.

KEY TO VOWEL SOUNDS, DIACRITICAL MARKS, AND SO ON

ā   as in acorn, date, late, mane.
ă   as in fat, bat, hat, have, man.
ah as in far, father, what.
aw as in awl, awful.
ē   (or e unmarked) as in eject, eternal, meat.
ĕ   as in end, met, net, check, peg, pen, her.
ī   (or i unmarked) as in ice, iron, pine, file.
ĭ   as in it, ill, pin, fin, fit, pick, admit.
ō   (or o unmarked) as in note, poke.
ŏ   as in not, pot, odd, frog.
oo as in ooze, spoon.
oi as in oil, boil, join.
ow as in how, plow, out.
ū   (or u unmarked) as in mule, mute, acute. If the u sound forms a syllable by itself, it is commonly spelled *yu*, pronounced *you*.
ŭ   as in tub, mud, us.
û   for a somewhat uncertain or obscure vowel sound, as in but and sun, known as the 'neutral vowel.'

Prolonged vowels are indicated by doubling the letter (as aa, ee, &c.)

Prolonged or trilled consonants are indicated by a double acute accent (").

The consonants, except c, g, and q, have their ordinary English values; c and g having in English both hard and soft sounds, require special treatment, q is not used. The q sound occurs only before u, and is better represented by kw (*kween* instead of *queen*).

---

* This statement reproduces the first page of Dr. Merriam's printed vocabulary forms.

Dr. Merriam's views on phonetic transcription are outlined in his paper, *The Classification and Distribution of the Pit River Indians of California*, Smithsonian Misc. Colls., Vol. 78, No. 3 (Publ. 2784), 1926.—Ed.

c is never used except before h, as in chin, chum, chap, church. It is commonly preceded by t to render the pronounciation more correct. Hence the usual combination is *tch*, as in *hatch*.

g is always hard, as in get, give, grind.

j is always soft, as in jet, jam, jelly, judge.

k has its usual value, as in kill, keep, king. It is also used instead of c for the hard sound of c in our words cat, cow, come, cold, cream, clinic, and the like.

s has its usual sound, as in see, sink, soft, &c, and is also used instead of c for the soft sound of c in our words cent, cinder, mice.

^{ch} (super) has the soft sound as in german *ach*, *büch*, &c. (In MS written ᴄ͟ʜ).

^{n} (super) is nasalized, and follows a nasalized vowel, as o^{n}. (In MS written ṉ).

An apostrophe (') after a vowel followed by another letter gives the long sound to the vowel, and may also indicate an omitted or silent letter.

An apostrophe (') at either end of a syllable calls for an exploded sound.

An exclamation (!) after a letter indicates that the letter is stressed.

BIBLIOGRAPHICAL ABBREVIATIONS

AA	*American Anthropologist*
BAE	Bureau of American Ethnology
–B	Bulletin
–R	Annual Reports
UC–PAAE	University of California Publications in American Archaeology and Ethnology

Contents

NOTES ON MATERIAL CULTURE

COMPARATIVE RECORDS

ILLUSTRATIONS

Map

Figures in Text

Plates

ETHNOLOGICAL ACCOUNTS

Tribes of Wintoon Stock

DISTRIBUTION

The territory of the Wintoon stock extends from the upper reaches of Sacramento River and the McCloud south to San Francisco Bay. There is conflicting evidence as to their extreme northern limit. Some say it was a line crossing the summits of Mt. Shasta, Wintoon Butte (known also as Muir Butte, Sugarloaf, and Black Butte), and Scott Mountain; others, that it was an east and west line crossing Sacramento River at Salt Creek, about two miles north of La Moine, the territory between Mt. Shasta and Salt Creek being the home of a tribe of Shastan affinities called Wi'-in by the Wintoon, A'-te by the Atchomawe, and Poo-e-soos by Stephen Powers.

The northern boundary of the Wintoon extends east from the high divide between the waters of Trinity River and those of Scott River to Black Butte and Mt. Shasta and passes a little north of Black Fox Mountain. The eastern boundary extends from near Bartles southwest to Grizzly Peak and continues south along the divide between Squaw Creek and the Big Bend of Pit River, not reaching Big Bend but crossing Pit River at a point about thirty miles above its mouth (or above the mouth of the McCloud). It follows the west side of Cow Creek, continuing south in a narrow belt along the east side of Sacramento River as far as Balls Ferry opposite the mouth of Cottonwood Creek. The western boundary extends south from the high divide between the waters of South Fork Salmon River and those of Coffee Creek, and follows Canyon Creek for its entire length to its junction with Trinity River. It is stated by members of the tribe that Weaver Bolly (Nor'-wahn Bul'-le) and Oregon Gulch were points on their western boundary and that their westernmost town was on Oregon Gulch a little east of the present town of Junction.

3

The Northern Wintoon (Wintoon proper) reached south from the upper Sacramento Valley and McCloud River region to Red Bank Creek, just south of Red Bluff (some say only to Cottonwood Creek). In the extreme southern part of this distribution, between Cottonwood Creek on the north and Red Bank Creek on the south, was a small division called Daw'-pum.

The Northern Wintoon were in contact on the west, north, and east with tribes speaking wholly different languages. On the west across Canyon Creek were the Che-mar'-re-ko; on the northwest over the mountains, the Ka-hoo'-tin-e'-ruk; on the north, the Shas'te; on the northeast, the Mo'dok; on the east the Ach'-o-ma'-we and Nōs'-se (Yah'na). On the south were related tribes of their own stock.

South of Red Bank Creek and north of Elder Creek was a small tribe called Wi-e'-ker-ril. Whether they were more closely related to the Northern Wintoon or to the Nom'-lak'-ke is not positively known, but the probabilities are that their affinities were with the latter.

The Nom'-lak'-ke had rather a large distribution area, extending south from Elder Creek on the north to Stony Creek and from about three miles east of Henleyville west to the summit of the high mountains that separate the drainage area of Sacramento River on the east from that of Eel River on the west.

East of the Nom'-lak'-ke were the Poo'-e-muk, a division inhabiting both sides of the Sacramento River from a few miles north of Tehama south for twelve or fifteen miles.

South and east of Stony Creek, extending from Elk Creek east to the sloughs of the Sacramento, and south to Grapevine Creek (2 or 3 miles north of Sites in the extreme northern part of Colusa Co.) was a division closely related to the Nom'-lak'-ke and perhaps best regarded as a division of that tribe. These people appear to have had no distinctive name for themselves. They were called Noi'-muk by the Nom'-lak'-ke on the north, and Dah'-chin-chin'-ne by the Choo-hel'-mem-sel on the south.

The Choo-hel'-mem-sel occupied a rather small area in the western foothills of Sacramento Valley, from just north of Grapevine Creek in extreme northern Colusa County south to a line passing a little south of Leesville and a little north of Venado (commonly known as Mountain House), the exact boundary apparently about a mile north of Venado. In an east and west direction their territory reached east from the divide between the headwaters of Stony Creek and those of Rice Fork of Eel River to the plain a couple of miles east of Sites.

The Chen'-po-sel inhabited the mountain valleys tributary to Cache Creek from a point apparently between Goat Mountain and Little Horse Mountain on the northwest, southeast to the junction of Bear Creek with

Cache Creek, about seventeen miles due east of the south end of Lower Lake, and reached east just far enough to include the valley of Bear Creek from its southern end north to a point nearly west of Venado.

The Ko-te'-nah or 'Klet'-win were immediately south of the Choo-hel'-mem-sel, east of the Chen'-po-sel, and west of the Sacramento River tribes known as Pat'-win and Ko'-ru. Their territory thus reached from the eastern edge of Bear Valley on the west to Sycamore Slough on the east, and from Venado (Mountain House) and Williams on the north, south to a few miles south of Arbuckle, and farther west to the ridge separating the headwaters of Sand and Cortena creeks from the head of Capay Valley immediately north of Rumsey on Cache Creek.

The Ko'-ru or Colusa people extended from just south of Princeton on Sacramento River south to include the sites of the towns of Meridian and Sycamore. Their northern line was approximately the present boundary between Glenn and Colusa counties. In an east-west direction they held the low flat valley country from a little east of Maxwell and Williams east across Sacramento River to the east side of Butte Creek and Butte Slough, including the western part of Marysville Buttes.

The Indians tell me that the barren part of the flat plain from Delevan south to south of Maxwell (and apparently nearly to Williams) was not claimed by either the Ko'-ru on the east or the Choo-hel'-mem-sel on the west, but was a desolate no man's land which at intervals formed the battleground between the two tribes.

The Pat'-win proper extended from the southern boundary of the Ko'-ru just south of Meridian and Sycamore, south to Knights Landing, covering a broad area on the west side of Sacramento River and a much narrower strip on the east side. In the northern part of their range Sycamore Slough was the boundary separating them from the 'Klet'-win, but south of Arbuckle their territory reached the foothills farther west. Knights Landing was on the boundary between themselves and the Poo'-e-win, but there is some uncertainty as to the exact course of this line to the southwest.

The Poo'-e-win territory extended from Knights Landing and Vernon on Sacramento River south to the north shore of Suisun and San Pablo bays and from lower Sacramento River west to include Yolo, Madison, Winters, Vacaville, and Suisun. On the southwest it reached Napa, Napa Junction, Suscol, Toluca (Tulokay), and probably continued to Sonoma. From the southern part of Napa Valley northeast to Winters the exact position of the boundary is unknown.

The Nor'-rel-muk, or Hay Fork division of the Northern Wintoon, occupied a mountainous area on the west side of the eastern Coast Range, which separates the headwaters of streams flowing into the Sacramento from those of South Fork Trinity River. Their territory covered the greater part of the drainage area of Hay Fork on the north and extended south to South Fork Trinity River. The western boundary, north of Plummer Creek (a tributary of South Fork Trinity) coincides very closely with the divide between South Fork Trinity and Hay Fork. The northern boundary is Miner Creek for its entire length, beyond which it follows the divide between Trinity River and Hay Fork to Soldier Creek, which it follows to its junction with Trinity River—where the Nor'-rel-muk are in contact with their close relatives, the Nor'-boss, the Trinity River subdivision of the Northern Wintoon. The eastern boundary, beginning on the north between Soldier Creek and Douglas City, passes southward, following in the main the summit of the eastern Coast Range to the headwaters of South Fork Trinity, at the north base of the lofty North Yolla Bolly. The southern boundary is formed by South Fork Trinity River from its headwaters to Forest Glen (otherwise known as Auto Rest).

The Nor'-rel-muk were in contact with four tribes: the Che-mar'-re-ko on the west and north, the Northern Wintoon on the east, the Set'-ten-bi'-den on the south and southwest, the Ni-i'-che on the middle west.

The Ni-i'-che were a small Wintoon tribe, the westernmost of the stock. They occupied a restricted area on South Fork Trinity River, extending from Plummer Creek on the north, south to the junction of Post Creek with South Fork near Forest Glen. Their western boundary was the summit of South Fork Mountain from a point west of the mouth of Plummer Creek south to a point approximately west of Forest Glen. The eastern boundary ran from the headwaters of Plummer Creek southeast to the headwaters of Post Creek, Post Creek forming the southern boundary on the east side of South Fork.

The Ni-i'-che were in contact with four tribes: the Athapascan Kos'-ten-ke'-ah on the west, the Che-mar'-re-ko and Nor'-rel-muk on the north, the Nor'-rel-muk on the east, the Athapascan Set'-ten-bi'-den on the south.

The tribe is said to be extinct. Information as to its boundaries and relationship has been given me by three tribes of Athapascan stock, namely, the Set'-ten-bi'-den ke'-ah, adjoining the Ni-i'che on the south, the Tsen-nah'-ken-nes' of upper Eel River, and the Lo'-lahn'-kok of South Fork Eel. Their language is said to be practically the same as that of the Nor'-rel-muk of Hay Fork.

DIALECTS AND DIVISIONS

A preliminary comparison of ten vocabularies which I obtained from as many tribes or bands of Wintoon stock (along with two others by H. B. Brown and Major P. B. Redding of which I have the original manuscripts written in 1852) brings out certain resemblances and differences and permits a rough classification of the tribes.

The various tribes and bands appear to fall into three groups.

1. The Northern Wintoon group, comprising the McCloud and Pit River, the upper Sacramento, and the Trinity River divisions; the Nor'-rel-muk of Hay Fork Valley; the Nom'-lak'-ke of the western part of Sacramento Valley between Elder and Stony creeks; and the Noema or Noimuk (called Nor'muk by the Hay Fork Nor'-rel-muk) of the Red Bluff region. There are three important divisions of the Northern Wintoon.

The Win-ne-mem or McCloud Division embraces the entire course of McCloud River and tributaries from its upper waters near Bartles to its junction with the Pit River, and also the lower course of Pit River from a point about thirty miles above the junction to its mouth in Sacramento River.

The Num-te-pom or Sacramento River Division comprises the drainage basin of the upper Sacramento, locally known as the "Little Sacramento," extending from the head of the river at Sisson down to its junction with Pit River. The term Cedar District is applied to the part of the upper Sacramento above Delta.

The Num-soos or Trinity Division comprises the drainage basin of Trinity River from its source southward and westward to Oregon Gulch, just east of the mouth of Canyon Creek.

2. The Pat'-win group, comprising three quite distinct tribes: the Patwin, occupying the western two-thirds of the flat Sacramento Valley from Stony Creek south to Knights Landing; the Win of the mountains, foothills, and included valleys bordering Sacramento Valley on the west from the neighborhood of Snow Mountain and Ladoga south over eastern Lake and Napa counties, and western Colusa and Yolo and northwestern Solano counties to near Napa and Vacaville; and the Poo'-e-win of the southern part of Sacramento Valley from Knights Landing to Suisun Bay and west along the north side of San Francisco Bay to Sonoma.

3. The Tehama group, comprising so far as known only the Tehama tribe, which, judging from the lamentably meager material available, cannot be classed with any of the others though its affinities appear to be toward the Nom'-lak'-ke of the Northern Wintoon group.

CLASSIFICATION OF TRIBES

GROUPS	TRIBES
Northern Wintoon	Wintoon proper
	Norrelmuk
	Nomlakke
	Normuk
Patwin	Patwin
	Pooewin
	Win
Tehama	Tehama

The members of the Northern Wintoon group are rather closely inter-related, although it is necessary to speak with caution as to the Noemuk or Noema, which appear to be two tribes called Nor'-muk by the Nor'-rel-muk of Hay Fork Valley. The only vocabularies of these tribes available are those obtained by the California pioneer, Major P. B. Redding, and the artist, H. B. Brown, who spent some time at Redding's ranch making sketches of Indians for J. R. Bartlett. Redding labeled his vocabulary "Noemuc and Wylacker," while Brown called his "Noema and Wylacker." They agree essentially. Both were written in 1852, evidently obtained from the same Indian or Indians. The dialect is rather close to Nom'-lak'-ke, but does not agree throughout. The proper name of the tribe is doubt-ful, and also its location, although it could not have been far from Major Redding's ranch, which was on the west side of Sacramento River a little north of the mouth of Cottonwood Creek.

That the difference in spelling of the tribal name ("Noemuc" by Red-ding, "Noema" by Brown) is of no consequence is shown by the circum-stance that while Brown wrote Noema on his vocabulary, he wrote Noemuc on his map. I am fortunate enough to possess the originals of both Brown's and Redding's vocabularies, as well as the map of California (published by B. F. Butler, San Francisco, 1851) which Brown carried with him and on which he indicated in colors his routes of 1851 and 1852, as well as the areas inhabited by the "Coluse" (Patwin), "Cushna" (Midoo), and "No-sah" (or Yahna) tribes. In addition to this important information, in acquiring which Brown evidently had the benefit of Major Redding's knowledge, there are on various parts of the map, in Brown's handwriting, the names of a number of other tribes. Among these are "Wylacker" and "Noemuc," one above the other, on the west side of Sacramento River—"Wylacker" written above Cottonwood Creek; "Noemuc" immediately south of "Red Bluff Creek," now known as Reads Creek.

This would seem to locate the "Noema" or "Noemuc" of Brown and Redding on the south side of Cottonwood Creek, extending as far south at least as Elder Creek. If we assume that the tribe was confined to a com-paratively narrow strip along Sacramento River, this would agree fairly well with territory assigned by the Nor'-rel-muk to the Nor'-muk.

But these people must not be confused with the Noi'-muk proper of Western Glenn County, thirty-five or forty miles to the southwest be-tween Elk and Briscoe creeks. The names unfortunately are practically identical ("Noemuc" of Brown and Redding being almost indistinguish-able from "Noimuk"). To avoid ambiguity and confusion I have adopted Nor'-muk for the tribe called "Noema" and "Noemuc" by Brown and Redding. Much remains to be learned of the names and distribution of tribes in this region. This applies not only to the Noi'-muk, but also to the

Dah'-muk and the Wi-e'-ker-ril, both of which are said by the Paskenta Nom'-lak'-ke to have inhabited the west side of Sacramento River between Cottonwood and Elder creeks. Other names also claim consideration, but in our present ignorance it is idle to discuss them.

These river tribes north of the Patwin appear to be extinct—at least, after considerable search I have failed to discover any members of them and am therefore obliged to rely on the short vocabularies of Brown and Redding, written seventy years ago. These appear to indicate that Nor-muk is a recognizable dialect closely related to Nomlakke but with a few words of Northern Wintoon and a few peculiar to itself.

Of the Patwin group, Win resembles Pooewin more than it does Patwin; the Pooewin words for the numerals 6 and 7 and a few other words differ radically from those of any of the related tribes, but the interrelations of the three are rather close.

Of the third group, which, lacking a better name, is called for the present Tehama, little can be said, the only vocabulary known to me being the short one collected by H. B. Brown in 1852, published by Stephen Powers[1] in 1877. A number of the words differ materially from corresponding words in any of the other known Wintoon tribes. Thus far I have searched in vain for a living member of the tribe, but still hope that something more may be learned about it.

In connection with the Tehama "tribe" the fact should be pointed out that we have no vocabularies—and practically no information save names alone—relating to several other river "tribes" which are said to have inhabited the borders of Sacramento River from Jelleys Ferry, twelve miles north of Red Bluff, south to Tehama. Names given me by adjacent tribes are Memwilakke (Mem'-wi'lakke) at Jelleys Ferry, Dah'muk at Red Bluff, Wi-e'-ker-ril between Red Bank and Elder creeks, and Poo'-e-muk and Poo'-e-soos for the Tehama region. The name Mem-pom-ways, published in Elliott and Moore's *History of Tehama County* (1880), may also apply to the Tehama tribe, but its source is unknown.

TRIBAL NAMES

The tribal names used by the Wintoon for the designation of other tribes are almost always compass names, indicating direction rather than tribal distinction. Thus the first syllable of the great majority of names is either wi', north; nor', south; poo'-e, east; or nom, west. The Shaste on the north are called Wi'-yu-ke, meaning "northern enemy"; the Nosse or Yahna on

---

[1] *Tribes of California*, 1877, p. 518; also vocabulary no. 6, pp. 521–529. The original is Smithsonian Collections No. 561, received from J. R. Bartlett, for whom it was prepared in 1852 by his artist H. B. Brown.

the east, Poo'-el-yu'-ke, meaning "eastern enemy"; the Modes'se of the Big Bend of Pit River, Poo'-e-soos.

Similarly, tribes and bands of their own stock are also mostly known by names indicating direction. Thus the Indians living toward Mt. Shasta are called Wi'-bos ("northerners"), those about Red Bluff Nor'-muk or Nor'-men Wintoon ("southerners" or "south-water people"), and so on.

To the word indicating direction is added a term which, although the exact meaning is not always clear, usually expresses the idea of home or the place in which the people live or speak. There are four of these terms: soos, bos, muk, and lak'-ke. The word bos means "home." The word lak'-ke is said by some to mean the "far limit" of the people (in the direction shown by the first part of the name); by others it is said to mean "speakers" or "talkers."

One informant states that the word soos indicates a tribe of another stock—people speaking a different language—while the terms bos, muk, and lak'-ke refer to tribes speaking dialects of the Wintoon language. But this is not always so, for the McCloud Wintoon call the related Trinity River tribe Num'-soos.

The name Wi'-bos is applied to the northernmost Wintoon—those occupying the upper waters of the Sacramento and McCloud rivers and Squaw Creek. Their territory is said to extend from Sisson east to Black Fox Mountain and Bartles. They are said to have intermarried extensively with the Modok—some say with the Shaste and Modesse also—and to have talked a mixed language. Some of the McCloud Wintoon regard the Wi-bos as a distinct tribe; Roland Dixon thinks they are a branch of the Shaste and calls them Okwanutsu, a term which, as I have elsewhere shown, is simply a Shaste word meaning "south people" and has no tribal significance. The Shaste call the Wintoon Hah-to-kwe-wah, and say that they held all the country south of Mt. Shasta and the upper Sacramento to Sisson.

The McCloud River Wintoon call their relatives at Red Bluff Nor'-bos and apply the same name to the people of Hay Fork Valley, who, they say, belong to the same tribe.[2] Other names applied to them are Nor'-men Wintoon ("south-water people") and Nor-kān-pom Wintoon ("south-and-down people"). The Hay Fork people, it is said, were in the habit of visiting Sacramento River near Red Bluff every summer to catch salmon. The chief of the Norbos tribe, Kob'-bun-ti'-e, lived at Red Bluff. His house was on high ground on what is now the main street of Red Bluff.

The name Pit River Indians has often been applied to the Wintoon.[3] There are to my knowledge two distinct tribes that inhabit the Pit River

[2] The Hay Fork people call themselves Nor'-rel-muk.

[3] Information in this paragraph is from Alfred Gillis, a McCloud River Wintoon.

country, the Wintoon on the lower Pit River, the Modesse on the upper Pit. It is a mistake to call these Indians the Pit River Indians for there is no connection between the Modesse and the Wintoon of the lower Pit.

GEOGRAPHICAL NAMES[4]

The term "Little Sacramento" was formerly used to designate the upper part of what is now called Sacramento River—the part between its source near Sisson and the junction with the Pit River. In early days the name Sacramento was applied to the longest course of the river, namely, the Pit and its continuation, the Sacramento. This was proper, in accordance with the customary usage in geographic nomenclature. At that time the northern tributary, extending from Sisson south to the mouth of the Pit, was called by some "Destruction River"; by others "Little Sacramento," a term still in local use.[5]

The old Wintoon trail along the Sacramento from Sisson down as far as Redding was divided into day's journeys, with regular resting-places where the night was spent. At each of these places was a small shallow hole in a rock—a hole apparently not more than a couple of inches in diameter and perhaps an inch in depth. The old Doctors used to go to these holes and pray for strength and success.

There was formerly a very large village on the west bank of Sacramento River east of Redding. It extended from the present concrete highway bridge on the road to Ingot all the way down to the red gravel bluff. The black earth and other signs of this village may still be seen at the west abutment of the bridge.

The largest village of the Pueta-pom Wintoon was at what is called today the Wellington Corral on the Pit River, some distance above the junction of Squaw Creek and the Pit. The Indian name for this village was Nom-dall-schet-el, meaning "village where the river bends to the west." This town, however, was not as far up the Pit as the Wintoon language extended. The Wintoon language was said to have been spoken thirty miles above what is now known as the "Silver Thorn Ferry."

Tah'-bot char'-row, meaning "serviceberry valley," was an extensive area extending southeast from Mt. Shasta to near Bartles. On Backbone Creek there is a fall about sixty feet high called Nawl'-te tā'-ke (nawl'-te means "across"). Copper City and Ydalpom are the same place. The Indian name is Wi'-dal'-pom, meaning "north camp ground."

The name of the Lewiston Valley was Wy-elte-pom, meaning "valley

---

[4] The information in this section, except the discussion of the names Kettenshaw and Kettenpom, was obtained by Dr. Merriam from Alfred Gillis.—Ed.

[5] The Wintoon of Lower Pit River made boats of skin supported by ribs. They are also said to have made, or lined, boats with pine needles and pitch.

of the northland." The Indian name of Hay Fork Valley was Norail-pom, meaning "valley of the southland." (Hyam-pom means "low land.") This valley was occupied by the Norail muck [Nor'-rel-muk] Wintoon. I have just received the information from Indians on New River, which empties into the Trinity near Burnt Ranch, that there were two languages of the upper Trinity, the Wintoon and the Hoopa.

There are two small valleys in the mountains of northwestern California whose names possess a certain interest for the anthropologist. These are Kettenshaw and Kettenpom (sometimes written with the initial letter H: Hettenshaw, Hettenpom). The tribe in whose language the names originated is uncertain but there is no doubt of their meaning and application. The word het'ten or ket'ten (pronounced 'ket'-ten' by the southern Athapascan tribes) is the name of the camas, an important food plant of many western tribes, which grew in abundance in both the valleys to which the name is applied. Kettenshaw, as printed on most maps, is a corruption of Ket'-ten chow', meaning "the camas dance." Similarly, Kettenpom means "camas place or valley." K'et'tenpom is a small valley a mile north of Hoaglin Valley.

The southern Wylakke of the region immediately north of Round Valley tell me that they think the name came originally from the Norrelmuk, a Wintoon tribe of the Hay Fork region. If this is true, it would indicate a former southward extension of the Norrelmuk, of which there seems to be no record; or, and more probably, it may mean that the Norrelmuk were permitted by the Wylakke or southern Athapascan owners of these valleys to visit them for the purpose of gathering camas or of attending ceremonies.

An old white man named Dave Wilburn, who has long lived in Hettenshaw Valley and has an Indian wife, tells me that in the old days some of the neighboring Indians pronounced the name Het-teen'-chow', but he does not know to what tribe they belonged.

WINTOON CHIEFS[6]

The Wintoon had seven great chiefs. These at one time were:

1. Num'-kaw-de (meaning "western hunter"), who lived on Clear Creek, between the Trinity and the Sacramento.

2. Pon'-te-tā'-wis of Trinity River near Lewiston.

3. Top'-pe-we'-tah of Trinity Center region. He always led in war and was the head war chief.

4. Sed'-dem-sā'-le of Antler on the Sacramento River. He defeated the

---

[6] The material in the following sections is noted by Dr. Merriam as told him by Alfred Gillis: "Wintoon Chiefs," "Warfare," "Weapons and Armor," "Massacre of the Wintoon on McCloud River," "Houses and Other Structures," "Plants and Animals," "Clothing," "Social Culture."—Ed.

Shaste and killed their great war chief in a battle at a place on the Sacramento River now called Antler. His home was at this place and he had a sweathouse just back of the site of the present hotel.

5. Sed'-de-poo'-e-we'-tah from Redding on the Sacramento.

6. Bes-soos'-kahl'-las (meaning "shining mink") of Pit River. He was a grandfather of informant Gillis; his son Billy Canyon is still alive.

7. Nor'-rel-poo'-tus, who belonged to McCloud River but at one time moved to Little Cow Creek to keep the Nôsse (Yahna) from encroaching on Wintoon territory. He later returned to McCloud River and was one of the signers of the treaty with the whites made at Redding. Nor'-rel-poo'-tus had two names. His original name was Nom-tā-roo-man. This was a great name and had been previously held by a great chief. It means "spirit of the west." He bestowed this name on his son and changed his own name to Nor'-rel-poo'-tus, meaning "south Indian summer."

Sed'-de-poo'-e-we'-tah (whose name means "Coyote man of the East") was at one time one of the seven war chiefs of the Wintoon; but he was only half Wintoon, the other half Nosse or Yahna. He lived at the old rancheria on the northeast side of the Sacramento River opposite the present town of Redding. His authority extended up Sacramento River as far as Kennett, and east and north of the Redding Bend covered the Stillwater Plains as far as Buckeye and Churntown.

It was his custom to take and train for his army all the strong boys in this area and to levy on the people for food and valuables for himself and for the support of his army, which is said to have numbered as many as six thousand warriors. He was a robber and helped himself to everything he wanted. As a result, the people under his domination were poorly nourished and lacked ambition; they were looked upon by the McCloud River Wintoon as inferior or of a lower class. The young men he took to train as warriors he taught dances intended to strengthen their muscles and make them agile and quick.

The Nosse wanted to push west to the Sacramento River because of the salmon and other fish to be had there. But the Wintoon held a narrow strip of land on the east side. Sed'-de-poo'-e-we'-tah made secret terms with the Nosse in the hope of driving the Wintoon from this strip and joined them with his army in an attack on the Wintoon at the junction of the McCloud and Pit rivers. They began the attack in the early dawn, shooting their arrows across Pit River. Sed'-de-poo'-e-we'-tah was seen with the enemy and his treachery was discovered. An effort was made to kill him, but he was very clever and escaped.

Sometime afterward he played a trick on the Wintoon which caused them to kill one of their own young men. He went to dance in a ceremonial house on the McCloud dressed in a large quantity of mem-pok, the clamshell-disk wampum or money of the tribe. He danced for a long time until dark. When ready to come out, he put his strings of mem-pok on a young man in the roundhouse and gave them to him. He then walked out himself and was not molested because the men lying in wait for him had seen him enter covered with the mem-pok and, when he came away in the evening naked, they mistook him for one of their own men. But when the young man to whom he had given the mem-pok came out covered with it, he was set upon and killed, the watchers mistaking him for Sed'-de-poo'-e-we'-tah.

Then a council was held by the three great chiefs of the northern divisions (Trinity, Upper Sacramento, and McCloud), and it was decided to challenge the treacherous chief.

So Dol'-le-ken-til'-lě-mah, head chief on the McCloud, went to Sed'-de-poo'-e-we'-tah's rancheria and called to him to come out. Dol'-le-ken-til'-lě-mah said: "You played a woman's trick in leaving your strings of mem-pok in the roundhouse and coming out after dark as if you were another person. Now come out and play a man's way." This was a challenge, but Sed'-de-poo'-e-we'-tah was a coward and ran away. His two sons came out and fought and Dol'-le-ken-til'-lě-mah killed them both. Then Dol'-le-ken-til'-lě-mah attacked Sed'-de-poo'-e-we'-tah's men. The fight began at what is now Reed's Ferry. Dol'-le-ken-til'-lě-mah won the battle and destroyed the villages. He then stayed all winter on the flat east of Redding.

Sed'-de-poo'-e-we'-tah finally came back and died at his home at the present site of Redding. His grave is there now—a large mound in a grove of oaks close to the river, across from Turtle Bay and near the highway concrete bridge leading to the McCloud.

In addition to the seven great war chiefs, there were chiefs of the three great divisions of the Northern Wintoon and a number of local chiefs. Ordinary chiefs are called wēh, head chiefs ti'-e. This designation commonly follows the man's name. Alfred Gillis, a McCloud River Wintoon, tells me that the word ti'-e is the name for chief in the Puget Sound country also; he suspects that his ancestors came from that region.

Dol'-le-ken-til'-lě-mah, chief of the McCloud Division, lived at Kal'-le ke'-le near Campbell's on the McCloud. He is said to have been a great orator; his name means "shining throat" or something of the kind. He was present at the McCloud River massacre of the Wintoon near his place.

Dok'-ke-che-re'-ke was a war chief who lived in the neighborhood of Castle Crags, where he defeated the Shaste in a great battle.

Wi'-el-poo'-tus (meaning "north Indian summer") was another war chief. He lived at the old rancheria at a place now called Gibson, just south of the railroad station Sims.

Kā'-ne (or Ken'-ne), meaning "dreamer," lived near Redding in a village at the west end of the bridge near the site of the present Shasta hospital.

A former chief named Nep' was a very intelligent and clever man. In the days when the early trappers followed up the Sacramento, they annoyed the Wintoon in many ways. Nep' told them that they would have to behave themselves and let his people alone or they would not be allowed to traverse the Wintoon country anywhere. He told them that they could follow up the Trinity if they behaved themselves, but they would not be allowed on the Sacramento.

Nep' was a good man. Because of his knowledge of the English language and of trappers and hunters some people believed that he had once been with the Hudson Bay traders. He was shot and killed at Redding by the whites when he tried to induce them to stop abusing his people.

WARFARE

The Wintoon had three notable enemies—the Shaste on the north, west of Mt. Shasta; the Modok on the north, east of Mt. Shasta; and the Nosse on the east. The Modesse, of the Big Bend of Pit River, and their near relatives the Atchomawe were not ranked as enemies, although at times there were intrusions or disagreements leading to battles. One of these was fought on Round Top Mountain (nearly south of Swobe and west of Bartles). It is said that the invaders were Atchomawe from Fall River.

The word for enemy in the Wintoon language is yu'-ke. The Shaste were called Wi' Yuke, meaning "north enemy"; the Nosse, Poo'-el Yuke, meaning "east enemy." A battle is called klik'-ā; a battleground, klik-ā-poo'-dǎ.

The Shaste and Nosse were hereditary enemies of the Wintoon and many battles were fought with them, each side making raids into the territory of the other.

Many years ago the Wintoon invaded Shaste territory and a great battle was fought in the foothills bordering the southeastern part of Scott Valley, near a place now known as Parker, about six miles northeast of Callahan on the road between Callahan and Gazelle. In this battle the Wintoon lost many warriors and appear to have been defeated.

The Shaste from time to time invaded Wintoon territory. On one of their raids they followed down Sacramento Valley to a Wintoon village on Salt Creek where they killed all the people and threw little children into the fire. This was an extraordinary and unprecedented act resulting from the desperation of the tribe. Usually they treated children kindly.

The big battle was fought at Castle Crags. The Wintoon fought under the leadership of a war chief named Dok'-ke-che-re'-ke, meaning "thick neck." It was a fierce battle and lasted a long time. The Shaste were defeated and most of them killed.

The last great battle was fought at Antler. A Shaste chief of the band called by the Wintoon Bul'-le-um ken'-te im-bos (meaning "living under the mountain"), whose home was close to the north side of the great Mt. Shasta, led a party of warriors south against the Wintoon in winter, when there was some snow on the ground and some ice in the river. He succeeded in reaching a point on Sacramento River now known as Antler and was crossing some of his war party on a raft when the Wintoon, under chief Sed'-dem-sā'-le (meaning "head of the Coyotes") suddenly attacked and destroyed them. The Shaste chief was killed by an arrow shot by Sed'-dem-sā'-le. This was the last great battle between the Shaste and Wintoon.

With the Nosse (Yahna) the Wintoon had many battles, some of which lasted for a long time. The Nosse coveted the narrow strip of Wintoon territory on the east side of Sacramento River, because it gave access to the highly valued salmon-fishing grounds along the river. The Nosse held Cow Creek. In order to keep watch over them and prevent them from raiding into Wintoon territory the Wintoon sent their war chief Nor'-rel-poo'-tus to the west side of Cow Creek, where he established himself and remained for a number of years, finally returning to McCloud River.

At one time there were a number of Wintoon on the north side of Pit River just below the mouth of the McCloud. One morning before it was fully daylight they were startled by a shower of arrows shot at them from across Pit River. They instantly seized their arms and rushed to battle. A number ran up Pit River and swam to the south side, thus getting behind the enemy; others crossed below. It was during this battle that they discovered the treachery of the chief Sed'-de-poo'-e-we'-tah, who was half Wintoon and half Nosse, but who had always pretended to stand with the Wintoon and had been recognized as one of their principal chiefs. He was defeated. But the Nosse kept on fighting, retreating to a small valley or flat south of Pit River and east of Bear Mountain, where the battle continued for some days. At times the Wintoon were hard pressed and sent runners for reinforcements, bringing warriors not only from the Trinity but also from points as far off as Hay Fork. Finally the Nosse were defeated. Ever since this great battle the place has been known as Klik'-ă-poo'-de, meaning "battleground."

The Modok and Wintoon had less cause for warfare than the other tribes mentioned, since the inhabited parts of their territory were separated by a broad stretch of inhospitable desert. Nevertheless the Wintoon occasionally invaded Modok territory as far as Glass Mountain in order to obtain obsidian for their arrow points and spearheads; and on the other hand the Modok now and then visited Trout Creek, about a dozen miles east of Mt. Shasta, for the purpose of securing the wood of the yew tree for their bows. But I have not succeeded in obtaining specific information concerning any of their battles.

Many writers have referred to the Indians of the McCloud River and the upper Sacramento as Modok or offshoots of the Modok. Joaquin Miller speaks of these Indians as "Modoc." He uses the name of an Indian boy Klamat, which is a Wintoon word meaning "give me." He also refers to the battle of the Castle Crags as a battle with the "Modoc." The attack on and robbery of the pack trains of which he speaks were the work of the Wintoon. These pack trains were captured on the trails between Trinity Center and Big Backbone Creek on the Sacramento divide. I know of a Wintoon woman who found six hundred dollars in gold and silver that the Indians had hidden after one of their raids.

There is also a chapter of Captain Drannan's book *Thirty-one Years on the Plains and in the Mountains* (1910) in which he speaks of a spirited fight with the Modok. The fight took place on a large creek flowing into the McCloud River.

So far as I have been able to learn there never were any Modok in this part of the country. They made raids into the Wintoon Country for the purpose of obtaining bow wood, koo-lul-chouse (yew wood). The McCloud bows were famous and were traded to other Indians farther to the south. It was against the Indian law, if we may call it such, to steal this wood, but they were encouraged to trade for it. The Modok living around the northern lakes made their bows of juniper, which did not have the strength or elasticity of the yew-wood bow.

The Pue-win [Poo'-e-win] of the Tehama district were not warriors. Their strategy in war was to run and cause the enemy to follow. When their enemies had been led on and were scattered over a vast area, the Pue-win would suddenly turn upon them from ambush, shooting them with arrows.

The people who lived west of the Nom-lacca had no war dance, nor did they scalp the dead. The Ylacca Nom-lacca and the Nom-elte-ylacca Wintoon danced the war dance and scalped their enemies.

The Indians of Hay Fork Valley were known to the Noy-muck Wintoon as Nom-elte-ylacca. The Nom-elte-ylacca Wintoon were unlike the Ylacca Wintoon of the McCloud River, the lower Pit, the Little Sacramento and the Big Sacramento, and upper waters of the Trinity in the fact that their fighting, no matter how fierce, always ceased at sundown. The Northern Wintoon made night raids, as did also the Modok to the northeast, the Shaste to the north, the Yahna to the southeast. The Upper Pits were not feared because they were not warlike.

There is a story told of a primitive war expedition against the Noy-muck by the Nom-elte-ylacca.

A Noy-muck of Grindstone having passed through the Nom-elte-ylacca country, being given all the courtesies of their custom, in a fit of anger killed one of the Nom-elte-ylacca's young men. A small force of warriors was assembled under a war chief. The Noy-muck hearing of their approach organized another body of warriors to meet them. But before the Noy-muck came in contact with the Nom-elte-ylacca the sun began to sink to rest behind the western mountains. The chiefs and their warriors, dressed in their elkhide cloaks and eagle feathers, with yew bows and skin quivers, lined up in battle array. The Nom-elte-ylacca chief observing the honor and moral code of their respective peoples began to speak to them:

"Warriors and Chiefs, one of your young men traveling through our country, partaking of our hospitality, murdered in cold blood one of our people. This and this only brings us to your country. We sought out the murderer, we found him; whatever you may think about him we do not know, but we don't think that he amounts to much. We have inflicted upon him the punishment he deserves. If you want him you will find him by a large rock just to the north of here, a place you all well know. I am done."

It was then the custom of the Noy-muck Wintoon to reply and they did, thus:

"We do not know that all that you say is true, but if what you say is so, then you are right because you have upheld the honor of the Wintoon, but on the other hand if what you say is not so then time alone will bring the truth to light. We Noy-muck do not travel far but we sometimes go to the great mountain [Mt. Shasta] to the north and also west to the Big Waters [the Ocean] and we may be passing through your country sometime and if what you say is not so, it will not be well with you. I am done."

These are stories told to me by the old Indians which show the real character of the old Indian type. They are the truth and should be preserved.

There is another short story of the Wintoon who did not believe in war. Many people think of the Indians as continually at war with each other before the white man came. The truth of the matter is quite the contrary. There were Indians who were warriors, orators, pacifists, and so forth. This is a story of a pacifist, or of an Indian who did not believe in war.

A certain young man of the north (Ylacca or Northern Wintoon) was courting a young Indian maiden. They had known and loved each other for many moons. The young man wanted her to go with him to his father's village to the north, to the McCloud River, but the girl thought too much of her father and mother whom she almost worshiped. They were getting old and she did not wish to leave them, though she loved this young man. In a heat of passion and mad jealous rage, rather than see his beloved become the bride of another, he shot her through the heart with his bow, killing her instantly.

The father of the girl—he was a village speaker or chief—spoke to his people in these words:

"I am a man who did not believe in war. I have talked against war. My people, you all know this, for many times you have heard me speak. I have slain thousands of deer, I have slain thousands of elk and have killed hundreds of bear, but my arrows have never touched human blood, nor did I ever in my lifetime intend they should. In all my hunting I have given the deer, the elk, and the bear but one shot and it has done its work.

"But all is over now. This young man of the north came and courted my only daughter and then slew her in cold blood. I will follow him, for vengeance shall be mine. Now I am out for war. I have now changed, for I am now a warrior, I shall follow him. I shall find him. He too shall receive but one arrow, and it will do its work."

Equipped with his bow and with his quiver full of arrows he bravely started on the hunt for the murderer of his daughter. After traveling many days, grieving under his heavy burden of sorrow, suddenly on the lone mountain trail he met the young man. They came closer and closer until they came within arrow shot of each other. Then quick as a thunderbolt from the sky the old man drew an arrow from his quiver and shot it through the breast of the murderer of his only daughter. To the youth the old man then spoke the thought of his heart.

"Young man, you courted my daughter. I thought you sincere and dreamed of many happy years for you and my only child, but all is over now. I have given you but one arrow. Arise if you can, pull the shaft from your aching body and go. I shall not harm you further. If you can pull that shaft from your breast, you will do the thing that no animal has ever done. The grizzly bear tried but failed. He died on the lone mountainside. Pull the shaft from your breast and go. You are a murderer. I have given you your chance, but you will not try. Die on the lonely trail, where the coyotes and wolves will consume the flesh from your bones. You are not fit for the trouble to bury you. I am going. I leave you to die."

WINTOON WEAPONS AND ARMOR

There are two kinds of bows—the long war bow, the ends of which turn back, and the ordinary bow which is straight. The war bows have sinew backs, glued on with skins of the silver-sided salmon. Many of them are decorated with the bright red bellyskin of the little red-bellied snake (*Storeria*), wrapped around the bow in a spiral—a very handsome finish. Bows are called koo'-lool'. They are made of yew wood, called koo'-lool choos'.

Arrows are called nawt'. The arrow points are of obsidian or flint. The common obsidian point is called dok'-kus; the long slender obsidian point used in war, min'-ne-les; the broad obsidian point, koi'-yu-mas; the red flint point, kah'-pit. The quiver is called ah-pe'-lis.

The war spear is called awl-wah'-nus, from awl, meaning "up" and wah'-nus, "to thrust." The blades are of obsidian seven or eight inches long. These spears are used not only in war but also in attacking grizzly bears forced out of their dens during hibernation.

Another kind of spear, with a short handle only about 4 feet in length, was used in close-up fighting.

The Wintoon warriors always carried, concealed in the hair on the back part of the head, daggers six or eight inches long; these were also sometimes covered by a conical hat of buckskin decorated with feathers. These daggers were usually made from the points or tines of elk antlers, but sometimes from the shinbone of the elk. They were handy in close-up fighting.

After the Wintoon were conquered by the whites and made peace, they buried in secret places their war-spear blades and the stone points of their arrows. Some of these caches have been accidentally discovered in recent years. Bucketfuls of spear and arrow points were dug up in making the railroad cut near the present station of Pit on the west side of Sacramento River nearly opposite the point where Pit River comes in; others have been found in potholes on Backbone Creek.

Jackets or cloaks of bearskin (or sometimes of elkhide), lined on the inside with fawnskin to be soft against the body, were worn in battle. While not absolutely arrowproof, they would lessen the force of the arrow and were a great protection.

MASSACRE OF WINTOON ON McCLOUD RIVER

In the 'fifties or early 'sixties there were a number of white hunters, trappers, miners, and soldiers in the Wintoon country. They established a camp on the middle McCloud at a place called Se'-de-tawn (meaning "pine needles"). It was near Campbell's.

They invited all the Indians of the region to a big feast and dance and told them not to bring their arms. They said they wanted to talk peace and make friends and have a "big time." Near the river they built long tables for the food.

About three hundred Indians came. Dol'-le-ken-til'-lĕ-mah, chief of the middle McCloud Wintoon, whose village was near Campbell's, was there with his men.[7]

They had been there several days, feasting and dancing, when some Num'-soos from Trinity Center came and warned them of danger, telling of a similar trick played on their people at a place called Kal'-lĕ-ke'-le, when many were slaughtered. Dol'-le-ken-til'-lĕ-mah replied that the whites had invited his people and had eaten with them, thus proving their

---

[7] His nephew, Willy Curl, is still living on the McCloud.

friendship. But the Trinity River Indians said this had been done in their case also and their people had been killed.

Then Dol'-le-ken-til'-lĕ-mah warned his people to be on their guard. The Indians began to slip away quietly until by the eighth or tenth day only forty-five warriors remained. The chief then noticed that whenever an Indian left the table, a soldier followed. This alarmed him, so he watched his chance and slipped down to the river. A soldier followed. The chief dived and when he came up the soldier fired at him, but he dived again and escaped. The forty-five Wintoon warriors remaining at the table were all massacred by the soldiers and volunteers.

An old woman named Sarah Barnes (a full-blood Wintoon) was a little girl at the time of this massacre and was there with her parents. She escaped by hiding in the willows.

HOUSES AND OTHER STRUCTURES

The old houses of the Wintoon, called kā'-wil or 'ki'-wel, were conical in form and were made of the bark of the large incense cedar trees (*Libocedrus*). The entrance or doorway is called pesh'; the bed, he'-nah; the tule mat, tā-nas-top'-pe; a ladder, dek'-kes top'-pe; a pole, tawl-lok. Sometimes a low brush fence is built around a house, enclosing a bare area called kum-kal-lǎ-no.

There were small individual sweathouses called kle'-doo-nas 'ki'-wel.

Arbors for shade, known as 'kles or 'klās, were common.

There were brush blinds for hunting, called boo'-hah, usually erected near a spring to which doves, quail, or other small game came to drink. Along the edge of the river were erected conical huts for spearing salmon. These were called bo-kā baw-mah. They were made of poles covered with fresh green boughs, usually of the Douglas spruce. They overhung the water.

Formerly there were menstrual lodges, placed on low hills near the village where everyone could see them. A woman, after her recovery, sweated in the sweathouse and then plunged into the river, after which she returned home and resumed her usual duties.

The large ceremonial house was called 'kloot' or 'klewt'. The floor was excavated to a depth of about three feet below the level of the surrounding ground. The house was domed, and seven supporting posts, connected by cross timbers, held up the roof, which was constructed of poles covered with brush and finally with earth. These houses were sacred; no one ever laughed there.

The great dance houses of the Wintoon were situated just between the junction of Spring Creek and the Sacramento River. There was another on the McCloud River, on the Copper City county road just about a mile from the McCloud River. This was a large dance house and the Indians from Chico and Paskenta were often called here to dance. The large excavation can be seen to this day. The Indian name of the village was "Dow-paukie-olale," meaning "the village of the great dam." It seems that they built a dam just below this village every year for the purpose of obtaining fish from the river. There was another on the McCloud River at Not-a-pawt-kody. Not-a-pawt-kody means "following down a trail through a cut, suddenly to your surprise entering onto a beautiful green flat." This place was the home of Dolly-ken-tillo-mar [Do'-le-ken-til'-lĕ-mah], war chief of the Wenem Mame Wintoon.

There was another large dance house at La Moine, on the Little Sacramento, the Indian name of this place being Tah-loy-ken-kody—the great "bowl in the rock." There was also another great dance house at Trinity Center; its Indian name, Nom-pta-nom-kane-pom, means "to the waste and down land."

There were other dance houses but I do not know just where they were located.

PLANTS AND ANIMALS

The lands and waters of the Northern Wintoon furnish an abundance of food, of which the chief are salmon and acorns. These are carefully dried and preserved for future use. Dried salmon, noor', is called di'-ye when pounded fine. It is rolled up and put into acorn mush.

Acorns and buckeye nuts are often kept over winter, being buried in cold, wet, swampy ground to free them from their bitter quality. In spring they are taken out and eaten. When boiled, they are like potatoes.

The Wintoon Indians of Trinity River roast and eat the nuts from the cones of the Digger pine (*Pinus sabiniana*). Sometimes they put them into a kind of candy. They also roast and pound for food the seeds of the narrow-leafed species of Wyethia, a composite plant related to the sunflower.

The Wintoon of Trinity River made arrows of the straight shoots of the common wild syringa (*Philadelphus Lewisii*). They use the buckeye (*Aesculus californica*) for fire drills, with an under block of juniper.

The black oak (*Quercus californica*) is called pen'-nel'-me. In many of the old trees the inside or heart turns yellow and crumbly and is partly decayed. This half-rotten heart wood is excellent to cook by.[8] It is called wen'-nem chen'-nis (meaning "middle waste"). The word chen'-nis is applied also to manure, meaning any waste material.

---

[8] Fire is called paw or 'haw; live coals, 'kah'-le; ashes, bo-kul; smoke, nook; the poker, 'klah'-pom; firewood, choos.

Willows, called moss'l-me, tell no lies. When their leaves begin to appear, it is really spring.

Deer and quail were plentiful, while in parts of the territory manzanita berries and other fruits, seeds, and food plants were obtainable in large quantities. It was the custom of certain bands to exchange foods with others. Exchanges of this kind were frequent between the Wintoon of the McCloud and those of the Trinity.

The Wintoon had regular deer drives in which hundreds of men took part, in order to drive the deer to prearranged vantage points. The favorite place of the Northern Wintoon was a bluff called Naup'-in tal'-lus (meaning "deer fall over") at the junction of Horse Creek with Squaw Creek about a mile east of Copper City or Ydalpom.[9] They were driven in a manner similar to that practiced by some of the Plains tribes in driving buffalo. Bones of hundreds of deer may still be found at the foot of this bluff.

Hah'-o or how', the gray fox, sometimes goes mad. Once, at a place a little south of Kennett where there is a red earth cut on the railroad, he bit a man. From this circumstance the place is called How'-por'-rit. Near by was a large village and a fine fishing ground.

The Northwestern Wintoon living on Trinity River near Lewiston (who call themselves Wintu) say that the condor used to be fairly common in their region and that, when feeding on deer, it would eat the flesh from the bones and pitch the bones into the air, catching and breaking them as they fell. Mol-luk, their name for the California condor, is the same as that used by all the Mewan tribes, an interesting point which would bear investigation.

Lool'-chit, the hummingbird, is the Doctors' messenger. He is the fastest of all and for this reason was chosen for important errands. Watch'-ut, the crested bluejay, is a robber, and also a great tattler. Still, he does some good, for he cries out when strangers are coming, thus warning the people. Both the crested bluejay and the coyote warn the Wintoon of approaching strangers. Lah-dit', the red-tail hawk, has a handsome red tail. His skin is worn on the back in some of the ceremonial dances.

CLOTHING

In early days the men wore breechcloths of buckskin called nahp'-ne-kow. The women wore short skirts of buckskin, called tā-rek, and aprons, called chah'-hi, of the inner bark of the maple. Moccasins, tam'-moos, were worn by both men and women; basket hats, tah-koos or tak'-ke, were worn by the women. The word for belts was lah-koom.

---

[9] Wintoon name, Wi'-dal'-pom, means "northern camp ground."

Robes or blankets were made of deer, bear, or rabbit skins. Rabbitskin blankets were extensively used by the Wintoon of the Redding region. The Indians living on Stillwater Plain were especially expert in making them. The skins were cut in strips and woven in checkerboard fashion.

The chin of married women was tattooed in three or four vertical bands—an emblem of loyalty.

NOTES ON SOCIAL CULTURE

The Wintoon have a tradition that their people came from the north and traveled south until they came to the Pit River, which they followed down to its junction with the McCloud. Then they saw the snowy peak of Mt. Shasta and followed up the McCloud toward it.

White men are called by two names—El'ete Win'too, meaning "far-off people," and Yah'-pi-too Win'too, meaning "poison people," because they poison the Indians with diseases.

The Northern Wintoon disapproved of inbreeding, feeling that the strongest children came from the crossing of men of one band with women from a distant locality. Hence in early days the McCloud Wintoon generally sought their wives from the Normuk of Hay Fork, or the Numsoos of Trinity River, whereas the Southern Wintoon sought theirs on the Mc-Cloud or Trinity. They say that in very ancient times, when the McCloud were at peace with the Shaste, they sometimes went as far as the Shasta country for wives.

There were high-class and low-class Wintoon, speaking different dialects. The high-class language is nearly extinct; it was spoken by the Doctors in conversation among themselves and was not understood by the common people. Doctors are called 'kloos-tawt; the Doctors' songs are called 'klah-he-chow; to doctor a sick person is 'klah-hah. The Doctors were very smart and practiced magic; some of them were also chiefs.

The old medicine men among the Wintoon used to make and shoot tiny poison darts called nem-klas; they were about two inches long, about the size of matches. They practiced a secret method of mixing deadly poisons with which they filled or saturated these tiny darts. With one of these concealed in the hand, a medicine man would clasp his hands behind his head and then, with a sudden movement, send the dart forward to a considerable distance, with remarkable accuracy of aim.

Every spring when the redbud is in flower the Dance to the Virgins is held. It is called wi-pah' nik-kah or the "dance to womanhood." The flowers of the redbud, called el'-lep, are used for decoration, tied in bunches and fastened to the shoulders and about the waists of the young girls. During this dance a song is sung in which occurs the phrase loi'-mes

lok'-kus awl we-na (loi'-mes, "virgins"; lok'-kus, "stars"; awl, "above";
win-nā, "look"), meaning "the stars above look at the virgins."[10]

In the game of sticks and basket, called bo-hā-mah choo-hā, a number
(20 to 40) of slender sticks about the size of straws and 10 or 12 inches in
length are used. Two of them (now called aces) are blackened in the middle; the others are not marked. Formerly an elkhide robe was spread on
the ground and the sticks were placed on it; now a cloth or gunnysack is
used. The slender sticks are tied together in four parcels, which are laid
side by side a short distance apart. The two aces (the marked sticks) are
concealed in two of these bundles. In placing them, a very large circular
flattish basket is held over them to prevent the people from seeing where
the aces are located. Sides are chosen as usual and the game consists in
guessing which package contains an ace.

The Northern Wintoon say they did not burn the dead, but buried in
the ground. The grave (ke'-lok) was dug deep in sandy soil and the body
(me'-nil) was placed in it in a sitting posture, but with the legs straight
out in front, the face toward the sun. The body and also the grave were
sprinkled with water. Then the grave was filled with sandy soil, and stones
were piled on top, making a mound. After the burial, the people went to
the sweathouse and sweated, and then bathed in the river, in order to
purify themselves before going back to their homes.

On the west side of the Sacramento River there was an old burial ground
at a place called Pas'-să-ken-kaw'-de, where the Copley Trail comes down
through a cut. The burial ground was on a small flat on Flat Creek.

In the old days, the Doctors, chiefs, and other high-class people were
sometimes buried in the ceremonial houses. The graves were dug just inside the wall of the roundhouse and were placed side by side, pointing
toward the center.

It is believed that, when a person dies, his spirit or ghost, called 'kles,
leaves the body and may become a source of annoyance or danger. Indians
who have associated with whites long enough to absorb certain religious
terms say that "ghost," "devil," "evil spirit," and 'kles are one and the
same; it is significant that the Wintoon word for shadow is also 'kles.

---

[10] Stars, frequently mentioned in the "Song to the Virgins," are looked upon as emblems of purity.
Some medicine men are spoken of as "Star Doctors"; in winter they tell the Star stories and sing the
Star songs. The 7 stars of the Pleiades are regarded as sacred and deeply influence the beliefs and rites
of the Wintoon. Thus there are 7 posts that support the roof of the roundhouse, 7 great chiefs of the
tribe, etc.

A Western Wintoon Ceremony: The Big Head Dance at Grindstone Creek

―――――――――――――――――――

[Plates 1–8]

*The Wintun Big Head Dance at Grindstone and the Stony Ford Pomo ritual,
the expulsion of Sahte (described in the next paper), are two closely related
religious ceremonies witnessed and photographed by Dr. Merriam. Similar is
the Hesi performed by the Cortina Patwin and described in 1919 by Barrett.*[1]
*These are the only three detailed and illustrated accounts of a series of native
religious revivals that began with the first Ghost Dance about 1869 or 1870
in Nevada, and were followed in California successively by the Earth Lodge
cult, 1871 to 1873, the Bole-Maru movement from 1872 or 1873 to well in the
present century, and the Big Head of 1874 to 1877. The diffusion, repercus-
sions, and modifications of these revivalistic Indian cults, as they have been
traced by Cora Du Bois,*[2] *form the background of a complex history—and in-
triguing psychology—against which Merriam's and Barrett's factual descriptions stand out sharply and with added significance.*

*Both the Stony Ford rite of 1907 and the Grindstone one of 1923, as well as
Barrett's Cortina account of 1906, combine elements of Caucasian origin, such
as flags and cloth shirts and dresses, with remembrances of impersonations
taken from the purely native Kuksu cult, especially its culminating Hesi performance. From this aboriginal cult derive the cloak-covered Moki or head
ritualist, the Tuya or Big Head, and the Dado or woman spirit, who wears,
besides a cloth shirt, a "redcap" visor (originally of scarlet woodpecker scalps)*

[1] S. A. Barrett, *The Wintun Hesi Ceremony,* UC–PAAE 14:437–488, 1919.
[2] Cora Du Bois, *The 1870 Ghost Dance,* UC–AR 3:1–152, 1939.

26

and radiating feather-tipped fan headdress (pls. 3, b, 4, c, 6, c, 12 right, 13 left, 17). The Big Head, on the contrary, represents a male spirit: he is distinguished by an enormous pincushion headdress of slender rods tipped with feathers or flowers and a sort of apron of shredded bark (pls. 2, c, 3, a, 4, a, b, 6, b, 8, b, 12 middle, 13 right, 14). Still other dance personages appear in plates 5, b, 7, 10, 11, 15, and 16.—Ed.

THE BIG HEAD DANCE

This dance is a Wintoon dance; from the Sacramento divide it has traveled west to Mendocino. The Big Head, or Bull Head, Dance was danced by the Indians of the Trinity and McCloud rivers many years ago. It has been over thirty-five years since it was danced by the Northern Wintoon. The last dance they had was held at the present townsite of Redding. There is only one place in the state where it is now being performed at this late day. The Indians of Grindstone Creek Rancheria, Stony Ford, and Cortina, Glenn County, have this beautiful dance every spring (May 15) when the wild flowers of their section are in bloom.

The Big Head Dance, or Bull Head as it is called by the Indians, is a dream, war, and ghost dance combined. The dancers are actors portraying in their costume and movement of their bodies the scenes of some Doctor's or Shaman's vision or dream.

The dance is performed in sets or pairs. Each set comes into the dance house dressed in gorgeous costumes. In each hand the dancers have clapsticks made from the elder, which are used to keep time and also to attract attention. Every movement of the feet or hands and the sound of the clapsticks are in time with the sound and syllable of the song being sung.

The dancers' costumes are very elaborate and beautiful. The head is covered with a grass mat fastened over the head, and in this mat or cap are placed many slender willow sticks plumed with various colored flowers tipped with white feathers. The dress is made of the inner bark of the maple and fits somewhat like the dress of the Hawaiian native; at the side hang, closely sewed or woven together, the red feathers of the wings of a yellowhammer that are fastened to a belt made of the red scalps of the giant woodpecker. These ribbons, as I might call them, hang loosely and sway as the performers dance. In all, it is a very beautiful costume.

Various sets, wearing differently colored headgear, perform in the same manner as described before. After the Big Heads are through with their dance, there enters the Red Cap, a woman dancer representing the old woman witch or Goddess of War. She is dressed the same as the other dancers except for the headdress, which is a mask of red that covers well the upper part of the head, allowing the dancer to look out from under her mask—downward, as it were. In her hand she holds a very brilliantly colored and striped bow about four feet long. Her performance is very graceful and artistic. Every movement of her body, and the rise and fall of the bow in her hand, is to the time and cadence of the beautiful song of the singers.

As the Goddess of War waltzes backward and forward waving her scarlet bow, a youth or young man with a headgear of yellowhammer feathers, a bow in one hand and a foxskin quiver full of arrows, runs backward and forward, dancing and following the old woman or witch. The old woman is beseeching the youth or trying to make a warrior out of him. This is the most dramatic and beautiful part of this wonderful dance.

The singers are chosen from the Indians with the best voices. The songs are beautiful, soft and low with several variations. The singers keep time with a piece of white oak, large at one end and tapering at the top so as to make it easy to hold in the hands. The movement of this stick is upward and downward on a box, keeping excellent time but not loud enough to be monotonous.

In front of the dancers are what are known as helpers, Indians who dance and shout while the song and the dance go on. The songs describe each act, explaining the various acts of the dance. This is a strictly religious dance and there are several very strict rules that govern the performance. The listeners or onlookers are required to be quiet and respectful to all within the dance house. Any violator of the rules is severely dealt with by being fined or punished.

The Expulsion of Sahte: A Stony Ford Pomo Ceremony

[Plates 9–16]

The ceremonies and dance costumes of the Pueblo Indians of Arizona and New Mexico have attracted wide attention, but it is not commonly known that some of the California tribes have ceremonial practices of almost equal interest and costumes even more elaborate and strange.

In California, as in the Pueblo region, each ceremony has a definite purpose and recurs at a particular time of year. Most of them last about four days, and the performances, usually given at night, consist largely in what, for lack of a better name, we call dancing. But it should be borne in mind that, whereas our dances are for amusement, these Indian ceremonies are of a religious character and are enacted with the utmost seriousness and with scrupulous attention to details, the violation of which would be followed, they believe, by harmful consequences.

While engaged in field work among the oak-dotted valleys and chaparral-covered foothills of the Stony Creek country, west of the great Sacramento Plain, my wife and I once had the good fortune to stumble upon a midsummer ceremonial[1] of more than ordinary interest—the routing of Sahte, the Devil—and we were granted the rare privilege of photographing some of the principal performers in their extraordinary costumes. The pictures taken at that time (pls. 9–16) show far better than any words can describe the aboriginal and spectacular appearance of the actors.

The plates show the five performers in the ceremony, which ends with

---

[1] The footnotes to this paper are extracted from Dr. Merriam's California Journal, pp. 76–83. They form the basis for the account of the "Expulsion of Sahte," but include pertinent material not there incorporated. The dates of the Journal entries which describe this ceremony are July 20, 21, and 22, 1907.—Ed.

29

the expulsion of Sahte, the Evil Spirit, as enacted by members of the Sho-te'-ah tribe of Pomo Indians on the last night of the ceremonies at their roundhouse near Stony Ford.[2] In return for the unusual privilege of photographing them in the sacred costumes I promised that I would not publish the pictures during the lifetime of the performers. That was in July, 1907. The actors are now dead, the ceremonies abandoned, the costumes burned in a fire that consumed the chief's house and no duplicates exist—so I am exonerated from further secrecy.

The ceremony was held a few miles east of Snow Mountain (Nakumtil) and given jointly by remnants of two tribes, the Sho-te'-ah (or Shamen)

Fig. 1. Elevation and cross section of the dance house, Am-mah'-sha-nah.

and the Western Wintoon, and was participated in also by the Ham'-fo' Pomo of Lower Lake and Sulphur Bank, and Win from Lolsel, Chenposel, Kabalmen and Kotena, not including representatives of still others present as invited guests, who took no part in the proceedings.[3] The four participating tribes danced in turn, each completing its series before the next began. In most of the dances three or four persons took part, although the wild War Dance (see fn. 8) was danced by only two, and a singularly slow and quiet act was performed by one man alone.

The ceremonies began at noon on Saturday and continued with brief intermissions until nearly daybreak on Monday. They were held in the roundhouse (pl. 9), a nearly circular domed structure covered with brush and earth, with the floor sunken four feet below the surface, and with two low elongate entrances—a front entrance looking east and a rear one looking west. Facing each entrance was a tall flagpole bearing a white flag marked by six vertical serrate bars in red. There were no windows, the only opening in the domed roof being the smokehole, which during the

---

[2] Visited the small rancheria of Shamen (Sho-te'-ah) Indians on a chaparral knoll on the north side of Stony Creek about 2¼ mi. west of Stony Ford, Colusa Co.

[3] The invited guests are continually arriving. The guests are Wintoon Indians from Grindstone Creek on the north, Win from Kabal'men and Cortina and Rumsey on the south, and Long Valley (Loh'-sel and Chen'-po-sel) on the southwest. There are also a woman from Coyote Valley on Putah Creek (O'-lā-yo-me) tribe, and the chief and others of the Ham'-fo' or Lower Lake tribe.

greater part of the day allowed a slanting bolt of sunshine to move part-way around the dark interior. At night the only source of light was the fire, which cast a flickering glow over the actors as they moved around it in the inner circle.

The roundhouse here (pl. 9; figs. 1–3) is different from others I have seen. It occupies an excavation varying from 1½ to 4 ft. in depth, according to the lay of the ground. The vertical wall of the excavation forms the outer wall of the round-

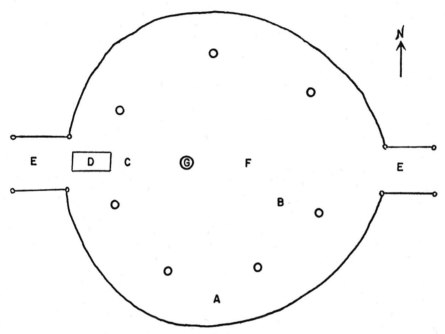

Fig. 2. Plan of the dance house. A, the outer space (for audience), ta-te'; B, the inner space (for dancers), lil-look'; C, singers' space, sa-ba-che-doo'-ah; D, the drum, chil-lo'; E, the doorways, how-wah; F, the fire, o'-ho; G, the center post, sah'-bah.

house, and is supplemented by a series of horizontal poles resting in forked posts about 4½ ft. high, on which the outer ends of the roof poles rest. These outer wall posts are called chi-ek-she-mah (fig. 3).

The center post is about 2 ft. in diameter, 18 ft. in height, and is forked at the top to receive the accumulated tips of the roof poles (fig. 3), which converge to this common center. The center post is called sah'-bah (fig. 2, G).

There are 7 posts in the circle separating the dancers from the audience—4 on the south side and 3 on the north side (fig. 2). These posts are only 5 or 6 ft. from the outer wall, giving just space enough for a person to lie down in the outer space. The 7 posts are called too-dit'-ke.

The drum is about 5 ft. long by 2½ ft. wide, its long axis agreeing with that of the roundhouse. It is of plank, elevated nearly 2 ft. in front (where highest), and 1 ft. behind. It is called chil-lo' (fig. 2, D).

The entranceways are about 4 ft. wide and 6 to 8 ft. long. They slope downward and inward from the outside level to the inside level. The doorways are called how'-wah.

The smokehole is rectangular (about 3 by 4 ft.) and is directly over the fire (between center post and east entrance). It is called o'-ho shut'-ko.

The floor is bare hard earth, swept clean and sprinkled; that of the outer circle (for the audience) is covered with fresh green willow boughs and leaves.

The long roof poles (about 34) converge to rest on the forks of the center post.

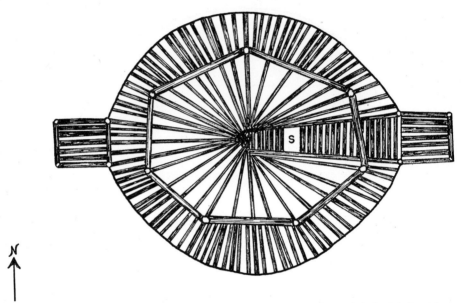

Fig. 3. Sketch plan of roof structure of dance house from below. S is the smokehole, O-ho' sut'-ko. Roof poles are called Hel'-la-ti'-ke.

On the basal part (resting on the horizontal poles which connect the tops of the circle of 7 posts) are many short poles, occupying the spaces between the spreading long roof poles. The roof poles are covered with tules and brush, making a compact thick roof, which is usually earth-covered, but here only a little earth has been put on. The roof and roof poles are called hel'-lā-ti'-ke (see fig. 3).

Outside the roundhouse and in the line of its long axis are 2 flagpoles, each about 30 ft. in height (fig. 1). The one in front of the east entrance is about 30 ft. from the outer end of the entrance; the one in the rear, 54 ft. west of the outer end of the west entrance. The inside diameter of the roundhouse (east and west), not including entranceways, is about 36 ft.; diameter, including entranceways, about 50 ft.; distance between flagpoles about 134 ft. (All distances paced.)

The two flags at the top of the flagpoles are just alike. The ground color is white. Upon it are six vertical bars of red, straight on the edge toward the pole and serrate on the edge away from the pole. The bars seemed to be about two and a half inches broad.

The dark outer circle was occupied by the onlookers, who sat or reclined on a carpet of fresh green willow boughs with their feet toward the center. Here the head chief made room for my wife and me, between himself and the widow of the chief of a neighboring tribe—which place we held till the end.

When ready for each performance, the actors assembled near the east flagpole, whence at a signal from the inside they ran through the low entrance and formed on the north side of the cleanly swept and sprinkled inner space, beating time by striking the hard ground vigorously with their bare feet[4] and singing or blowing low musical strains on their bone whistles—slender hollow bones of the wild goose or the golden eagle, which they held in the mouth and blew gently, producing a pleasing and harmonious chorus of sounds. Besides those of the dancers who sang, there were several special singers who, stationed between the drum and center post, sang and beat time with clappersticks of the sacred elderberry wood while the dances were progressing.[5] The time and rhythm of the dancing were perfect; the singing was weird and full of melody.

At intervals the old chief of a distant tribe, the Ham'-fo' of Sulphur Bank, climbed the low roof of the long east entrance and sang a sort of chant, accompanied by the measured shaking of a pair of feather-covered double-headed rattles, held one in each hand.[6] Shaking his wrists to vibrate the rattles, he raised his arms slowly above his head, brought them against the sides of his chest, thrust them horizontally forward to full length, and carried them down along his thighs. At break of day he sang his chant to the rising sun, then turned and seemed to harangue the people in the roundhouse. Before descending he again faced the sun, now risen above the eastern hills, and sang another chant, with the rattle accompaniment as before.

As a rule each tribe had its own set of costumes, differing materially from those of the other tribes; usually they were changed with the dances, but in a few instances the same one appeared several times. They consisted chiefly of feathers, which with surprising ingenuity were wrought into aprons, back-pieces, girdles, belts, collars, headbands, and headdresses. The headdresses, like the hats of some of our women, were truly marvelous creations—some, indeed, actually startling—as can be seen from the pictures (pls. 10–16).

---

[4] The dancers also sang and beat time with their bare feet. The head dancer struck the ground furiously with his feet, and kept it up so long each dance that one was amazed that a human being could stand so much strain and jarring, not to mention the physical endurance necessary.

[5] Throughout all the dances the singers stood at the end of the plank drum (between the drum and center post) and sang and beat time with the elder clappersticks, while the drummer stood on the raised plank and beat it with the big end of a thick manzanita club ($2\frac{1}{2}$ in. in diam.), pounding straight down (instead of beating with his feet).

[6] All of the dancers carried something in their hands—rattles, wands, feather tridents, or bows and arrows.

Most of the dancers were naked except for breechcloth, feather belt, and headdress, though a few had skirts or aprons and the flag dancer and one other wore robes that completely covered their bodies. The feather belts, some of which are shown in the plates, were six or eight inches wide and of varied patterns worked in brilliant colors—red from the crown of the California woodpecker, yellow from the breast of the meadowlark, blue from the back of the California bluejay, and green from the neck of the mallard duck. Some were made of skins of heads of the California wood-pecker arranged in squares, with the bills attached, but most of them were of closely woven fibers of milkweed or Indian hemp with the individual feathers tightly bound in so that only the colored tips projected, as in the

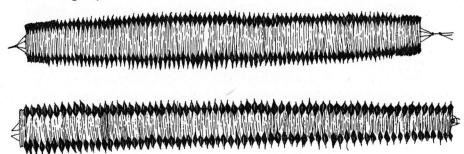

Fig. 4. Flicker-feather headbands.

well-known feather baskets. Great skill and patience as well as time are required in their manufacture, and they are valued accordingly.

Several of the men wore splendid broad red ribbons made of a multitude of the glistening red quills of the California red-shafted flicker (*Colaptes cafer collaris*), evenly trimmed, with the black pointed tail tips projecting on both sides so as to form peculiarly handsome borders (see fig. 4). The flicker ribbons were of three kinds: short ones, about two feet in length and of equal breadth throughout, worn across the forehead with the free ends meeting in front or curving behind according to the position of the head; longer ones, broadest in the middle and worn as belts; and still longer ones, often five feet or more in length, attached to the back of the head and hanging loosely down the back. They were in themselves ex-ceedingly beautiful and, when waving in graceful undulating curves with the movements of the dancers, produced truly gorgeous effects.

The head dancer (pls. 10–13) had on his head a frontal band of the red flicker feathers, a closely fitting skullcap of white down, three snow-white feather tridents, and an occipital piece of black feathers with a few white ones protruding, from which dangled several bits of abalone and small red quill pendants. Lying loosely against his dark skin, sometimes on the breast, sometimes between the shoulders, were two wing feathers of the broad-winged hawk suspended from a cord around the neck—the cord concealed by a handsome necklace. Encircling his waist and overlapping the red breechcloth was a broad and richly colored feather belt; tucked under it in back hung the skin of a gray fox (*Urocyon*), tail down. In his right hand he carried a full quiver made of the skin of a red fox; in his left a strung bow and two loose arrows (pl. 11). In some of the performances the red breechcloth was exchanged for a black one, while a new feather belt gave a different combination of colors.

Three of the actors (pls. 12–14) had headdresses of surprising originality and extravagant proportions, consisting of a mass of white feathers stuck full of slender plume-bearing rods which stood out so far that the wearer could not pass through an ordinary doorway.[7] The plume tips of two head-dresses were white with a few red ones intermixed; in the third, that of the flag dancer, they were red and blue. Most of the dancers had the back of the head covered with a large occipital piece of dark feathers, from which the red flicker ribbons hung down.

The flag dancer (pl. 15, *a*) was clad in a loose robe or tunic of white, orna-mented by vertical chains of diamond-shaped markings in greenish blue arranged in regular series, held in around the waist by a broad feather belt of woodpecker heads alternating with areas of inset feathers. His headdress was of a rod-and-plume style with a pair of red flicker ribbons trailing down his back; and he carried in each hand a white flag marked with serrate bands of blue.

One of the most striking figures was that of a little man in an aboriginal skirt composed entirely of strips of soft wavy inner bark of the California maple (*Acer macrophyllum*) the dangling strands of which, rubbing to-gether as he moved, made a low swishing sound (pls. 12, 13). The top of the skirt was hidden in a broad snowy white girdle of large feathers of the snow goose, supplemented by collar and wristlets of the same material, an elegant rod-and-plume headdress, and two pairs of red flicker ribbons, the free ends of which were looped up to the sides of his belt. In his hands he carried a pair of musical clappersticks of the sacred elderberry wood.

The head chief (pl. 15, *b*), a well-built and rather heavy man with the most beautiful glossy skin I ever saw, held in his left hand a strung bow, in his right a handful of loose arrows. He was dressed in a handsome feather belt and red breechcloth and on either side of each knee had a large square red spot. His head was adorned with a red flicker frontal band, two white

---

[7] Some of them wore headdresses of feathers stuck full of slender rods about 2 ft. long, each having one or more tufts or plumes of red and white feathers, so that the diameter of the headdress is fully 4 ft.—so great that the wearer cannot get through the entranceway of the roundhouse except by backing in with head bowed, so as to bring the rods in base first (pls. 12–16). Only 2 dancers wore robes—most curious affairs. One wore a red skirt, with white border and zigzag decoration at the bottom.

tridents, and the usual occipital piece with three orange tassels attached, while a rich necklace of brilliant abalone pendants served to heighten the color of his broad, handsome chest.

Perhaps the most fantastic of all the costumes was that of Sahte (pls. 12, 13, 16), an aboriginal Deity who, it is believed, became the evil spirit and was finally banished from the country. Sahte was clad in a short yellow skirt with two red bands at the bottom, a broad feather belt, a white collar of stiff projecting feathers of the snow goose, the usual occipital piece, four red flicker ribbons, a curious bonnet turned down at the sides and surmounted behind by a huge fan-shaped framework of slender pink rods, each of the twelve diverging rays of which carried a similarly colored goose feather. The side hair fell in long locks over the otherwise naked breast, while thrust horizontally through the coiled back hair was a straight smooth stick about fourteen inches in length—the most ancient style of hairpin known to the Indians of California. In the long, long ago this magic hairpin, according to the creation myth, was used by Sahte to set fire to the world.

During the act in which this evil genius figured the head dancer repeatedly came close, as if drawn by some irresistible charm, gazed intently into Sahte's face, and then with dramatic effect shook his head, turned quickly about, and ran away. The scene closed with the expulsion of Sahte.[8]

From first to last I was impressed by the intense earnestness of the actors, each straining every nerve to play his part without slip of omission or commission, each seeming to gain inspiration from the appreciative enthusiasm of the audience.

To be permitted to join the eager Indian onlookers in the dark outer

---

[8] Under the Journal entry for July 22 is the description of another dance, not mentioned in the previous account.—Ed.

July 22. The Indians went home today—those visiting Stony Ford for the ceremonies.

The ceremony last night was full of interest and different from the others. The Stony Ford Sho-te'-ah (or Shamen) tribe danced. The chief (San Diego) and two other men and two women danced strange and weird dances, one of which was wild and fierce. This last very oldtime dance (War Dance) is called Kek'-o-de by the Stony Ford tribe, and Hin'-te-lak'-ke by the Putah Creek Ola-layome. They say it is the oldest and most ancient of all the dances.

The men were naked except for the headdress and breechcloth, and the Golden Eagle aprons two of them wore. The suits of eagle feathers had three long plumes standing up against the back—one in the middle and one on each side—and a full apron of eagle plumes worn over the buttocks and hanging down behind (only the breechcloth in front). Each man wore a red flicker band on his forehead, the long projecting sides flapping, and each carried a trident of three white plumes which he held outstretched in front, or depressed to the ground, with muscles rigid while he danced and stamped and leaped about violently, often crouching. They danced around the fire and also around the center post. They blew bone whistles. The two dancing women kept on the north side. They wore beautiful feather headbands and belts, and each held a colored handkerchief in her hands as they stood side by side and beat time with their feet, swaying their bodies to and fro and singing.

The man on the drum beat time with his manzanita club, and three men standing at the end of the drum sang and beat time with the split elderberry clapper sticks. The singing was particularly fine.

circle of the roundhouse, listening to a symphony of strange and weird music—a harmonious blending of the measured beating of the drum, the rhythmic stamping of the feet, the tuneful play of the bone whistles, and the rich melody of the voices trained to songs foreign to our ears—while the ancient ceremonies were being enacted only a few feet away by fantastically attired actors, intermittently illumined by the fitful glow of the fire, was indeed a rare privilege, and one which is daily growing rarer, for in the very near future these aboriginal observances will have disappeared completely from the earth.

The Yokiah Pomo:
Miscellaneous Notes[1]

The word Pomo means "red clay," a substance much prized by several divisions of the tribe; ordinary earth or ground is called mah. This red clay was mined by the aborigines and there is a mine of this kind in Potter Valley, another in Lā'-mah Valley (called Lema by the whites). The red clay was used chiefly for mixing with acorn flour to make acorn bread. It was dissolved in water and the finely ground acorn flour was mixed with it, giving the bread a flavor and a color desired by the Indians.

There is a red mountain east or southeast of Ukiah called Mah-ke-sit-tildan'-no, meaning "red eastern mountain." The ordinary word for "red" is tahs, but "red earth" is mah-ke'-sil. The term ke'-sil is not applied to any red except red earth.

The Yokiah built small brush blinds called p'sh-ah-chah close to small springs in order to shoot with bow and arrow such animals and birds as came to drink. One of their men in this way killed seventy-five California woodpeckers in one day.

The sling for throwing stones is called um'-she'-uk; it consists of a small piece of buckskin attached to a cord of sinew or plant fiber. Curiously enough the same term applied to a plant means "wilted."

Snares were used for catching birds and animals. The bird snare is tahm-nahm; the deer snare bă-de'-uk. Usually several deer snares were set near together. They were made of Indian rope and were very strong; so strong, we are told, that they sometimes caught and held bears. The act of snaring was called um'nahm'.

---

[1] Information from Stephen Knight.

Acorns and other kinds of food were kept in very large storehouse baskets called e-tēt, which stood on a low scaffold called ho'-chom. The acorn
leach is called sh'ā-oo-mo; the act of filtering acorn meal, sh'ā-oo.

Nets called yet were used, as well as the large carrying baskets worn on
the back. The nets were carried in the hand or hung by the side.

In years of scarcity of food toasted grasshoppers were eaten. Grass fires
were set in large circles and, as the fire burned toward the center, the
grasshoppers' wings were singed so that they dropped into the burning
grass and were slightly roasted.

The word for ashes is no, but the word for the falling of ashes and
burned leaves from a large fire is no'-te (from no, "ashes," and te, the
small woolly feathers of birds, commonly known as "down"). The Yokiah
appear to have no specific word for hungry. They say "Mah-ah chum-
dahl'," meaning "I am dying for food."

Pipes were called sak-kah' kah'be. They were straight and made of the
wood of an ash tree. Tobacco was not cultivated. Wild tobacco was called
sak-kah'. It was usually carried in weaselskin bags called sak-kah ho'-lah,
meaning "tobacco sack."

In the early days the men had blankets called steet', made of the skins
of cottontail rabbits. The women wore deerskin robes called pe-shě' kā-
too. Deer skins were tanned to make them soft, but the hair was not removed. Such tanned deer skins with the hair on were called shěs'-te.

Moccasins were not worn by either men or women. There were no hats.

No belts were worn except for ceremonies and dances. There were two
kinds—a bead belt called nah-kaht' and a belt called sh'boo', finely woven
and decorated with red feathers of the woodpecker's head and quail
plumes. These were very costly and were worn only by the rich.

Ear pendants, called smah'-che'-ah kol-le ("ear run through, to do
with") were worn on occasion. They were of curious construction, consisting of the finely carved or engraved leg or wing bone (5 or 6 in. long) of a
large bird, usually the turkey buzzard. They were decorated at both ends
with quail plumes and tufts of bright red feathers from the crown of the
California woodpecker. They were suspended horizontally from a hole in
the lobe of the ear.

The women tattooed their faces with three straight lines, one descending
vertically from the middle of the lower lip to the chin, the two others running out diagonally from each angle of the mouth. These marks were
called oo'-e-che'. There was no tattooing on the body or arms. The material used for tattooing was juice from green oak galls. After this juice
had been put in the scarified lines to produce the desired color, poison oak
was rubbed in to make the cuts sore so that the markings would be more
distinct.

The dead were burned, not buried. The dead person, called chah kah-low', was wrapped in his best and most valuable skins and wampum. An excavation, called chah ho'mo ("person's fire hole") was dug and the wood for the funeral pyre was arranged in it. The burning of a dead person is called chah ho'-nā-o. The mourning ceremony at the time of the burning is Ho,chah moo-low, meaning "fire, persons go around"—in reference to the mourning relatives going around in a circle.

The spirit or ghost of the dead person is known by two names, koo'-yah and chah' doo-wel. The ghosts remain on earth. The burned bones and ashes of the dead, called chah yah ("person's bones") are not preserved in a basket or otherwise. After burning the body, the mother and sisters rub ashes of the burned person on their faces, but the widow is not required by the Yokiah law to do this.

The regular word for unhappy is mah-tsōts'-mahn; but if a person, usually a child, has been scolded, the word for his unhappiness is mah-tsā'-ge-doo.

In the old days there were certain people or secret societies called Yum'-tah or Yom-tah. Usually there was only one in a tribe, sometimes one in several neighboring villages. This person knew the sacred ceremonial songs of the cult. There is still an old Yokiah woman who is acquainted with some of these secret formulas but will not tell them even to an Indian of her own tribe.

Fifty or sixty years ago (date forgotten) a new religion was brought in from the east and extended as far west as Stony Ford, at the base of the inner Coast Range in Colusa County. Where it came from is not positively known, but it is said to have come from the Sioux chief, Sitting Bull. During its prevalence the Doctors who preached it said that a terrible wind was coming—a wind so strong and violent that it would destroy all living things—and that the only way to avoid it was to dig underground refuges. Under their direction large sweathouses, about fifty feet in diameter and ten feet in depth, were dug in the ground, the roof being laid flush with the ground. The sweathouses were entered by means of a tunnel thirty or forty feet long, which sloped gradually from the surface of the earth to the floor level of the sweathouse. The religion taught by these Dream Doctors was a fake religion and had nothing to do with the original religion of the people.

In the genuine Ghost Dance (called Koo'-yak-ke) the old chiefs used to meet together in one of the ceremonial houses. It was their custom to smoke four times before saying a word so that they would have time to think before speaking. In trivial matters they spoke quickly but when they were discussing serious or religious matters they spoke with great deliberation.

YOKIAH POMO BUILDINGS

The old-time community houses of the Yokiah, called chah, were circular and stood on top of the ground; the ground was not excavated. The houses were made of long willow sticks thatched with straw. The sticks were set in the ground with the tops incurved so as to form a large domed structure, with a large opening in the center which was not roofed over.

The houses were large, some of them forty to fifty feet in diameter. A number of families, usually relatives, occupied the house; from seven to twelve families usually lived in each house. Each family had a small fire for its individual cooking, and each had an entrance of its own.

The large circular area in the center was used for community cooking, as well as for making acorn mush and bread and roasting meat. The acorn mush was cooked in baskets by means of hot stones in the usual manner; the acorn bread was baked in ground ovens, the meal or flour being mixed with red-clay water to give it flavor and color.

A few years ago one of these community houses was still standing at Shă-nel (Hopland).

The large ceremonial houses were called shah'-ne; the sweathouses ho shah'-nĕ. They were similar in many respects. Both were circular and domed; both were excavated to a depth of three or four feet; both had a single doorway, a large center pole, and a fire between the center pole and the door. The roofs of both were supported by either six or eight posts (informant was not sure which) and were covered with brush overspread with earth.

The ceremonial houses were very large—about sixty or seventy feet in diameter—big enough to hold several hundred people. In addition to the doorway and smoke hole, they had small openings around the sides for ventilation. The door, if the informant remembers correctly, was on the south side. The hollow drum-log was suspended over an excavation by means of stout buckskin ropes from four posts so that no part of it touched the ground. It was near the back side of the house, opposite the doorway.

The sweathouse, which in most respects was similar to the ceremonial house, was smaller, though still large enough to accommodate forty or fifty people at a time. The door was on the east or the west side; the informant thinks usually the east.

It was the custom of the men to go to these houses twice a day, morning and evening. Each man carried a log or an armful of sticks for the large fire. The heat soon became very intense. When the men had stood it as long as they could, they ran out, lay on the ground awhile to cool off, and then plunged into the river.

The men were divided in two parties or sides—one on the north, the other on the south. This division is hereditary, not optional, and is of deep significance, suggesting the curious division of the southern Mewuk into similar sides.

While the men are lying on the ground in the heat of the sweathouse, a man from each side, provided with a pole to which is attached a deerskin or blanket, steps to the other side and fans the heat against his opponents, the effort being to make the place so hot that it cannot be endured. When a man runs out, unable to stand it any longer, his side is declared vanquished, the other side the winners.

Women did not go to the sweathouses.

The Tuleyome

WITH SPECIAL REFERENCE TO THE LOKNOMAH (MEWAN STOCK)

Grouped around Mt. St. Helena within a radius of a dozen miles from its broad summit and only sixty miles north of San Francisco are Indians belonging to four linguistic stocks—Pomoan, Mewan, Yukean, and Wintoon.

The mountain itself lies wholly in the territory of the Miyahk′mah division (commonly called "Wappo") of the Yukean stock, though on the north and northeast the Lōk-nō′-mah[1] band of Tu′leyo′me—a tribe of Mewan stock—encroaches upon its basal slopes. The Miyahk′mah, as is well known, comprise three bands or subtribes: the Misha′wal of Alexander Valley; the Moo′tistool′ of Knights Valley, and the Miyahk′mah proper of the upper two-thirds of Napa Valley.

A supposed fourth division, the Lōk-nō′-mah, has been claimed by some authors.[2] But Lōknō′mah is not a Yukean band; it is merely the Yukean Miyahk′mah name for the Middletown and Dry Creek Valley band of Mewan Tu′leyo′me. This was told me twenty-seven years ago by old men of both Tu′leyo′me and Miyahk′mah tribes, and has since been verified repeatedly by several headmen of the Tu′leyo′me tribe, including old Salvador Chapo, his grandson John Sebastian, Henry Knight, and others. The fact is that although the Tu′leyo′me name for Middletown Valley is Lah-ki′ yome, most of the few survivors of the tribe have adopted the Miyahk′mah name, Lōknō′mah.

[1] C. H. Merriam, "Distribution and Classification of the Mewan Stock of California," AA, n.s., 9:338–357, 1907; the Loknomah, p. 353.
[2] S. A. Barrett, *Ethno-geography of the Pomo*, UC–PAAE 6:273, 1908; A. L. Kroeber, *Handbook of the Indians of California*, BAE–B 78, p. 219, 1925.

43

Four years ago I asked the old Miyahk'mah chief, Joe McCloud, what his people call the Middletown tribe. He replied, "Lōk-nō'-mah, E, Lōk-nō'-mah" (meaning, "Lōknō'mah, yes, Lōknō'mah"), thus reaffirming his former statement and adding that both his people and the Middletown people use the same name for Middletown Valley and its people. He stated further that the Lōknō'mah Indians were the same as the Coyote Valley Indians (Olayome band of Tu'leyo'me), speaking a language wholly different from that of his people. I then inquired about the boundary between his people (the Miyahk'mah) and the Lōknō'mah, and he located it precisely as it had been previously located for me by the Lōknō'mah and Olayome bands of Tu'leyo'me.

Lōknō'mah was the ruling village of Middletown and Dry Creek valleys and is said to have been situated on ground now covered by the northern part of Middletown. Its full name in their own language (Tu'-leyo'me) is Lōknō'ma yo'me poo'goot, with ko added for the inhabitants.[3] In the Miyahk'mah language the word for village is no'-mah, the village name becoming Lōk-nō'-mah no'-mah, and the full tribal name Lōk-nō'-mah no'-man-nok—the last syllable, added to the word for village, being the word for tribe.

Since the name Lōk-nō'-mah is in the Miyahk'mah language, one wonders why it was adopted by the Middletown Tu'leyo'me. The reason would appear to be that the two tribes were in contact immediately south of Middletown and that both were familiar with both names. And some of the Tu'leyo'me Indians still call Middletown Valley by their own name, Lah-ki' yome, after their village Lah-ki' yome poo-goot (from Lah'-kah, "goose," yome, "home place," and poo-goot, "village"), for both names mean the same thing, "goose valley village."[4]

A century ago the Mission *padres* were familiar with the name Lōknō-ma, for it appears in the Sonoma Mission books of 1824–1837, though always without information as to locality or tribal relations. And in recent times Fr. Zephyrin Engelhardt, in specifying the tribes formerly at Sonoma Mission, includes both "Locnoma" and "Loaquioni" (Lah-ki'-yome) but, like the Mission books, gives no reference or other information.[5]

The earliest mention of the name subsequent to Mission times, so far as known to me, was by Mariano G. Vallejo, who, in enumerating the several

[3] The word Lōk-nō'-mah means "goose valley"; yo'me, "home" ("home place"); poo'-goot, "rancheria" or "village"; ko, "people." So a literal translation would be "goose valley home village people." Strictly, the word poo'-goot means the mound or little hill on which a rancheria stands, but in common usage it means the rancheria itself.

[4] The location of Lah-ki' yome poo-goot was given me as on a small creek a short mile east o. Middletown—the creek flowing northwest to enter St. Helena Creek about a mile north of Middletown.

[5] Z. Engelhardt, *The Franciscans in California*, p. 451, 1897.

tribes and bands attacked and massacred by his brother, the brutal Salvador Vallejo, during his raid on Clear Lake Indians in March, 1843, specifically mentions the "Tuliyomi,"[6] but fails as usual to say just where they were encountered.

In the early 'seventies Stephen Powers learned that a tribe speaking a language different from its neighbors had formerly lived in Coyote and Pope valleys, but did not succeed in finding out who they were.[7]

It remained for S. A. Barrett to discover that the Indians in these valleys belonged to the Mewan stock. This he announced at the close of the year 1903,[8] but he gave no name to the tribe or to any of its villages. Five years later, however, in his highly important volume, *The Ethno-geography of the Pomo,* he indicated the boundaries of the tribe and located eight village sites, one of which, Tuleyome, is in what he calls the Lower Lake Division; another, Oleyome, in the Putah Creek Division. In neither case was particular stress laid on the name, and no name was proposed for the tribe as a whole other than "Northern Dialect, Moquelumnan."[9]

While working with this tribe in August, 1905, three years before the appearance of Barrett's volume, I obtained the names and localities of their principal divisions and of thirteen of their villages,[10] and secured also some very interesting myths, published in 1910.[11] At that time and during subsequent visits it was ascertained that the tribe had no generally accepted name for itself but consisted of two principal divisions, each named from a ruling village: Tuleyome po-koot and O-la-yome po-koot.

Tuleyome po-koot is in a small valley (Excelsior Valley of the whites) about three miles south of the town of Lower Lake; Olayome po-koot is in Coyote Valley six or eight miles northeast of Middletown. Tuleyome is the most ancient settlement of the tribe and the seat of the major part of their mythology. Its people were the ones attacked by Salvador Vallejo in 1843, and its name is the one most often mentioned by the survivors as the proper designation for the tribe as a whole.

Another name sometimes applied to the Coyote Valley band of Tuleyome (Olā'yo'me) is "Guenock." In 1860, Alexander Taylor, in his "Indianology" (a series of newspaper articles on California Indians) mentioned the "Guenocks" of Coyote Valley but had no knowledge of their relationships.[12] Twenty-one years afterward L. L. Palmer remarked: "The

[6] M. G. Vallejo, MS, Doc. XI, p. 354, quoted by H. H. Bancroft, *History of California*, 4:362–363 (fn.), 1886.

[7] *Tribes of California*, p. 218, 1877.

[8] "A New Moquelumnan Territory in California," AA, n.s., 5:730, 1903.

[9] S. A. Barrett, *Ethno-geography of the Pomo*, pp. 314–318.

[10] C. H. Merriam, "Distribution and Classification of the Mewan Stock," pp. 352–353.

[11] C. H. Merriam, *The Dawn of the World: Myths and Weird Tales of the Mewan Indians of California*, pp. 138–151, 212–214, 1910.

[12] *California Farmer* (March 30), Vol. 13, No. 7, 1860.

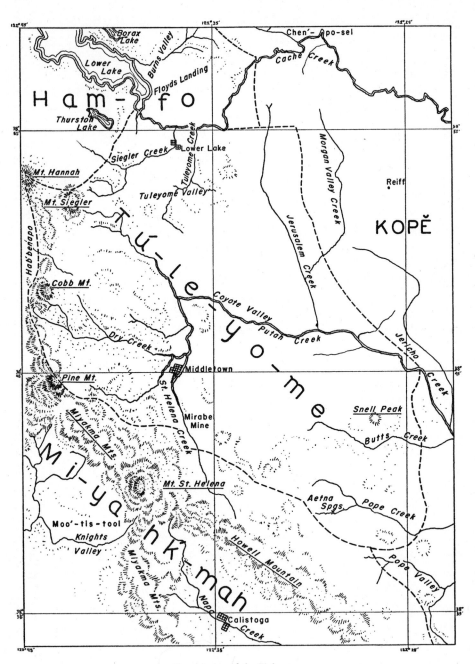

Boundaries of the Tuleyome

Guenocks had their home in the valley of that name in Lake Co."[13] And much more recently Kroeber mentions Guenoc as an Indian place name, "but unidentified."[14]

Guenock is the white man's name of a ford and abandoned postoffice on Putah Creek in Coyote Valley, and also is locally applied both to the valley and to the native Indians—as I have been told repeatedly by neighboring ranchers.

There has been some discussion of the origin of the name. Barrett was right in considering it not Spanish, but wrong in thinking it was never used by the Indians themselves.[15] It is merely a rendering in Spanish of the native Indian term wen'-nok—their name for a picturesque little valley encircling a small lake in the hills six miles due east of Middletown. The place was a famous winter resort for geese and ducks, and the lake abounded in fish—suckers, catfish, minnows, and "pike" of two kinds, large and small. Trout also were mentioned, but I am not sure that they were from this lake. Because of the good hunting and fishing there, the valley was important enough to contain three "villages." These were Kā-boot'-poo-goot, on a knoll or low point east of the north end of Wennok Lake; Sahl'-sahl poogoot, on a small flat on the southeast border of the lake at the base of Cone Peak (Loo-peek' powwe); and Hawl'-hawl poo-goot, on the outlet only a short distance below the lake. This last, which may have been only a winter camp, owes its name to the fish trap, hawl'-hawl, a long cylindrical wickerwork basket which, in winter, the Indians used to set in the near-by outlet to catch fish.[16]

BOUNDARIES AND NEIGHBORS OF THE TU'LEYO'ME

The Tu'leyo'me occupy a rather small area between Mt. St. Helena and Lower Lake (southern arm of Clear Lake) in the mountainous region known as the Coast Ranges of northern California, and are entirely surrounded by tribes speaking widely different languages. They are the most northerly group of Mewan stock and are completely isolated from other tribes of the stock—as pointed out by Barrett in 1903.

Starting from Mt. Hannah (locally known as Bogs Mountain), the western boundary of Tu'leyo'me territory runs south to Cobb Mountain; thence it turns southeast and, becoming the southwestern boundary, passes just east of Pine Mountain Flat and south of Helena Mine, crossing

[13] *History of Napa and Lake Counties, California*, p. 45 (Slocum, Bowen and Co., San Francisco), 1881.

[14] *Handbook*, p. 895, 1925.

[15] *Ethno-geography of the Pomo*, p. 317.

[16] C. H. Merriam, "Distribution and Classification of the Mewan Stock," pp. 352, 353.

St. Helena Creek about a mile south of the old Mirabel Mine and continuing in the same direction, passing a little south of Oat Hill and Aetna Springs to the northwestern part of Pope Valley.

The northern boundary runs east from Mt. Hannah to Mt. Siegler and thence northeast to the southern extremity of Lower Lake, thence east along the south side of Cache Creek and beyond to the dividing ridge between Jerusalem Creek and Morgan Valley Creek, where it turns abruptly south to become the east boundary.

The eastern boundary runs southeast along the ridge beyond Jerusalem Valley for ten or eleven miles to a point just west of Devils Head where, apparently following the west side of Putah Creek for two or three miles, it turns almost due south to the northern part of Pope Valley—a distance of about seven miles—where it meets the southwestern boundary already described.

The intertribal boundary between the Mewan Lōk-nō′-mah and the Yukean Miyahk′mah, as told me in complete agreement by headmen of both tribes, begins at the summit of Cobb Mountain, runs south and southeast to the east side of Pine Flat or Mountain (thus enclosing the whole of Dry Creek and its headwaters); then, turning southeast, it passes just south of the Chicago and Helena mines and continues to St. Helena Creek, which it crosses at the head of Mirabel Valley (a little more than a mile south of the old mine); continuing in the same general direction, it passes a little southwest of Oat Hill and Aetna Springs to the northwest part of Pope Valley, where the territory of the Tu′leyo′me comes to an end.

The neighbors of the Tu′leyo′me tribe are as follows: on the northwest, north of Cobb Mountain, the Pomoan Hab′-be nap′-po; on the north, the Pomoan Ham′-fo; on the northeast, east, and southeast (in Morgan, Pope, and Berryessa valleys), bands of foothills Wintoon; on the west, the Yukean Miyahk′mah.

The Mourning Ceremony or Cry of the Mewuk

[Plate 17]

This is an account of a four-day ceremony of the Miwok taken from notes and an incomplete manuscript of Dr. Merriam. The sequence of ceremonies described below is as follows: the nights of October 9 and 10, the Yum'-meh, or Nah'-choo-wah (mourning or "cry") ceremony; the morning of October 11, the Mo-lah-gum'-sip (washing) ceremony; the night of October 11, the Kal-lā-ah (fandango or Acorn Dance) rite; the night of October 12, the Wok'-ke-lā (War Dance).—Ed.

THE MOURNING CEREMONY AT RAILROAD FLAT, 1906

During the nights of October 9 and 10, 1906, and the morning of the eleventh I had the good fortune to witness, in its entirety, the Yum'-meh or Yum'-me, the mourning ceremony of the Mewuk (Me'-wuk). It was held at Hā'-cha-nah (called by the whites Railroad Flat, after an abandoned mine), in the lower part of the yellow pine belt in Calaveras County, California.

I reached the place the night before the ceremony began—in time to witness the preparations[1] and see the guests arrive.

---

[1] The following account by Dr. Merriam describes preparations for a "cry."—Ed.

On Sept. 17, 1905, while sitting talking with the chief at West Point at his place I saw an old man from Railroad Flat ride up and dismount and walk straight to the rear of the "roundhouse" where an old woman had died two or three weeks ago. The chief told me to listen, as the old man had come to cry. I looked at my watch; it was four o'clock. The old man began in a low voice a low wailing howl, not unlike the wailing of a small dog, only much lower. As he cried, he put his arm around the daughter

49

The resident Indians and those from the neighboring rancheria at West Point were camped around the ceremonial house—or "roundhouse"—in temporary brush shelters of fresh green manzanita and oak boughs.

The ceremonial house, called hang'-e by the Mewuk, is a circular structure of variable size but usually about 40 ft. in diameter. It consists of a single chamber formed by an enclosing wall of vertical boards or slabs 5 or 6 ft. high, with a high conical roof supported from the inside by 4 tall posts, arranged in the form of a square, which serve to define an open central area, thus dividing the interior into an inner and an outer space. During the ceremonies and dances the performers occupy the smaller inner space, called kal-loo'-tah, the spectators the larger outer space, called et-chat'. The fireplace is in the center of the floor, and over it, in the peak of the conical roof, is a circular hole for the escape of the smoke. The door fronts the north or northeast.

Formerly the ceremonial house was partly underground and its roof was domed and covered with earth. In the Mewuk territory this type is now rare and is replaced by the conical structure here described. The modern form is easier to build and appears to be borrowed from the Ne'-se-non tribe on the north.

Two of the resident women took forty dollars' worth of gold dust, obtained by washing the river gravels, to the nearest store and traded it for flour, sugar, tea, coffee, and crackers.

On the morning of the ninth a small group of women went to the hung-oi'-yah—the place where the acorn flour is leached and the mush cooked—kindled a fire of manzanita wood, and covered it with stones to be heated. The acorn flour was put on the circular leaches, of which there were two, each about four feet in diameter, and warm water was poured on till the bitter was washed out. It was then cooked in large baskets by means of hot stones, in the usual way. (See pl. 17.) Enough was made to fill four large and several small baskets.[2] The large ones held from one to two

---

of the dead woman and patted her on the back. After keeping this up at intervals for half an hour, always in the same low key, he came over to us and handed the chief a milkweed cord about 10 inches long, knotted with 7 knots, indicating the number of days before a mourning ceremony (commonly called the "cry") would be held at his place at Railroad Flat. The chief must untie one knot every day; when the last one was untied, he would know it was time to go to the cry. The old man had a number of these strings and gave one to the headman of each Indian village.

The daughter of the dead woman—a young woman about twenty-two—had painted a red mark on each cheek.

The "cry" for the old woman probably began Sept. 24. I was not there, but Ed McLeod, who visited the place while the Indians were gathering, told me that they had hollowed out a manzanita bush near one of the houses as a receptacle for gifts for the dead. They had cut out the middle part of the manzanita and stiffened the outer branches by interlacing with splints and sticks and had put a binding around the outside, leaving a large cavity. Into this had been placed the clothing and other presents brought by the mourners to be burned.

[2] Only a few of the baskets in which the mush was cooked and served were made by the Mewuk; the greater number were Ne'-se-non, including a large, handsome one decorated with the han'-pi bo'-no-ho design. Two were Washoo, from across the mountains. One of these, a fine big one, was used more than all the others for the cooking.

bushels each, so the total quantity was considerable—and more was cooked each day for three days. Two kinds were made—the thin porridge called oo-lā', and the thick mush called nu'-pah, which jellies when cold.

The women who were not engaged in making the acorn mush were busy all day baking bread and preparing other food for the expected guests; and in the afternoon the men killed a beef and cut it up. Most of it was cut into strips.

For several hours the young men were occupied cutting and carrying into the ceremonial house armfuls of pine boughs, from which the old people inside tore off the tufts of long needles and scattered them over the earth floor until it was completely and thickly covered with the fresh green needles, filling the house with the welcome fragrance of the pines.

The guests began to arrive on the afternoon of the ninth. They came from the rancherias at or near Oleta, Mokelumne Hill, San Andreas, Sheep Ranch, Murphys, and one family from as far south as Bald Rock near Soulsbyville. As they arrived, they were housed in the ceremonial house, where most of them took places on the west side. Baskets of bread and acorn mush and vessels of tea and coffee were carried into the cere-monial house by the resident women and set before them. This was done not only when the guests arrived, but also three times a day during the four following days. All meals for the visitors were served inside the cere-monial house; but all food, except the meat, was cooked outside. The beef was distributed raw in strips, and the guests broiled theirs on the coals inside.

When eating the oo-lā', the thin mush or porridge, three or four persons sat on the ground around each basket and ate it by dipping their fingers into it, the thumb folded back out of the way, the other fingers collectively making a sort of spatula which was turned in the porridge, rotated when lifted out, and thrust into the mouth.

First Night: The Yum'-meh Ceremony

The ceremony began before it was quite dark, about six o'clock, and lasted an hour and a half, when it was followed by sermons or harangues from the principal chiefs. The head chief of the tribe, a very old and rather feeble man known to the whites as "MacKenzie," officiated as master of ceremonies. He sat on the ground at the foot of the southwest post, which position he retained as his station throughout the ceremony. At the begin-ning the principal mourners, called naw'-chet-took and loo'-wah-zuk, were seated in a semicircle on the west side. When all was ready, the old chief spoke a few sentences that I did not understand, whereupon the mourners, without rising, immediately began to mourn and wail. In a few minutes the old chief arose, carrying a long staff in his right hand, entered the inner space, and began a slow march around the fire, taking very short trotting steps and uttering a prolonged sad cry in musical cadence, in which the others joined. The words most often repeated were, "Hā-hā-hā-yah, hā-hā-hā-yah," pronounced simultaneously and in perfect time by all. Some of the women mourners—the number varied from four to seven—now arose and followed the old chief in single file. They were soon joined by three mourning chiefs, and the procession continued to circle from left to right around the fire for an hour and a half with slight intervals, the old head chief always in the lead.

During the entire ceremony the Indians not engaged in the mourning chant occupied the outer space, sitting or reclining in little groups on the carpet of pine needles that covered the hard ground. Now and again a dusky figure arose and moved noiselessly from group to group or passed in or out of the gloom; at intervals sorrowing women burst forth in dismal cries, while solicitous mothers gave breast to eager children, and a hundred hungry dogs wandered back and forth to lie down sooner or later beside their silent masters.

Save the dull light from the fire, the smoke-blackened interior was absolutely dark, forming an appropriate background for the solemn rite. The smoke rose fitfully, at times diffusing itself through the room, at times ascending to the roof hole in a pulsating column, reddened intermittently by the glow of the coals. The flickering fire disclosed at intervals the forms of the people reclining in the outer circle and cast a dim and lurid light on the band of mourners as they continually circled round it. All was silence save the steady rhythmic chant of the marchers and an occasional muffled sob from the obscurity of the outer space.

At one time the march stopped and the mourners faced the west and cried; then they faced the north and cried, meanwhile wailing and swaying their bodies to and fro. At another time three women from the outer circle stepped forward and each took hold of one of the women marchers and led her to one of the four inner or central posts where they immediately sat down cross-legged in facing couples—one couple at the foot of each of three of the posts. They then grasped each other by the elbows or shoulders and swayed their bodies backward and forward, sometimes stopping to caress each other on the face and neck, but still sobbing and crying.

While this was going on the others continued the march. Sometimes the leader halted and seemed to utter commands, whereupon the marchers faced about, changed the words of the cry, and gesticulated in a different manner. At times the head chief looked down at the ground, with his arms and the palms of his hands extended toward a spot on the earth floor, around which he moved in a semicircle, addressing it as if speaking to a dead person or to a grave. Sometimes all of the women simultaneously extended their arms forward and slightly upward with open hands, as if in supplication, sobbing and wailing as they did so. One of the mourners, a woman with hair clipped short and face blackened in memory of the recent death of her husband, did not join the marchers but throughout the ceremony remained sitting on the west side of the outer circle with her face to the wall, uttering continually a peculiarly sad and at the same time plaintive musical lament, in slow rhythmical cadence. It was a beautiful strain, full of pathos and melody. She was very much in earnest and was so exhausted by the excitement and effort that, when the march was over, she fell on her side and remained motionless in that position for more than an hour.

When the march was over, the mourners retired to the outer circle, and So'-pi-ye, the old blind chief from Murphys, delivered a solemn oration. His voice was remarkably loud, deep, and clear. Another chief, who sat on the ground at his side, joined in from time to time.

At daylight on the following morning, the head chief harangued the people again for a long time, speaking until he was completely exhausted. A kindly old woman brought him coffee and a small basket of food but it was a long time before she could persuade him to take anything.

SECOND NIGHT

On the second night, October 10, the proceedings began shortly after dark and lasted about two hours, when the old head chief fell from exhaustion and the affair came to an abrupt end.

The character of the performance differed materially from that of the first night. In the beginning, the head chief faced the south, standing with his staff in his right hand. He then turned and faced the north, speaking and exhorting. Then a woman on the east side of the outer circle began sobbing. Then two women on the south side stepped out and sat on the ground with their arms around one another, sobbing and crying. The head chief remained standing on the south side of the inner space, facing in; he then turned and faced out, continuing his exhortations. After this he moved to the east and kneeled by the side of So'-pi-ye, the blind chief, who was sitting on the ground with his legs crossed. Immediately two other chiefs took places facing each other, squatting close together on the ground, and both couples moaned and cried. At the same time the women in the outer circle were wailing and sobbing. The chiefs who were squatting on the ground facing each other rested their hands on each other's arms and shoulders. The four chiefs then changed places and partners, everybody crying, after which three of the chiefs arose and began a slow

dancing march back and forth from the west side of the inner space, singing, "Hā-hā-hā-hā, hā-hā-hā-hā." While this was going on the women
mourners were squatting on the ground in facing couples, crying and sobbing as before.

The old head chief, leaning on his staff, next approached one of the
couples to the south and seemed to address them personally, while another
chief continued the dance alone, moving slowly around the fire. Then the
wife of one of the chiefs went to So'-pi-ye and sat down facing him; they
placed their hands on each other's arms and shoulders. There were now
three chiefs standing near the fire. Then another old woman danced once
around the fire alone, slowly swaying her body and arms, and sat down
facing one of the chiefs who was a mourner, so that there were two couples
kneeling or squatting on the ground, each consisting of a chief and an old
woman. At this time the old head chief was slowly moving around the fire
with one of the subordinate chiefs. The march stopped and the head chief
kneeled by an elderly woman mourner and placed his hands on her head
and she hers on his shoulders, both kneeling and weeping. The local chief
danced slowly around the fire alone, bending his body and pointing to the
ground in various directions with his wand. He then squatted on the
ground, and an old woman put one hand on his heart and reached over
with the other and patted him on the back.

The three chiefs and three old women exchanged partners and continued
to sway their bodies and mourn as before. Then the local chief arose and
went to the fire, and three of the chiefs took places on the south side,
facing outward. Another old man squatted by one of the old women as
before, and the local chief danced slowly around the fire, facing first to
the right, then to the left, motioning with his wand. He then sat cross-
legged on the ground by the side of a visiting chief who was one of the
mourners. This left the head chief the only man standing. He continued to
face the south, speaking and gesticulating. Two women knelt by the
visiting chief, who knelt down and placed a hand on the shoulder of each,
and all three remained kneeling. The old head chief continued to exhort,
still facing the south, but showed signs of great fatigue. Then the wife of a
local chief approached the fire, stood close to it, and, swaying her body
back and forth, pointed across it. Another woman began the slow dancing
march around the fire alone. A young mother, not a mourner, went to a
woman at the fire, led her away, and they sat down together, facing each
other, sobbing and rubbing one another with their hands.

The local chief now faced the fire and exhorted. He was soon joined by
two other chiefs and the three stood in a row, while one of the women continued the march alone, swaying her body and arms and sobbing. She was
soon joined by another woman and the local chief took his place at the

head; a third woman followed at the rear. The head chief beat time and moved slowly back and forth on the east side of the fire. He then, in spite of his obvious exhaustion, led the dancing march and was followed by two other chiefs, after which he again faced south and continued to exhort, while the local chief stooped low, with hands extended, facing alternately in different directions but continuing to move slowly around the fire. The old chief again led the march, then halted and called out; the others also halted and swayed their bodies and arms.

The old chief now moved alone to the north side of the inner space and exhorted, his voice becoming feebler and feebler. The others faced him, standing on the south side. A few minutes later seven persons were marching around the fire, when the head chief stopped them by putting his hands on the old women and men. Again he led off, and the marchers were joined by others, until there were in all eleven persons marching around the fire, the largest number at one time during the ceremony. The head chief then stopped and sang out, "Hi-hā-ho-ho," and everyone stood still. He then faced the west, and the women continued the march alone, soon joined however by two of the other chiefs, while the old head chief continued to exhort from the north side. The dancers fell away until only three were left. By this time the old head chief's strength was gone and he fell to the ground exhausted. He was carried to his place at the foot of the southwest post by a local chief and an old woman, and it was a long time before we were sure whether he would live or die. This put a stop to the proceedings.

At intervals throughout the ceremony of the second night, as on the first, the woman mourner with the cropped hair and blackened face, who sat on the east side of the outer circle with her back to the others, remained in her position and continued to wail, keeping up her peculiarly pathetic musical lament.

THE MO-LAH-GUM'-SIP

The ceremony of the second night, so abruptly ended, recommenced before daylight the following morning, when the final act, known as the Mo-lah-gum'-sip, or "wash," was performed.

Since the old head chief was too ill to take part, his place was taken by a local chief, Pedro, who at half-past five addressed the mourners in the roundhouse. He finished sometime before daylight, after which there was an interval of silence. Shortly before sunrise, some of the women brought out a large basket, set it on the ground near a small fire about forty feet north of the entrance to the ceremonial house, filled it with water and heated the water in the usual way by means of hot stones which had previously been put into the fire. When the water was hot, the chief ("eph") from the neighboring village at West Point and an old woman who had been designated for the place, each holding a cloth in the right hand, took positions facing one another, one on each side of the basket (called choo-soo-ah').

Then there was a stir inside the ceremonial house, and a local chief led out three of the women mourners and brought them to the basket. As each in turn leaned over it she was seized by one of the washers, who immediately proceeded to wash her face vigorously with the cloth, which was frequently dipped in the hot water. After the women's faces had been washed, their wrists and hands were treated in the same way, but were held outside so that the water would drip away from, not into, the basket. When these three had been washed, a chief and an old woman led out two old men chiefs, also mourners, and they were washed in the same way as the others. Then two more mourners, both old women, were led out and washed. After this one of the local chiefs went to a place in the chaparral, at some little distance, where a middle-aged couple were sleeping, grasped the woman by the hand, and led her all the way back to the choo-soo-ah' or hot-water basket, where she was treated as the others had been before.

This completed the ceremony of the Mo-lah-gum'-sip or "wash," and was the last act of the Yum'-meh or mourning ceremony. It also ended the period of mourning for those who had been washed, thus freeing them from the restrictions imposed upon them during its continuance.

It should be stated however that mourners who have lost a husband or wife a short time before the Yum'-me are not expected to accept liberty at that time but continue in mourning till the "cry" of the following year. A mourner who takes advantage of an opportunity to terminate the mourning period within two or three months after the death of husband or wife is not well thought of by the people.

In the ceremony under consideration, the woman mourner who took no part in the march but remained throughout facing the outer wall singing by herself in a remarkably sad and sweet voice was washed with the others at the Mo-lah-gum'-sip, but declined her liberty and expects to give a Yum'-me at her own home next fall.

The ceremony being over, all returned to the ceremonial house, where they were harangued by So'-pi-ye, the old blind chief from the settlement on the hill near Murphys.

The sun now rose above the mountains in the east, and the feeble old head chief got up slowly from his place at the foot of the southwest post and with his staff walked out to an open place on the west side of the ceremonial house, where he stood in silence for a long time, facing the sun.

After this, breakfast was served, consisting of coffee, acorn mush, and biscuit. I ate with the others. Each of the mourners who had been washed gave a silver fifty-cent piece to the local chief in charge of this part of the ceremony.

The chiefs, when speaking, shouted the first syllable of each sentence or clause, and sometimes of each word, thus: "TEN'-ni-ah; NAT'-too'-nă-tah, POO'-soo'-ne," and so on. This they did uniformly in all their addresses and sermons; So'-pi-ye the blind chief did it with great vigor. At the close of each speech, and at some of the pauses, the audience sang out "Hoo'-oo'-oo."

So'-pi-ye in his last address spoke of some of the old chiefs who had passed away—notably of Teniah of Yosemite Valley, whose youngest son was brutally murdered by the whites. He spoke also of various tribes from the village of Poosoone at the mouth of American River to the Natoona-tah on lower Kings River.

At the end he said, "Me'-chet me-chet'-te, woo'-te woo'-te. Koo-nahs" —his voice falling with the last word. The words mean, "What shall we do, what shall we do? Let's go, let's go. That's all" or "I'm done."

The Yum'me held at Hā'-cha-nah October ninth to eleventh, 1906, consisted of three quite distinct parts: (1) the mourning march of the first night; (2) the mixed ceremony of the second night; and (3) the Mo-lah-gum'-sip or "wash," which took place at daybreak on the morning of the third day. The Indians say that the ceremony often occupies four nights instead of two.

In the ceremony I witnessed, the operations of the first night consisted mainly of a nearly continuous slow trotting march in single file around the fire, broken by two conspicuous acts—one in which the old head chief appeared to address the graves of the dead, the other in which the old women danced slowly around the inner space with their arms and hands held forward as in supplication. On the second night the marching was reduced to brief intervals and the principal part was made up of a number of separate acts, the most prominent of which were the frequent assembling of the chiefs and principal mourners in facing couples squatting, sitting, or kneeling on the ground; the dancing march of solitary individuals; the impressive act of the old woman who, bending forward, with outstretched arm and finger, pointed across the fire; the curious stooping dance of the old chief who, with body bent low and arms extended, faced out in different directions in turn while dancing slowly around the fire.

Throughout the period covered by the mourning ceremony and subsequent festivities the greatest respect and affection were shown the old head chief. His speeches and sermons, and those by So'-pi-ye, the blind chief from Murphys, are worthy of permanent record, but my knowledge of the language is so exceedingly meager that I was able to understand only disjointed fragments. It was evident however that the addresses

were of two kinds—the one historical, dealing mainly with the distribution and relations of the tribes, the conditions under which they lived, and
the succession and characteristics of the great chiefs; the other advisory,
exhorting people to do right. The young men were admonished to let drink
alone, to keep away from quarrelsome people, to be slow to anger; to
avoid hasty replies, particularly when talking to white men who might
say exasperating things; to be kind and good and follow the example of
the old people.

The foregoing account is hardly more than an empty skeleton of the
ceremony—a skeleton divested not only of the life, but also of the meaning
of the several acts. It is submitted as a fragmentary contribution to the
life history of a little known people.

Third Night: The Kal-lā-ah or Fandango

The mourning ceremony of two nights' duration was immediately followed
by the dancing ceremony, Kal-lā-ah, also of two nights' duration. The
first night of the dance, October 11 (the third night of the ceremony), the
performers were as follows: one too-mop'-pĕh or drummer, who beat the
large plank drum with his feet; one mul-lip'-pĕh or singer, who stood with
his back to the dancers, facing the drummer and beating time with a pair
of clappersticks of elderwood, about fifteen inches long; and eight kol-
lep'-pĕh or dancers, five of whom were men, three women.

The five men dancers wore tum-mah'-ke-lah—broad red headbands
made of the red shaft-feathers from the tails of the red-shafted flicker
(*Colaptes cafer*). These headbands are worn horizontally across the front
part of the head and project on each side so far that, when the two flaps
are brought forward, they meet on the middle of the forehead. Most of
them were solid red, with a black border formed by the tips of the tail
feathers. One was interrupted by black vertical bars, and all were black
at the ends. Three of the dancers had, projecting horizontally from each
side of the head, chah'-le-lah, two large white feathers. The two remaining
men dancers had other feathers standing up on the top or back of their
heads, and one wore a white side feather also. The so-pop'-pĕh or head
dancer, wore, in addition, a sol'-lah or large feather apron, which hung
from his hips and reached nearly to the ground. It was made of feathers
of hawks and turkeys, and had the tail of a red-tail hawk in the center.
It was fastened on by a cord passing under the arms and around the back
of the neck. To the sides of this cord were attached obliquely on each side
several long, dark feathers, giving the appearance of ribs. Each dancer
carried in his hand a sort of feather wand. (They complained that they
should have had complete feather suits, but did not possess them.)

The three women dancers wore no feathers, but each had a handkerchief tied tightly around her head and each carried in her hand a long handkerchief or piece of cloth. The women stood in a line between two of the posts, at first between the two on the east side, later between the two on the west side. The men dancers occupied the space between the drum and the two rear or south posts, from which position they danced toward or around the fire and back, the inner circle being their dancing ground.

The first dance began at eight o'clock and lasted till ten-thirty. The three women dancers stood in a row between the two posts on the east side and did not move out of their places, their part consisting in swaying their bodies and heads and beating time with their feet, while, at the same time, they made curious movements with their hands. The handkerchief held in the hands was at first passed around behind the body, the ends held in the hands just over the hips. While the dance was going on, the hands were repeatedly pushed forward and downward, moving the handkerchief in a sawing motion across the back.

The women were not painted. The men dancers had their faces painted in horizontal black bands, but each dancer was decorated differently from the others. The leader had two broad black horizontal cheek bands, one passing backward in continuation of the moustache, the other about half an inch above it. Each band was about half an inch in width. Another dancer had a single black band passing entirely around the front of the head, just below the level of the eyes. The leader had two black rings painted around his ankles.

The singer stood with his back to the dancers, between them and the west end of the drum. He sang in a rather low voice and beat long clapper-sticks, held in his right hand, against the palm of his left hand. The drummer beat time with his feet, keeping time with the singer. The men danced in perfect time and with remarkable vigor, stamping the ground hard with their bare feet; the pine needles that covered the ground had been swept away from the dancing circle immediately around the fire. During the first dance the men jumped with both feet together; during the others they usually danced two-step, stamping each foot twice, first one and then the other.

The leader was a ventriloquist, and from time to time uttered smothered sounds which led the audience to believe that a man was hidden in the hole under the drum. He and the others, when dancing, made a hissing, expiratory sound, said to be in imitation of the bone whistles they formerly used. All said repeatedly while dancing, "Hoo-hoo-hoo'-e." Each dance was repeated four times, and at the end the dancers turned and faced the drum and danced for a short time longer, then stopped suddenly and all together; the time was perfect throughout. During the progress of the dance, which I shall not attempt to describe in detail, the leader often left the others and ran back and forth in a zigzag course about the fire, frequently crouching and leaping as if escaping from or pursuing an enemy. Once he danced for a few minutes by alternately squatting and leaping with great vigor, a very difficult procedure and one requiring great strength. At the close of each dance the audience, which occupied the outer circle where they sat cross-legged on the ground or reclined in various positions, uttered a low "Hoo-oo, hoo-oo-oo."

Before the dance the dancing circle was sprinkled with water, and one of the old women threw acorn meal into the fire and uttered four times a peculiar wailing cry, facing the drum as she did so.

The dance on the first night of the ceremony was borrowed from the north and is known collectively (for it consists of 6 or 7 separate dances, each repeated 4 times), as the acorn dance. It is supposed to bring a good crop of acorns the following year. The original or aboriginal dances of this tribe were danced by couples, male and female, with a clown between each two couples. About one hundred people were present, in the outer circle.

FOURTH NIGHT: THE WOK'-KE-LĀ OR WAR DANCE

The dancing space about the fire was carefully swept and sprinkled as before. Then a woman stepped forward and sprinkled acorn meal on the fire. After she had done this several times, an older woman, wife of the local chief, came forward and in like manner sprinkled acorn meal on the fire, and then sprinkled the heads and bodies of the dancers with more of the same meal. Shen then uttered a prolonged wail in a single key. This she repeated at intervals four times, sprinkling the dancers and casting meal into the fire. The dancers then crossed the ceremonial house and went outside for a few moments, each turning a complete circle just before he passed outside. Returning, each turned around again after entering the house before crossing to the place at the rear. This was done in order to propitiate the spirits and secure permission to open and use the feather dresses without danger of serious consequences. As one of the Indians told me, this war dance, called Wok'-ke-lā, is the most particular and dangerous of all the dances and has to be done just so, or the dancers would be very sick.

Before the dance began (at 7:30) the door was tightly closed and a guard placed beside it. Then the singer began to sing in a low voice and beat time with his clapper, holding the clapper in his right hand and striking the palm of the left hand. The drummer at once began to beat time on the plank drum with his feet in the usual manner, stamping hard and in perfect time, and the dancers followed singing "Hoo-e, hoo-e, hoo-e."

Five men and four women took part in the first dance. One woman stood alone between the posts on the east side, the other three in a row between the posts on the west side. The women held their hands in front, each holding her handkerchief between her hands. At first the leader of the men danced by the side of the solitary woman on the west side, the other four men dancing in two rows between the south posts, each man holding feathers in his hands and moving his hands tremulously (the feathers in the hand representing the bows and arrows formerly held during the dance). The leader carried a bunch of feathers, each of the others two white feathers in each hand. During the first dance the movements were made in a succession of jumps, both feet moving simultaneously, the heels striking the ground vigorously and keeping perfect time with the drum. The expiratory hiss in imitation of the bone whistle was prominent throughout this dance. During the second dance the lone woman on the east side did not take part; she reappeared in the third dance. Ventriloquial sounds were made by the leader at intervals.

Some of the dancing was done in a circle about the fire, but most of it back of the fire or between it and the drum. The women remained in their places throughout, swaying their bodies and moving their hands. Between the dances the dancers sat in a semicircle between the drum and the rear posts, with their backs to the audience, and sang and beat with three or more sets of clappers. Originally this dance had to be continued for four nights.

THE MOURNING CEREMONY AT BALD ROCK RANCHERIA, 1907

A Yum'-meh, the "cry" ceremony for the dead, was held at Bald Rock Rancheria, Tuolumne County, on the night of October 3, 1907, followed by the Mo-lah-gum'-sip, "washing" ceremony, at daylight on the morning of the fourth. It was originally intended to continue the Yum'-meh the second night, but for some reason this was given up.

PREPARATIONS

All day long on the third and fourth the old women cooked acorn mush, nu'-pah, and acorn bread, oo-lā', and they made a most astonishing quantity, fully a ton, all cooked in the handsome large cooking baskets by means of hot stones.

There were two cooking places—one in the rancheria, the other on the bank of the creek, below. About five women worked at each place, and they worked hard and continuously from morning till nearly dark. There were three leaches (each about 4 to 4½ ft. in diameter) at the upper cooking place and two (one 4 ft., the other 5 ft., in diameter) at the lower. A big fire to heat the stones was kept going all day at each cooking place, large sticks of Ponderosa pine being used for fuel. About two bushels of stones, averaging six to eight inches in longest diameter and about four inches thick, were heated in each fire.

Twenty or thirty baskets were in use at each cooking place, about half of which were the large 3-rod cooking bowls, holding from one to two bushels each. About half of these were of Nis-se-non make, a few of Washoo, the rest their own manufacture.

The baskets in which the cooking was done—three or four were kept going at each place all the time—were set in depressions in the sand. At the upper camp these depressions were lined with wet gunnysack; at the lower camp with wet pine needles and willow twigs and leaves.

The filters (leaches), four to four and a half feet in diameter, were circular depressions of coarse sand on a foundation of creek gravel, the stones averaging about an inch in diameter. Those at the upper camp were permanent and had an under foundation of rocks a foot or more high on the downhill side—for they were on sloping ground. The filters were lined with coarse cloth and wet.

A large quantity of freshly pounded acorn flour of the black oak (*Quercus californica*), made from new, hardly ripe acorns, was piled on each filter, wet, and spread out evenly. Then a fan or mat of fir boughs (of *Abies concolor lowiana*) was laid on each to spread evenly the warm water poured on it. The water was heated in a big basket in which a few hot stones had been dropped and was warm, not hot. (Blue-oak acorn flour is leached in cold water.)

In cooking the mush the baskets were filled about half-full of the hot stones—not at first but gradually, as new stones were taken out of the fire and put in. Small basketfuls cooked in six or ten minutes, but the big baskets took about half an hour each. When the mush was beginning to cook and was still thin, it was skimmed from time to time with a small scoop-shaped skimmer basket called chah′-mi-yu to remove ashes, cinders, and other foreign matter appearing on top.

When the mush was thick and cooked enough to begin to set or jelly, it was dipped out in a small basket and carefully emptied in the creek on some leaves or a coarse cloth, where it hardened in the cold water.

The loaves of bread thus made, called oo-lā′, are exactly alike and look like a lot of turtles. They are flat on one side, convex on the other, and measure about eight by six inches in diameter and three inches in thickness. In color they are pale grayish pink or pinkish gray—some cookings being grayer than others. In two cookings at the creek, twenty-three loaves were made in each cooking, or forty-six in all. These were left in the cold running stream for a couple of hours; then were carefully lifted out and put in two large baskets, in which they were carried on the backs of the women to the upper camp, where all were kept together until suppertime. Then they were carried into the roundhouse and placed before the guests. After the first cooked mush was made into oo-lā', the baskets were filled again and the mush called nu'-pah was made. Almost a ton and a half, all told, was made in two days.

The Yum'-me Ceremony at Bald Rock Rancheria

Shortly after sundown on October 3, 1907, the speaking began.[3] Two or three of the older men spoke at intervals, standing in the roundhouse. The actual ceremony commenced at nine-thirty when a woman mourner with cropped hair, sitting at the southeast post, began to wail and cry. After a few minutes she was followed by several other women with cropped hair, who arose and fell into line and marched in a circle round the fire. They were joined by others till all the women mourners were marching and wailing. From time to time the mourners dropped out in two's and squatted at the base of the northwest post, just outside the inner circle, usually in facing couples.

The march was a slow shuffling trot, each advance carrying the moving foot less than half the length of the other foot. Soon after it started, a bearded old man from Chicken Ranch, who had taken a position midway between the two west posts, began to talk and exhort, which caused the wailing to increase.

One old woman then led off and moved completely around the circle several times in a series of low jumps, swaying her body and uplifted arms from side to side, followed by the others. Then the jumper stood still on the north side while the others continued to march. Then three facing couples squatted at the northwest post, and the marchers massed on the north side and beat time with their feet.

Then a woman on the southeast began wailing louder and the march continued. A new exhorter appeared on the east side.

The marchers broke into two divisions, lined up, and halted—one line on the north, the other on the south.

The march was resumed, and the men fell in until there were fourteen men and women marching. They stopped on the south side facing the fire.

The marching began again, led by an old woman mourner with cropped

---

[3] This account, found in Dr. Merriam's files as a completed manuscript, is based on observations at Bald Rock, Tuolumne Co., in Oct., 1907.—Ed.

hair and blackened face who threw up her arms alternately and shouted
"Uh'-ŭh-ŭh'" in a rather high voice, at which the circling march stopped.
(This she did later at intervals, always uttering the same cry and always
stopping the march for a few moments, after which it continued.)

Again the march began, at first with three men and three women. Then
more women joined until fourteen women and three men were marching;
the women increased to eighteen, making twenty-one persons marching.

There was an intermission of nearly an hour.

The speaking commenced again, with two speakers on the east side.
Before they had finished, the march began, and soon seventeen women
were marching. While the march went on, three women stood side by side
on the south, swaying their bodies and arms and singing and from time
to time holding their hands straight out in front toward the fire and the
marchers. Lined up behind them were three men, blowing in an expiratory
fashion. One of these, the leader, stood at the east end of the line and
clapped his hands once for each change. There were now eighteen marchers,
mourning in a low voice so that the voices of the singers were heard above
them. After a time they stopped marching so as to leave an opening on the
north side.

Then the old Heampoko, of Bald Rock, sitting at the northeast post,
exhorted the people. The march was resumed, the mourners chanting a
low mournful song. Again the three women with swaying bodies and outstretched arms took positions on the south side, and in line behind them
stood the three men blowing in expiratory fashion.

The marchers again halted, and opened the circle on the north side, the
low mournful wail continuing. A man led around once alone, beginning on
the south and circling to the north, followed by the marchers. Then the
men fell out, leaving only women.

The expiratory blowing by the three men and the swaying by the three
women with outstretched arms continued in the south background. The
leader clapped hands once and the marchers halted, lined up on the east
and west sides. The greater number remained on the west, marking time
with their feet, while those on the east (4 women alone) went on marching.
The leader in the rear clapped once and all were silent, the marchers forming in a semicircle on the south side, open at the north.

The expiratory blowers began again, the three women swaying as before, and the march was resumed, moving always from right to left. The
bearded man on the west spoke again while the march continued. The
singing leader clapped once and all halted, the circle opening on the north.
The three swaying women dancers continued to sing and the three men
behind them continued the expiratory blowing. The leader clapped, and
the march halted, to begin again soon.

Exhorters spoke on both east and west sides, and the march and mourning cry continued while they were speaking. Again the circle opened on the north, and the marchers marked time with their feet as usual.

There was a second intermission.

The march began again with eight men and thirteen women. The exhorter (the bearded man on the west) spoke again and continued through the first part of the march, uttering a succession of sentences ending in "chah."

The marching stopped, and all the people sat or squatted on the ground. A man on the south sang, "Hā'-e-hā, hā'-e-hah', ā-ha'-e-hā, ā-hā'-e-hah"; a sitting woman on the east mourned musically.

There followed an intermission, shorter than the others.

In the fourth and last act of the night's ceremony two women (instead of 3) took positions in the singers' space on the south side, singing and swaying their bodies and arms and from time to time raising their arms and holding them forward toward the fire. Behind them were the three men in a row, blowing in an expiratory fashion as before.

The women marchers fell in again, and the bearded man on the west exhorted again. Men now joined the march, followed by more women, until there were seven men and eighteen women circling, making in all twenty-five persons, all mourners.

Then an old woman went alone to the northwest post, leaned against it, and cried. The circling march halted, opening east, and the mourning song continued while at the same time the singing women swayed their bodies and arms and the men behind them continued the expiratory blowing.

This ended the exercises of the night. At daybreak next morning the people assembled for the final act, the Molagumsip, consisting of the washing of the twenty-five mourners.

The Mewuk:
Miscellaneous Notes

AUTUMN CEREMONY IN YOSEMITE VALLEY

The last ceremony I saw was on the night of October 10, 1910. The performers (dancers) consisted of four men and three women, all in costume. Both men and women wore flicker headbands with two tufted rods sticking upward and forward, one on each side of the head. The men were naked, with breechcloths and beadwork belts, and all but one carried in their hands bow and arrows and a gray foxskin quiver. One of the men carried tufted wands.

At this ceremony there were present Chief Kelly and one or two others from Kalarow, near Mariposa, and also a few Piute from Mono Lake.

They sang during the performance. The various motions, the stamping on the ground with the bare feet, the bending of the bodies forward, and the loud expiratory breathing were essentially the same as those I have repeatedly observed in ceremonies of this tribe and of their relatives, the Northern Mewuk.

The women, like the men, wore flicker headdresses and bead belts, but unlike the men each carried in her hands a handkerchief or a piece of cloth held by the upper corners. They swayed their bodies from side to side while singing in the usual way.

This dance is called Kal'-ling-ah. Normally a clown called wah-cho'-le takes part in this ceremony. He wears a tail, acts funny, and mimics the dancers. He carries a carved wooden bird's head in his hands and helps himself to anything he takes a fancy to about camp. In early times in connection with this ceremony there was a dance very early in the morning

66

before eating; another at four or five o'clock in the afternoon, but the main one was always held after dark at night. The early morning dance was called Poos'-ne.

This ceremony is said to be one of the oldest held by the tribe. People with children were afraid to dance it, and threw pieces of money and acorn meal into the fire.

Chief Kelly made the address. The ceremony closed prematurely because of rain at ten o'clock at night.

COOKING ACORN MUSH AT CHEROKEE, TUOLUMNE COUNTY[1]

One of the families at Cherokee is preparing to give an acorn feast tomorrow and I arrived there in time (7 A.M.) to watch an old woman cook two large baskets of acorn mush. She put four or six large hot stones in each basket and stirred the stones with a ladle so they would not rest long enough in one place to burn the basket. She took them out of the fire with the usual two long straight sticks, not with a loop stick.

When the mush was done, she took the hot stones out with the ladle, lifting them one at a time, tilting them over the edge of the basket and letting them drop into a basket of water held close under, in which they were rinsed. They were then pitched back into the fire. The rinsing water, now rich with mush from the stones, was emptied into the big mush bowls—each holding about a bushel. When the mush (or soup, the consistency of thick bean or pea puree) was cooked, a number of small and middle-sized bowl baskets were filled and put aside to cool. A small 1-rod basket was used as a dipper.

I saw also some loaves of acorn bread, called oo-lā'. Some were cooked, others standing in a basket of water waiting to be cooked. They were like large thick pancakes in form. Some they called ma-soo'-tah instead of oo-lā', but I didn't find out just how they differ. The ma-soo'-tah are sweet, whereas the oo-lā' is slightly sour. The mush or soup they call nup-pah'.

Only old—very old—baskets of their own make were used. The cooking baskets were large, deep, and rather coarse 3-rod bowls called him-mah, ornamented with simple designs. The baskets filled with the mush were 3-rod coiled bowls called pul-lē'-sah. The basket used as a dipper was a 1-rod coiled bowl called keng-ah-kah'. A somewhat larger and shallower 1-rod bowl was called kāy-wy-you.

Some of the 3-rod coiled bowls of oldtime make have very little design but are extraordinarily hard, strong, and compact and are well made.

---

[1] Observed at the Indian village near Cherokee, Tuolumne County, Aug. 21, 1903.

They are made of sprouts of Digger pine (*Pinus sabiniana*). I have one I got at Grapevine Lodge a mile west of Sonora a year or two ago.

There are many circular winnowers here (het-tal-ăh) mostly made by the Mariposa and Chowchilla Me'-wa. There are also a few of the deep round openwork bowl baskets made at Chowchilla for filtering manzanita cider. These Indians call them ō-wy'-you and use them also to gather acorns in—hanging them on the arm.

The Me'-wa apparently make only one type of conical burden basket— of open slender rods brought together in couplets at alternate crossings of the transverse strands. Since small seeds would fall through the interspaces, the baskets are coated with a white mucilaginous paste from the soaproot (*Chloragalum pomeridianum*). This species is regarded as poison and never eaten, although an allied but much smaller species is eaten.

A big rock on a stream between Cherokee Camp and Tuolumne station has the top pitted with about twenty mortar holes. There are also plenty of mortar holes in rocks about Cherokee Camp; and others at and near the Bald Rock rancheria.

I saw a woman and her little girl, both wearing necklaces unlike any I have seen before. They consisted of small bundles (each, say, 1½ in. long and ¼ in. thick) of a form of sage herb (*Artemesia ludoviciana* subsp.), simply tied with thread and strung on a string about two and a half inches apart. The woman told me her eldest daughter had died a few months before and she and her remaining child were wearing these to keep disease away.

Both species of blue manzanita occur here, *Arctostaphylos viscida* and *A. mariposa*. In *A. viscida* the bracts, berries, and pedicles are glandular-viscid and sticky, and the terminal twigs and leaf stems are conspicuously glandular-pubescent. In *A. mariposa* all these parts are smooth-glabrous. I was surprised to find that the Indians discriminate them. They call *A. viscida*, a'-yah, and *A. mariposa* muk'-ka-zoo'. The berries of both are edible and used for cider, some people preferring one, some the other. They say muk'-ka-zoo' berries make darker cider with stronger taste.

COOKING HOLES FOR TRIPE AND CLOVER

The Northern Me-wuk have two kinds of cooking holes. First, there is hoo'-pah-o-lah, which is dug in the hot ashes of the fireplace after the fire has been burning a long time and the ground is thoroughly hot for some depth. The hole is lined with wet earth or clay. Deer tripe and blood are put in, then covered with more wet clay. Coals are put on top and the fire is kept on top all day. The hole is opened in the evening, when the food is ready to eat.

The second cooking hole, oo'-lik-kah, is a hole two and a half feet deep, dug in the ground and walled around with stones like a well. Fire is built until the stones are very hot. Then the fire is taken out and the hole is filled with alternating layers of clover and hot stones. The clover is left about half a day and then the hole is opened. The cooked clover is called pahj'-jah-ku. Three kinds of wild clover are used. When done, the cooked clover is dried and keeps a long time. It is sometimes eaten dry, but is usually stewed in a basket with hot stones just before eating.

WILD TOBACCO

Wild tobacco of two species (*Nicotiana attenuata* and *N. bigelovi*) is culti-vated about many of the old rancherias. At the Aukum rancheria near the South Fork of the Cosumnes River, which I visited on August 8, 1907, the large flower species (*N. bigelovi*) was common and an old woman had already picked a quantity of the large leaves and had spread them out to dry. Some of the leaves that were completely dry she had pounded ready for smoking. This tobacco is called kah'-su.

TUOLUMNE MU'-WAH DOCTORS[2]

The Tuolumne Mu'-wah had three kinds of Doctors or "medicine men": Koi'-ah-pe, the Witch Doctors; Too'-yu-goo, the Dance Doctors; Wen-nĕh'-hoo-ne, the Medicine Doctors.

Doctors are usually men, but there have been women doctors of each of the three kinds. The office is not hereditary, but the persons are selected and trained by the old doctors.

The Koi'-ah-pe or Witch Doctor is by far the most powerful of the three, and is the one usually called when a person is very sick. He is well paid for his services. He never gives medicine and never dances. His method is to scarify (or make cuts over) the affected part and suck out the cause of the disease. He also makes magic and can kill people at a distance. The people are afraid of him. He practices his art at night only, never in the daytime, and never works over a person less than four consecutive nights.

The Koi'-ah-pe has the power to kill people at a distance by finding their spit and putting something in it. When he does this, the person takes sick and dies. He kills people also by the use of poisons. He has some medi-cine that he rubs on a pin or small stick or piece of grass stem which he can shoot (throw) to a great distance to kill a person. The old people have seen him stick a small peg in the ground and then go off thirty or forty yards and throw these tiny sticks (smaller than a white man's match) at

---

[2] Observed at Bald Rock rancheria.

it and have seen them all go right to it and hit it or strike the dust close against it.

The Too'-yu-goo or Dance Doctor heals by dancing and does not give medicine or suck out the evil. But he has the power and may poison or kill at a distance.

The Wen-něh'-hoo-ne uses herbs and medicines only. He does not suck or dance nor does he make magic, and he cannot kill people at a distance.

These people say they did not kill a doctor even when he lost three consecutive cases.

The Mono Paiute

[Plates 18–23]

For a distance of five hundred miles the State of California is divided into two parts by a great range of mountains—the Sierra Nevada—a range so broad, so high, and so rugged that it forms an almost impassable barrier between the activities of the two sides. On the west is the main part of the State with its busy cities, its commerce, its principal industries; on the east is the desert—the beginning of a series of arid valleys and barren mountains, known as the Great Basin, which stretches east across Nevada and far into Utah—a curious region whose waters instead of flowing to the sea disappear in alkaline sinks and lakes. Of these, the largest and the best known is Salt Lake in Utah; the most picturesque and romantic is Mono Lake, just within the eastern border of California.

Mono lies at the base of the lofty Sierra, overshadowed by snow-marbled, glacier-bearing peaks that tower six thousand feet above its placid waters (pl. 18, *a*). It is surrounded by desert, but on the west side sparkling streams, born of melting snows, dash down the steep slopes, plunge into the narrow canyons, and emerging on the plain below, carry slender lines of trees to its very shores.

The foothills of the mountains are dotted with evergreen trees, the piñon or nut pine, sometimes mixed with juniper; the lowlands are sparsely covered with olive-gray sagebrush and other desert bushes. A noteworthy feature of the region is a group of barren ash-colored volcanic cones known as Mono Craters, whose summits, capped with surprisingly perfect and symmetrical craters, rise to a height of nearly three thousand feet above the lake. The points of eruption were so near together that the ejected materials had not room enough to form independent cones, hence the resulting volcanoes are crowded and fused into a continuous mass or

71

wall, which rises boldly in impressive desolation above the barren sage-brush plain (pl. 18, *b*). Seen across the shimmering desert, through the hazy wrinkled undulations of the superheated atmosphere, their gray sides and black rims have a weird look, justifying the superstitious awe in which they are held by the Indians. This feeling of the supernatural is strengthened by the existence of a strange freak near the south end of the craters—a veritable "Devil's Cauldron," perhaps two hundred feet in depth and a quarter of a mile across, with sides so steep one can hardly climb in or out.

From time immemorial Mono Lake has been the home of Indians. These Indians call themselves Mono Paiute and are a branch of the great Paiute family or stock. How numerous and how powerful they were in the past I do not know; at present they consist of a few small bands living in rude brush huts in widely separated camps.

During several visits to Mono Lake it has been my fortune to meet nearly all of the Mono Indians. They are skillful horsemen, brought up in the saddle, and most of them are well-formed, good-looking, and intelligent. Like other Indians they are reserved and reticent in the presence of strangers, but when satisfied that the visitor is a friend, they answer and ask questions and sometimes take a leading part in conversation. Usually their first question is "Where you come from?"; the second, "Where you go?" When told that my home was in Washington, one of them said he had heard of the place and asked how I came. They have a keen sense of humor and both men and women laugh heartily at droll incidents and at jokes that do not involve them in ridicule; but they are highly sensitive and dislike exceedingly to be made fun of by white men. Some of the squaws tattoo their faces, usually with a vertical line on the chin and an interrupted or zigzag horizontal line on each cheek.

These Indians, like many others in California and Nevada, are self-supporting. They are not on any reservation and receive no assistance from the government. That some of the men are lazy goes without saying, but most of them are industrious and work by the day or month. They make good teamsters and farm hands and are employed by ranchmen at the west end of the lake for nearly all kinds of work. I have noticed them particularly in haying, at which they labored steadily from daylight until dark—more than twleve hours a day. I was told that they work also at the lumber business at Mono Mills, a sawmill in a pine forest south of Mono Lake.

The women, in addition to their family duties—gathering roots, seeds, berries, nuts, and firewood, and preparing food and clothing for their families—harvest the grain, cutting it with knives and winnowing it with large snowshoe-shaped baskets (pl. 23, *c*). Some of them are employed at the ranch houses to do washing, cooking, and other kinds of housework.

The older women and a few of the younger weave baskets and make beautiful beadwork—the latter chiefly for belts and hat bands.

In summer they live in open brush huts called wickiups, in front of which is a cleared place fifteen or twenty feet in diameter, which may or may not be completely enclosed by a rough fence of uprooted sagebrush (pl. 19, b).

The winter huts are conical or dome-shaped and are completely closed. Some have low projecting entrances through which one must crawl to enter—a feature suggesting the igloo of the Eskimo. Some are of thatched straw or tule, like the one shown in plate 20, a; others are of slender upright willow poles interwoven with small brush.

At meals the Indians gather around the fire, sitting, squatting, or reclining on the ground. After supper, which in summer is eaten late when the long day's work is over, they enjoy the white man's luxury of a smoke before rolling up for the night in their rabbitskin blankets. These blankets are worthy of remark. They are made by sewing together a multitude of spirally twisted strips of fresh skin that look like little cylinders of fur. The skins used are those of the cottontail rabbit, jack-rabbit, and, more rarely, the bobcat or lynx. The blankets are exceedingly soft and warm and are highly prized—as well they may be in view of the immense number of skins and the great length of time necessary for their construction. In several instances I have known one to serve as bed and covering for an entire family—man, wife, and children.

Once the Paiute were famous hunters and wandered far and wide in pursuit of game. They hunted with bows and arrows, in the use of which they are still surprisingly skillful. The shafts of the arrows are straightened, smoothed, and given the proper form at the tip by means of a piece of pumice stone grooved on one side and perforated by a tapering hole. The rough grain of the stone acts like sandpaper in rounding and polishing the wood.

The points of some of the arrows are made of obsidian or volcanic glass, a substance that occurs in great cliffs and masses on Mono Craters. Among these craters are probably the largest aboriginal obsidian quarries known, quarries containing millions of tons of the variously colored glasslike material—some white, some black, some banded—enough to supply arrows and spearheads to all the Indians of the world till the end of time. That they have been used for countless ages is indicated by the abundance of arrowheads and chips strewn over the ground throughout the region, particularly along the trails. Chunks of the rough obsidian were sometimes carried long distances to be worked, and doubtless also to be bartered with other tribes, as shown by accumulations of stone flakes and "rejects" in remote spots, even on the faraway west flank of the Sierra. The site of one of these ancient workshops may be seen today on a commanding eminence a little north of the Yosemite. It is where the trail from Mono Pass and Lake Tenaya breaks through the dark green forest of pines and firs and suddenly comes out on a ridge of bare rock overlooking a new world—a world of granite domes, yawning chasms, and lofty mountains. The abruptness of the transition is startling. The bewildered eye looks up at the lofty peaks of the upper Merced and down into the mysterious hazy abyss of the Yosemite. Let one gaze for a moment at the wondrous panorama here spread before him and tell if he can what manner of man it was who chose this enchanted spot for his workshop! Yet there are people who say that Indians have no soul and no appreciation of the beautiful or sublime!

From childhood to the grave the life of the desert Indian is a continuous struggle for food. The Paiute are desert Indians, but the Mono Paiute, owing to the more favorable situation of their home, have less difficulty than the other bands in obtaining subsistence. Before the invasion of their country by whites, game was abundant and easily secured. Deer and blue grouse were plentiful in the mountains, antelope, rabbits, and sage-hens were common about the lake, and the waters teemed with ducks and other wild fowl. Many kinds bred there in numbers, and during the migrations ducks, geese, swans, and shore birds literally covered the water. Even now the lake is no mean resort for waterfowl, though it must be admitted that the kinds frequenting it in summer, except certain wary ducks, are hardly such as tempt the palate of the epicure. The Indians however are quite willing to dine on gulls, grebes, or such other species as they are able to secure. Along the borders of the lake they build rude brush huts or blinds in which they conceal themselves and wait patiently for the birds to come within reach of their arrows. On the east shore, about the middle of last August, I found several of these blinds in use, and the number of wings of gulls dangling from the wickiups near by bespoke the success of this primitive method of hunting.

In August a small fly accumulates in incredible numbers about the edges of the lake, forming a black band a foot or more in width for miles along the shores and resting in masses or rafts on the surface of the water. Thousands of grebes and gulls, and hundreds of thousands of phalaropes, congregate to fatten on the flies, and the birds as they drift lazily past the blinds, afford easy targets for the well-directed arrows of the Paiute boys.

In the fall the larvae of the flies are thrown up by the waves in countless myriads, and in places on the south shore are piled up in long windrows (pl. 21, *b*). Professor I. C. Russell, while studying the geology of Mono Basin, once had the good fortune to visit the lake at such a time. He found picturesque groups of squaws gathering the larvae and preserving them for food. When the worms are partly dried and the outer skins removed by rubbing and winnowing in scoop-shaped baskets, the kernels or bodies are tossed into the conical burden baskets that the women carry on their backs. On the same shore I found the large wickiup shown in plate 21, *a* and, close by, a heap ten or twelve feet in diameter of the empty skins or "cases" of these larvae, which had been dumped there by the Indians. Professor William H. Brewer, who visited Mono Lake in 1863, says that after the worms are dried in the sun, the shells are rubbed off with the hands, leaving a yellowish kernel which looks like a small grain of rice. This material, called koo-chah'-bee, is oily, very nutritious, and not unpleasant to the taste. "If one were ignorant of its origin," adds the Professor, "it would make nice soup."

But far the larger part of the food of the Mono is of vegetable origin. Buffalo berries (pl. 22, *c*), serviceberries, wild peaches, and other berries and fruits are dried for winter use; seeds of a great variety of plants are gathered and roasted or pounded into meal; and diverse roots, some from the desert, others from remote parts of the mountains, are collected and cooked. Of all the native foods however, the rich oily nuts of the piñon or nut pine hold first place (pl. 22, *a*, *b*). The piñon is a characteristic tree of middle altitudes in the desert ranges of California and Nevada, and near the west end of Mono Lake it grows conveniently on certain outjutting spurs of the Sierra. The crop of nuts—the seeds from the pine cones—is usually ample, which is fortunate for the Indians, as many birds and mammals are alert in gathering and hoarding them for winter. The ground squirrels and chipmunks begin before the nuts are fully ripe, coming singly and working in silence, stuffing their commodious cheek pouches as full as they will hold before running off to unload in their storehouses. The piñon jays and Clark crows come in noisy flocks, making the hills ring with their cries; and while they have no pockets in which to tuck away provisions, they carry off by force of numbers full as many as the squirrels.

The nuts ripen in September, and if the near-by supply is inadequate, the Indians make long journeys on their ponies to mountains where the crop is better. Usually several families join in these excursions, which are made the occasion of special festivities and jollifications. The places where the pines grow are often a long way from water, so that water enough for all must be carried. It is brought in narrow-mouthed baskets called water bottles, of which there are several kinds and sizes.

Sometimes the cones are gathered green, before the scales have opened to set free the seeds, and are piled in heaps on the ground and burned until the heat causes them to open. In preparing the nuts for food the Indians first roast them slightly by shaking them with hot coals in a flat winnowing basket; they are then pounded or ground into meal, which is made into bread, mush, and soup, and eaten alone or mixed with dried berries, fruits, or other delicacies.

Besides the nuts of the piñon, which grows so abundantly in their own country, the Mono prize the acorns of the California black oak, which is found far away on the other side of the High Sierra. To obtain these acorns special trips are made over the rugged mountain passes and down the west slope to the lower or yellow pine belt in which the oaks grow. In former years some of these trips led to bloody wars with the Yosemite Mi-wa and other bands of so-called "Digger" Indians, whose territory includes the black oak belt; now they are the occasion of friendly visits with the few survivors of these interesting people.

The Ko-too-mut Ke-hi-ah or Fiesta for the Dead

A MORTUARY CEREMONY OF THE TONG-VA OF TEJON[1]

[Plate 24]

The Ko-too'-mut Ke-hi'-ah is an elaborate ceremony sacred to the memory of the dead. It lasts eight days and is always given by a person of wealth and prominence.

The length of time elapsing between the death and the ceremony varies from one to three or even four years, depending on the time necessary for the giver to accumulate the necessary means—food, clothing, baskets, wampum or money, and other needed articles. To this end he makes every sacrifice.

The person giving the fiesta is called mah-ne-sas or master of ceremonies. He contributes the feast and most of the baskets to be sacrificed, furnishes all the food to be eaten by the guests during the eight days of the ceremony, invites such of the neighboring tribes and bands as are desired, names the principal participants, and chooses from each tribe or village a prominent man to serve as captain for that tribe or village. These captains, called to-me-arr', must be actual mourners—persons who have lost a near relative within the period covered by the fiesta. It rarely happens therefore that the to-me-arr' is the real chief of the tribe or band which he represents. Each to-me-arr' selects from his relatives two or three men (if

---

[1] Presented by Dr. Merriam at the 390th regular meeting of the Anthropological Society of Washington, at the Cosmos Club, April 24, 1906, under the title, "Fragments of Californian Ethnology: A Mortuary Ceremony, Kotumut."

77

possible, a son, brother, or uncle) to do the necessary work. These workers are called wor-ro'-rhat [wo-ro'-rhat, war-ro'-rhat], and, like the captains, must be actual mourners.

When the mah-ne-sahs, or master of ceremonies and host of the feast, has everything in readiness and has fixed the date, he notifies the to-me-arr' or tribal captains, and these see that the workers are ready and present at the appointed place and time. The place is his own home.

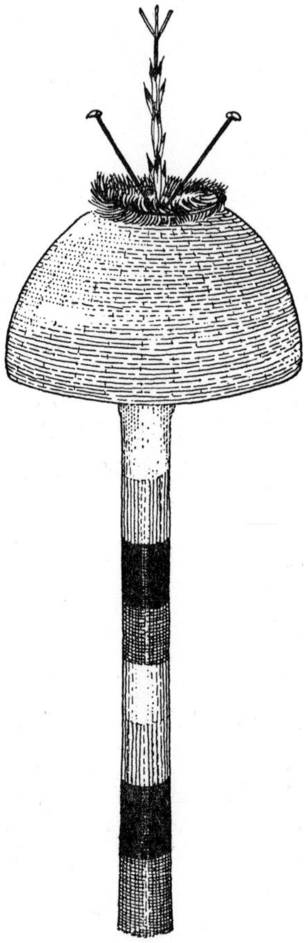

The master of ceremonies has previously invited a number of women mourners (called taw-to'-kow) who are expected to bring offerings of clothes, beads, food, money, and baskets for the sacrifice. But they must not bring more than two or three baskets apiece as the main supply is furnished by the mah-ne-sas. He may have bought all of these. Baskets made for this purpose are of the best workmanship, and are sold by the makers to the mah-ne-sas at a very low figure, usually about one-tenth of their real value.

When the day has arrived, the people assemble at the house of the master of ceremonies. First to appear are the wor-ro'-rhat, or workers, who come early in the morning, are given a dinner to take with them, and set out at once into the mountains to cut and fetch a pine tree, which must be at least forty or fifty feet in height. When the tree has been felled and the branches lopped off, the trunk is carried on the shoulders of the workers to the fiesta ground, where the bark is peeled off and the pole is polished with pumice stone, painted, and adorned with baskets.

Fig. 1. Top of Ko-too-mut pole.

It is then called Ko-too'-mut, and becomes the central figure of the ceremony. The paint is put on in bands or rings about six inches wide, in four colors arranged in the following order: white, red, black, and gray, each of which has a particular significance. These rings are repeated from top to bottom until the entire pole is covered.

[A letter to Dr. Merriam from Constance Goddard Dubois, dated March 7, 1907, comments as follows.]

On looking over your last letter I see you mention the Kotumut pole. Is it not remarkable that I had exactly that word for this fiesta? It was called *Nortish* or

Kutumit (so I spelled it). Was your word supposed to be Luiseño? The connections of these Indians with other tribes prove to be very interesting.

The pole itself was called Kee-mul Che-ha-nish [in Luiseño]. Baskets were hung on top to be reached in a contest of skill.

It is as high as the house, and painted with different colors. It represents the dead man, the spirit. Different parts of the pole are painted in different colors to refer to different parts of the body. It is not painted in the shape of a man, but one part means the knee, another the arm, etc. The top, for the head, is always painted white. On top is fastened the dressed raven's skin.

This fiesta came [to the Luiseño] from the north, but was performed at San Luis Rey within the memory of Lucario, an old blind man.

When the Ko-too'-mut pole has been trimmed and painted, and a hole dug in the ground for it to stand in, the baskets are put on. These are mainly the beautiful mortuary urns and the handsome choke-mouth receptacles called by the Mexicans "guaritas." Both kinds are richly ornamented with symbolic designs in red and black. They are put on bottom-side up, the smallest at the top, the largest at the bottom. The bottoms are cut out to admit the pole; and in most of the urn-shaped baskets the top has to be cut out also since the pole is too big to pass through the natural opening.

The top basket, which must always be the same in form and design, is called tso-po'-tat; the second ko'-maht; the third and all the others ho-ko'-pe-tat.

The top basket, as already remarked, must be of a particular kind, and always the same. When it is turned bottom up over the pole it is decorated in this wise: a small stick dressed in feathers is stuck up vertically in the center of the bottom, and two sticks painted red are fastened obliquely one on each side of it, as shown in figure 1. To the top of each of these sticks is fastened a small shell. The middle stick is decorated with feathers for its entire length and at the summit are three white quills, cut from the butt ends of eagle plumes. An eagle plume, dyed red with red earth, is wound round the bases of the three sticks. This completes the decoration of the top basket.

Captain Gaspar de Portola and Father Juan Crespi in their diaries of the Portola Expedition, 1769, write of the high poles in the Indian cemeteries of Santa Barbara Channel.

Portola says: "In all these towns they have cemeteries, in which poles are raised over the graves with the distinction that for the chiefs they raise a higher pole, and, if it is a woman, they hang baskets or wooden bowls on the pole, if that of a man, the hair, sacrificed by his relatives."[2]

Crespi says: "They explained to us that they had one [cemetery] for the men and another for the women, and that before each grave is placed a very high pole

---

[2] Publs. Acad. Pacific Coast History, I (no. 3):29, 1909.

painted in several colors, on which is hung the hair of the men, which without doubt is cut from the body before burial. On the poles for women there are wicker baskets."[3]

Miguel Costanso, in his *Narrative of the Portola Expedition*, writes: "They bury the dead and their burying grounds are within the town itself. The funerals of their chiefs are conducted with much pomp, and they erect over their bodies some very high rods or poles, on which they hang a variety of articles and utensils which they used. They also place on the same spot some large pine boards with various pictures and figures, representing no doubt, the achievements and valor of the individual."[4]

THE MOURNERS

The principal women mourners, those who sing and dance during the ceremony, paint their faces red in regular designs and wear ornamental skirts reaching halfway from knees to ankles, with eagle down on the breast, and on the head a broad band of eagle down or rabbit fur dyed pink. They wear necklaces and belts covered with beads and wampum, and carry in their hands strings of bear's teeth and claws to jingle as they dance.

The men paint their arms and bodies and have a special mark in the middle of the breast. The medicine men dress in a short skirt of feathers reaching to the knees and wear anklets that jingle as they dance. They wear also high caps and eagle plumes sticking up all round and a cleverly made collar of beads, stones, and bear claws.

While the baskets are being arranged on the pole, which is held in a slanting position, the butt resting on the ground, the mourners bring their offerings of food, clothing, baskets, beads, and money and toss them against it in such quantities that it is nearly buried, at the same time wailing, crying, and singing their mournful chants to the dead.

Then the workers slowly erect the pole and stand it in the hole dug for its reception. While this is going on the mourners shake shallow baskets of pine nuts and other edible seeds and shower them against the pole, singing the Che-ā-ē[ch] Ke-hi'-yah:

CHE-A-E[ch] KE-HI'-YAH

1. Wā'-mi wo'-vā-nah[ch] Ke-hi'-yah
2. Wā'-mi wo'-vā-nah[ch] Ke-hi'-yah Ke-hi'-yah
3. Po-kah'-vo yah'ng-o yā-ro
4. Po-kah'-vo yah'ng-o yā-ro
5. Ah-soo'-no ah-soo'-no Ke-hi'-yah Ke-hi'-yah
6. Po-kah'-vo-yah'ng-o yā-ro
7. Po-kah'-vo-yah'ng-o yā-ro

[3] Palou, *Noticia de la Nueva California*, II: 144 (Mexico), 1874.
[4] Publs. Acad. Pacific Coast History, I (no. 4):47, 1909.

Lines 1 and 3 translate thus, word for word:

1. All-together lifting, Ke-hi'-yah
3. Give-some-[seeds]-to-me to-throw

When the pole is in position the men give three loud yells or whoops, pressing the fingers over the mouth and vibrating them rapidly so as to produce a trembling sound. This is repeated on the last (eighth) day, when the pole is transferred to the graveyard and erected again.

THE KO-TOO'-MUT SONG

As soon as the yells have been given, the singers form a circle around the pole and, keeping step, forward and backward, sing the Ko-too'-mut song—a pretty little melody—to the pole. The words are as follows.

Non wī"k mah
Non wī"k mah
Non wī"k mah

Ko-too'-mut-tah

During the continuance of the fiesta the Ko-too'-mut song is repeated three times a day—morning, afternoon, and night.

THE SOO-E'-SOO-E^CH

Once each day while the ceremony lasts, as each invited to-me-arr', or visiting chief of the Kotoomut, brings his people to the Ke-hi'-ah, he and they, on entering the fiesta ground, sing together the Soo-e'-soo-ē^ch, the words of which, as sung for me by Mrs. J. V. Rosemyre at Bakersfield, July, 1905, are as follows. (Her father was a Serrano, her mother a San Gabriel.)

Po'-mo we'-ween	po'-mo we'-ween
Po'-mo we'ween	po'-mo we'-ween
They [are] beginning	they [are] beginning
Po'-mo wī'k-mah	po-mo'-tah he-tah'-rah
Po'-mo wī'k-mah	po-mo'tah he-tah'-rah
They [are] measuring	they why (?)
Māh-rah'k'-mahm	che-wā-nah^ch
Shall tell him (?)	explain it
Māh-rah'k'-mahm	too-ko'-pe-tah
Shall tell him (?)	the sky above

Then, at irregular intervals a light melody is sung.

> To'-ve-mah to'-ve-mah pan'-nah hah'-re
> To-ve-mah to-ve-mah pan-nah hah-re
> To-ve-mah to-ve-mah pan-nah hah-re
> To-ve-mah to-ve-mah pan-nah hah-re
>
> To-vē't-ke pan'-nah hah'-re
> To-vē't-ke pan'-nah hah'-re
>
> To'-ve-mah to'-ve-mah pan'-nah hah're
> To-ve-mah to-ve-mah pan-nah hah-re
>
> To-ve't-ke pan-nah han-re   (twice)
> To'-ve-mah to'-ve-mah pan'nah hah're   (twice)
> To-ve't ke pan'-nah hah'-re   (twice)
> To'-ve-mah to'-ve-mah pan'-nah hah'-re   (five times)
>
> To-ve't ke pan'-nah hah'-re
> To-ve't ke pan'-nah hah'-re

On the eighth and last day the workers take up the pole and carry it on their shoulders to the koo-nahs'-gnah, or burial ground, where it is erected among the graves and allowed to stand forever, the baskets slowly going to pieces as the years roll by.

When the pole is stood up in its final resting-place, the men give three loud tremulous yells, as when it was first erected. Then the singers gather around it and sing again for the last time the Ko-too'-mut song.

THE CHI'-E-VOR

Then all return to the Ke-hi'-ah ground where the last and most remarkable part of the ceremony is enacted. The tribal captains (to-me-arr')[5] take from the pile of offerings enough silver to give three or four dollars to each of the workers (wor-ro'-raht); all the rest of the presents (se-ō^ch-he) are gathered together into as compact a mass as possible and put into a large bag made of seal skins brought from the coast, and shaped like some huge animal. This effigy is decorated with beads, shells, and feathers, and trimmed along the borders with eagle plumes. All this is done by the workers, in the house of the mah-ne-sahs (the person giving the Ke-hi'-yah). When stuffed and sewed up ready for the final act, the effigy is called Chi'-e-vōr, and is a most sacred object.

It contains hundreds of dollars worth of beautiful baskets, and large quantities of beans, bread, grain, acorns, pine nuts and other food, clothing (including in recent times whole pieces of new cloth), long strings of

---

[5] Hugo Reid says the chief's oldest son is called tomear, eldest daughter, manisar. (*Los Angeles Star*, 1852); Taylor, *California Farmer*, June 11, 1861.

beads and wampum, handsome abalone shells, and even silver and gold money—all given freely to be sacrificed as a burnt offering to the dead.

The effigy or Chi′evōr is now brought out of the house and carried to the center of the fiesta ground by a number of old men, preceded by a man, curiously painted and in strange attire, who walks backward uttering "Hŏh′, hŏh′, hŏh′." Following him is an old man with hands extended in front (palms down) who, waving his hands downward and walking backward, says in a solemn voice: ah^{ch}-ah^{ch}-ah^{ch} (expiratory breathing). Meanwhile everybody wails, and the relatives follow with their hair down.

A large fire is now kindled, the Chi′evōr is placed upon it, and more wood is thrown on, until the whole is consumed. Some of the hair of the dead, carefully preserved for the purpose, is burned with the effigy.

It should be remembered that the people who bring the offerings for this sacrifice are themselves very poor and need everything they have. Their generosity is a pathetic illustration of the intensity of their devotion to the memory of the dead.

THE TOV-TOO-E^{CH}

After the burning is completed the to-me-arr′, or chiefs, of the Kotumut sprinkle earth on the ashes and trample the place down hard by stamping with their feet.

Then a young unmarried man called to-vē′t, son of a chief, is carried by three of the workers from his home to the place and is paid for dancing. He is curiously dressed in feathers, wearing a large feather headdress called hah-rah′-rum which comes down to his shoulders and is crowned with eagle plumes and set with beads, wampum, and gold, and a short feather skirt, the upper part white, the bottom black. The sacred funeral rope (hō-yow't we′-vōr) is wound spirally around his naked body, which, with his arms, is painted red, white, blue, and gray, each color having a special significance. He carries two sticks, about two feet in length, which he beats together to make a noise and keep time, striking them over his head, around his legs, and so on. On each shoulder he wears a curious object called ah-ū′-in (noise), covered with feathers and containing something which, when he dances, makes a noise like a bell or rattle. These shoulder pieces are tied on with (or to) the same sacred rope (hō-yow't we′-vōr), which is wound around his body.

When everything is ready, to-vē′t, the dancer, begins to dance, and the surrounding circle of men singers sing:

Het-tā-pah′-se   (4 times)
Hoo′-e, hoo′-e, hoo′-e
[Lower]   Hŭh′, hŭh′, hŭh′

He then dances violently on the spot where the fire was, whirling rapidly and irregularly, while the singers, surrounding him in a circle, address the dead, singing:

> Tor'-kwah-po uk'-ko ho'-yo wah'-we we'-wah yow'm-ne   (3 times)
> Ho'-yo wah'-we we'-wah yow'm-ne
> Tor'-kwah-po hah-rah'-rum hah-rah'-rum tah'-met pahm-se-ō't ne-pah

These song words mean:

tor'-kwah-po	beneath
uk'-ko	lie down
ho'-yo	the sacred we'-vor
wa'-we	alone
we'-wah	you are following me
yow'm-ne	catch me
hah-rah'-rum	feather headdress
tah'-met	the sun
pahm-se-ō't	big bird
ne-pah	my brother

This ends the fiesta.

While here at Bakersfield this October 11–15, 1903, I have spent about five hours each day with an old Indian woman, Mrs. James V. Rosemyre, whose father was a Serrano and whose mother was a San Gabriel. She speaks both languages and I got very full vocabularies of both. She was a "singer" in early and middle life and still remembers a number of songs in San Gabriel—particularly funeral songs and songs sung during the Fiesta for the Dead.

This fiesta was given by prominent mourners in several tribes inhabiting the San Bernardino and Tejon mountains and neighboring valleys—particularly the Serrano and San Gabriel tribes. Some years ago Mrs. Rosemyre gave two fiestas, one in honor of her father, the other for her mother. The Tejons, Tulareños, and others were invited.

Following are the words used in this Fiesta for the Dead.

	In San Gabriel	*In Serrano*
fiesta	ke-hi-e	wah-kats
burial place	koo-nahs'-gnah	nah-kah'-me-ă-nā-ve-ah
effigy burned	chi'-e-vor	chi-hé-vot
woman captain, hostess, and master of ceremonies	mah-ne'-sahs	ke-kaah'-an-nă-me-hoon
tribal captains	to-me-ar'	ke'-ki
workers	wor-ro'-rhat	pah-pah'-cho-kum
mourners	taw-to'-kow	no-nōm
pole	ko-too'-mut	ko-too'-mut
cylinder	ho-yow't	hoo'-yah-ot
entering song	soo-e'-soo-ēch	hoo-e'-ko-man-nits

Sometimes the fiesta is called Chiebor (or Chi-e-vor) in Gabriel (and Chi-he-bot in Serrano) after the burned effigy.

Among several tribes, including the San Gabriels and Serranos, it was a common practice to put and leave on the graves beautiful urn-shaped and choke-mouth baskets (*guaritas*), just as we use tombstones. Sometimes they are filled with food.

Both Mr. J. V. Rosemyre and Mr. Lopez tell me that they have seen three or four poles standing in the old burial ground at the "Monte" near Tejon, representing as many Fiestas for the Dead. They were impressed by the beauty of the baskets, as only the very best were used on the poles.

A common design on baskets in this region is this:

Fig. 2. Ko-too-mut basket design.

In different tribes it means different things. Here, Mrs. Rosemyre tells me, it means an artificial "bird" used by the Serranos and San Gabriels at funerals. This "bird," called Ho-yow't, is a cylinder covered with feathers, white in the middle, red at the ends. It is strung on a rope or long cord (called Ho-yow't we'-vor) carried by two men alongside the funeral procession, and is thrown forward and back on the we'vor by the men holding the ends of the rope. It is so constructed as to make a mournful sound, and this is its function. This song, called We-vo'-e-naht, after the mystic we'-vor, was sung by Mrs. Rosemyre herself and by her grandfather. It is sung at the burial, in presence of the body; not part of the Kotoomut fiesta.

WE'-VO-E-NAHT

Si'-woh! Si'-woh! Ah' soon po'ro soo'e-no ka'-ro (7 times)
    Si'-woh! Si'-woh! ah'-soon po'ro
Nu'-re! nu'-re! ah'soon po'-ro
So-aht'-po so-aht' wah-ne'-vo

Yi'-vo yi'-vo kah' soon po'-ro soo'e-no ka'-ro
Si'-woh! si'-woh! ah'soon po'-ro soo'e-no ka'ro   (twice)

    Si'-woh si'-woh ah'soon po'-ro

ADDENDUM

PUBERTY SONG OF THE TONGVA

This is called Sā-wē^{ch}. It is sung by the mothers while dancing in a circle around a group of young girls twelve to fifteen years old. It was sung for me by Mrs. J. V. Rosemyre at Bakersfield, July, 1905.

Hah'-ming-mi^{ch}	yow'k mi	sŏw'-ā-to-tah'-rah	(3 times)
Where do they	get it	the singing stone	
We-soo'-rah	pi'-e-sŏw'-tah	yā-wā'k	tow-sŏw-tah
Magic	drink this tea	again	the stone
Ham-me-mah	yow'k mah	sŏw-ā-to-tah'-rah	(3 times)

A curious porous stone called to-sow't came from the sea. It belongs to the chief but is borrowed by an old woman who gives the Puberty dance. The old woman makes a very bitter tea of the large seeds of the manroot vine, *Echinocystis macrocarpa*. The vine and seeds are called e'-hi-e'^{ch}. The tea is called pah-e'-hi^{ch}. The stone to-sow't is put into a basket of hot water, when it at once begins to gurgle and sing. The girls stand around it looking down at it. Then the stone is taken out of the water and a small bowl-shaped basket of the bitter tea is placed upon it. Then each girl's mother (or aunt) puts a valuable thing (shell or money) under a small cup and the old woman takes and keeps the money and gives each girl a cup of the bitter tea to drink. After the ceremony the chief announces that the girls are women.

The Luiseño: Observations on Mission Indians[1]

We visited three bands or settlements of the San Luis Rey or Luiseño Mission Indians—Rincon, La Jolla (pronounced La-ho-ya), and Pauma. There are two or three other bands which we did not visit, namely Mesa Grande, Agua Caliente (Warner Ranch), and San Luis Rey Mission.

I was fortunate in having my cousin, Harry S. Merriam, with me, as he not only speaks Spanish fluently but also is personally acquainted with all the Indians of the three settlements visited. This enabled me to learn in a short time more than I could possibly have accomplished in weeks by myself. Only a few of the younger Indians whom we encountered could speak English.

In all three of the settlements the people live in well-made adobe houses, many of which have a willowwork room and willow- and brush-covered shelter outside for summer use. The houses are not near together but scattered about, usually an eighth or a quarter of a mile apart. Most of them are provided with wells, though some are so near the base of the mountain that they have small streamlets of running water.

They cultivate peaches and figs, and the fruit of both was drying on flat baskets (*batéas*) and scaffolds at all the houses we visited. Fig and to-bacco trees grow about the houses, and great masses of the giant tuna cactus are often near by. Usually the house stands on a small cleared place surrounded by chaparral.

Most of the families cultivate wheat and barley—barley for their horses and wheat for themselves.

---

[1] Extract, dated Sept. 24, 1901, from Dr. Merriam's California Journal, Vol. II.—Ed.

They all have stone mortars and metates for hammering and pulveriz-
ing the grain and acorns, and some of them have large upright cylindrical
willowwork storehouses for the grain, called mus'-co-nish. These storehouses are really fine pieces of work. They are three to four feet in diameter and four to six or seven feet high and are made by winding the willows, with the leaves on, around and around in a close spiral and weaving
in the ends.

Many of the houses have brush roofs, and some have thatch-roofed
piazzas in front; in one house (that of Pesqual and Appolonia, his wife) the
front of the piazza is covered with vines.

All of the families have large home-made clay water bottles called *ollas*.
These are usually covered with a piece of cloth, wet to keep the water
cool; some are set in the ground and others are stood in a box of earth on a
bench or rest of some kind to keep them at convenient height. The earth is
kept moist and the water is deliciously cool.

At many of the houses the women were sitting on the ground, usually
under a brush-roofed shelter, winnowing grain. They thresh the grain by
piling it around a post and driving or riding horses (usually 3 horses)
around and around over it, a man riding one of the horses and driving the
others, while old women work over the straw and pitch it where it will be
properly trodden as the horses go round.

After the grain is threshed the women gather it up in big baskets and
bring it to the house, where they winnow it by rocking it in flat or nearly
flat (slightly concave) baskets which they call, in Spanish, *batéa*. These
baskets are circular in outline and vary from fifteen to seventeen inches
in diameter. They are plain or decorated. The most common design consists of from one to three black rings around the outer third. Some are
much more elaborately ornamented. The Indians' name for this basket is
tuk-mal. In shape and size it resembles the het-al, or winnowing basket,
of the Mariposa Mew'-wah Indians, but in weave and design of ornamentation the two are widely different.

The old Luiseño women agitate these baskets full of wheat with double
motion—a rotary and at the same time a pitching movement—so that
the chaff gathers on the top where the wind carries it off (or if no wind,
they cuff it off) and the sand in the grain comes to one place on the edge.
They then smash the grain in their stone mortars and grind it to flour on
their stone metates.

In Rincon I discovered at two houses, legged metates—metates with
three legs hewn out of the stone on the underside of each. These legs are
at the ends, those at one end being larger than at the other, in order to
give the metate the proper slant. The stone they work back and forth in
their hand to do the grinding is flat on one side (or really slightly concave

lengthwise) so as to conform to the trough of the metate. I purchased a
fine old one, but not without difficulty, as they are loath to part with
them. I got it at Pauma, where I found still another, making four in all
that I actually saw. There are doubtless others. The ordinary common
metates one sees at all the houses have no legs but lie flat on the ground.

The stone mortars, like metates, vary greatly in workmanship. Some
are neatly rounded outside; some nearly globular; some handsomely
quadrangular with beautifully rounded and smoothed top, while others
are merely rough rocks with the regulation mortar hole on the top. One
(which I examined at the house of Louis Majado at La Jolla) had a flaring
basket rim five or six inches wide fastened with a resin or pitch to the
inside of the top of the mortar, so as to catch the spattering grains. I shall
try to secure it.

In the late fall all of these old Indians go to Palomar Mountain to
gather the acorns of the black oak (*Quercus californica*) from which they
make mush and soup, usually mixing fresh meat or pork and chile with
the acorn meal. The old women call the black oak acorn we'-ut. The
acorn of the mountain live oak (*Q. chrysolepsis*) they call que'-la. The
latter they say is too hard to smash and grind to be available to any extent
for food. The acorn of the valley live oak (*Q. agrifolia*) they call we-as-'el,
but I did not learn that these are ever used for food.

These Mission Indians still make many baskets, but of few kinds. I
found nothing among them corresponding to the big cornucopia carrying
baskets of the northern tribes (the che-ka-la of the Mew'-wah or the wo-na
of the Piute), nor to the large compact baskets in which acorn meal is
cooked by means of hot stones.

The baskets I saw and talked to them about (and purchased examples
of) belong to six classes, as follows.

1. Large bowl-shaped baskets with flat bottoms, for holding grain, fruit, acorns,
   etc. (some nearly or quite 3 ft. across). Called in Spanish *cora*, in Luiseño bak-ut
   (or pac-kwut; or pa-cot).
2. Small bowls, usually shaped like wash basins. Spanish name *corita*, Luiseño
   bak-qua-mal (or pac-kwa-mal).
3. Circular winnowing baskets (15–17 in. diam.). Spanish *batéa*, Luiseño tuk-mal
   (or took-mul).
4. Subglobular baskets with flat bottoms and mouth smaller than bottom (usually
   6–8 in. diam.). Spanish *guarita*, Luiseño pay-yayo-mal. Larger baskets of this
   kind are called in Spanish *guare* (warra), in Luiseño pay-yayo-la.
5. Hat baskets (truncate cones), now rarely worn. I could find only one. Name in
   Luiseño chel-koot (or chel-kwut).
6. Acorn-gathering baskets, of open work, usually subglobular or subcylindrical,
   with rounded bottoms. Usually rather small, holding two to six quarts. Called
   char-ra.

For carrying burdens the old women have open-mesh nets, which they carry on their backs, supported by a band across the forehead. I saw them carrying heavy loads of squashes in these nets. They also carry their big ollas full of water in the same way, and loads of acorns (first enclosed in a sack or basket) and other heavy matter. They call these nets ul-cot (or ool-koot). In all these names it is difficult to determine the exact pronunciation.

Practically all of the baskets are straw color, with designs in yellowish brown and blue-black or purplish black. No other colors were seen by me.

All of the baskets (except the openwork acorn-gathering basket) are coiled, and the coil is made of a bundle of grass. The body work which covers the grass coil both outside and inside (of pale straw color) consists of split (peeled) twigs of the squaw bush (*Rhus trilobata*) which they get on the mountains—mainly on Palomar where I found it growing in abundance. When fresh it has a strong aromatic odor.

The yellowish brown material, which usually has a glossy surface, is a slender bulb-rush, split. It is past maturity and has assumed the yellowish or golden brown tint when gathered, and is a natural color, not dyed.

The black or purple-black material is the same bulb-rush, gathered younger (when still whitish or pale straw color), dyed, and afterward split. The women told us that they color it by burying it in a certain kind of mud for one or two days. Some say there is iron in the wet mud. The rushes grow in San Luis Rey Valley.

I was told by Harry Merriam, and also by the teacher of the Indian school at Rincon, Miss Ora Salmon, both of whom have witnessed the ceremony, that just a year after the death of an Indian a mourning "fiesta" is held, at which relatives and friends of the deceased build a long fire and throw into it clothing and fine baskets woven for the purpose— baskets they will not sell. The other Indians, invited guests, are placed on the other side of the fire, and if any of the baskets fail to lodge in the fire but roll on their side, they are at liberty to take and keep them. Miss Salmon, who has been a teacher among them for fourteen years, tells me that the baskets burned at these death anniversaries are often of the best workmanship and most sacred designs—the baskets into which they weave their lives.

The graveyards, two of which we visited, are curious affairs. They are enclosed by some kind of a fence—usually wire or wire and pickets—and are merely flat bare places cleared in the chaparral. The graves are mounds a foot high, marked by a wooden cross of some kind, usually low, and almost completely covered with glass and crockery, mostly broken. Most of them have an eviscerated clock (commonly a Waterbury or something of the kind) with the hands set on the hour of death, hung from the headboard. On the middle or other end of the grave is a lamp, usually a glass kerosene lamp. The rest of the grave is covered with cups and saucers, tumblers, beer bottles, teapots, pitchers, and bits of broken crockery and glass. Several had old tin cans, and one had an earthenware spittoon. The name and date of death are cut or written on the crossbar of the headboard.

These Indians are very fond of fiestas and go from camp to camp and tribe to tribe to take part in them. Most of them have just returned from a fiesta at Saboba, and in a week or two they are going to another, to be given by the Indians at Cahuilla (pronounced Ka-we′ah) or at Pichanga. They dance a great deal and decorate themselves for the occasion. In the house of Appolonia Omish I saw a feather belt, consisting of tail feathers of several golden eagles. Each feather was attached to a hemp cord and the cords were woven into a hemp belt, finely made. This is worn around the waist. I saw also a woman's belt with a shredded bark (like inner bark of cedar) dangling a foot or fifteen inches from the front part of it. They used to dance naked, except for these belts, but now are said to wear underskirts and drawers, with the belt put on afterward.

The young men have organized rabbit hunts in which they choose sides and run the rabbits on horseback in the chaparral and kill them by throwing sticks at them. Harry Merriam showed me a stretch of "wild buckwheat" chaparral, mixed with more formidable kinds, in which hunts are held nearly every Sunday. Usually the Rincon boys play against the La Jolla boys. They hunt in pairs, one man of each side riding together. The one whose turn comes first gives chase to the first rabbit started and rushes his horse after it at full speed. The horse is said to take an active interest in the sport and do his best to get over the rabbit. As the Indian rides up alongside he throws his stick violently down and usually kills the quarry. If he misses, his fellow rider of the opposite side takes up the chase and tries his hand. When all the rabbits have been killed, the sides count the results and the side having the largest number gains the game. The rabbits are then roasted entire (without opening) in the ashes and feast ends the sport.

In several places we found large flat rocks perforated by the old mortar pits of the Indians. One of these is between Valley Center and Rincon, but the best is on Palomar, right among the black oaks whose acorns were hammered up in them. This one is in Doan Valley and there are at least twenty mortar holes in the one rock. It is the finest I ever saw.

Most of the Luiseño have several children. The men and women are usually rather large and good-looking. The women tend to grow stout with age. The old people are numerous and look strong and healthy.

The children are very apt to develop tuberculosis and die between the ages of sixteen and twenty-five. The deaths greatly exceed the births. Most of the deaths are of young people, and many of the young men and women we saw were coughing sadly. We were told that there have already been fourteen deaths of young people this year (1901); a girl of nineteen died the day before we reached La Jolla. Most of the inhabitants were at her house, leaving their own locked. A girl recently returned from an Indian school at Carlisle, Pennsylvania, had a dreadful cough and apparently a short lease on life. She died the same year.

Apparently all the families have small iron stoves, most of them outside the houses now, under the brush piazzas or shelter, but they are brought inside as winter approaches. On nearly all of these stoves I noticed the home-made clay ollas containing boiling water or some kind of soup or stew, cooking. Many of the baskets about the houses contained figs, peaches, red peppers, onions, and the like, and some held grapes.

The Beñemé of Garcés

On March 8, 1776, Padre Francisco Garcés, while plodding his weary way over the Mohave Desert, discovered an Indian village belonging to a tribe which he called Beñemé (Chemeweve). He was traveling west from the country of the Mohave Indians on Colorado River and was quick to observe that he had encountered a different people, for his journal of that date contains the following entry: "I arrived at some very abundant wells which I named Pozos de San Juan de Dios, and there is sufficient grass. Here begins the Beñemé nation."[1]

The place was identified by Coues as Marl Springs.[2] Marl Springs is shown on the U. S. Geological Survey's map of "Desert Watering Places in the Mohave Desert," as about twenty miles east of Soda Lake—otherwise known as the Sink of the Mohave.[3]

From these springs or "wells" Garcés continued west five leagues to an arroyo of saltish water which he named (Arroyo) de los Martires (probably the arroyo leading into the Sink of the Mohave), and next day followed the windings of the river in a general west-southwest direction, camping on the same arroyo in a place with "cottonwoods, much grass, and lagunas," identified by Coues as in the vicinity of the Caves, "a usual first stopping place in going up the Mohave from Soda lake."[4]

A day later (March 11), the entry reads:[5]

Having gone one league eastsoutheast I arrived at some rancherias so poor that they had to eat no other thing than the roots of rushes (*rayzes de tule*); they are of

---

[1] *On the Trail of a Spanish Pioneer, the Diary and Itinerary of Francisco Garcés, 1775-1776*, trans. and ed. by Elliott Coues, 1:238, 1900.

[2] *Ibid.*, p. 258, fn. 10.

[3] U.S.G.S. Water Supply Paper 490-B, pl. 12, sheet 4, 1921.

[4] *On the Trail of a Spanish Pioneer*, p. 239, fn. 18.

[5] *Ibid.*, pp. 239–241.

the Beñemé nation and there were about 25 souls. I gave them my little store (*los regale con mi pobreza*), and they did the same with their tule-roots, which my companions the Jamajabs [Mohaves] ate with repugnance. The poor people manifested much concern at their inability to go hunting in order to supply me, inasmuch as it was raining and very cold, and they were entirely naked. Here grows the wild grape; there is much grass; also mezquites and trees that grow the screw. This nation is the same as that of San Gabriel, Santa Clara, and San Joseph. They have some baskets (*coritas*) like those of the Canal (de Santa Barbara). They have coats of otter, and of rabbits, and some very curious snares that they make of wild hemp, of which there is much in these lands. As a rule are they very effeminate, and the women uncleanly, like those of the sierras; but all are very quiet and inoffensive, and they hear with attention that which is told them of God.

On March 12, still journeying along the Mohave River for two leagues farther to the west-southwest, he came to an uninhabited rancheria where, while waiting for his Mohave Indians to kill and eat one of their horses, he remarked:[6]

The rain, the cold, and hunger continued, for there were no roots of tule, and the remaining inhabited rancherias were afar (*largo trecho*). In which emergency I determined that my companions should kill a horse to relieve the necessity; not even was the blood thereof wasted, for indeed there was need to go on short rations (*ponor cóto en las raciones*) in order to survive the days that we required to reach the next rancherias. On account of the severe cold turned back from here one Jamajab Indian of those who were accompanying me; of the other two Indians of his nation I covered the one with a blanket, and the other with a shirt (*tunica*). As there was much to eat of the dead horse, they would not depart hence until the 15th day [of the month—which was 3 days later].

On the fifteenth he followed the river for another league and a half to the northwest, and on the sixteenth two leagues more. Then, quitting the river, he traveled southwest until he met it again and continued, with some inclination to the south, for four leagues to a point where "there were good grass, large cottonwoods, cranes, and crows of the kind that there is at San Gabriel."

A day later, while crossing the river, his mule mired down, wetting all that he was carrying, so he remained at the place and dispatched his Indian Sevastian and another Indian to seek inhabited rancherias. The next day (March 18) Sevastian "returned without mishap, praising the kind reception that had been given them [himself and his companion] by the Indians whom they had seen"; whereupon Garcés went five leagues southwest up the river, there arriving "at a rancheria of some forty souls of the same Beñemé nation," where, he says, "they regaled me with hares, rabbits, and great abundance of acorn porridge."

---

[6] *Ibid.*, p. 241.

Next day, when one league farther on, he writes:[7]

I ... arrived at the house of the captain of these rancherias. He presented me with a string of about two varas of white sea-shells; and his wife sprinkled me with acorns and tossed the basket, which is a sign among these people of great obeisance. In a little while after that she brought sea-shells in a small gourd, and sprinkled me with them in the way which is done when flowers are thrown. Likewise when the second woman came she expressed her affection by the same ceremonies. I reciprocated these attentions as well as I could (*del modo que pude*), and marveled to see that among these people so rustic are found demonstrations proper to the most cultivated, and a particular prodigality (*magnificencia*) in scattering their greatest treasures, which are the shells.

Continuing, he appears to have remained in the territory of the same Chemeweve tribe until near the head of Cajon Canyon.

On his return more than a month later he was with them again. The exact location is uncertain, but he states:[8] "The Indians were very affable, and the women cleanlier and neater than any I had seen before of this same Beñemé nation."

In regard to the relationship of the Beñemé, Garcés says, "This nation is the same as that of San Gabriel, Santa Clara, and San Joseph."[9] This of course is not in accord with present-day knowledge; but it must be remembered that Garcés before setting out on this expedition had been traveling northward along or near the lower Colorado River, where he was continuously in Yuman territory; therefore after leaving the Mohave and encountering a tribe—the Beñemé—who spoke an altogether different language which he recognized as similar in general to that of San Gabriel and other San Bernardino Valley languages (for he naturally had in mind gross resemblances), it is not surprising that he regarded them as the same as those at that Mission.

Garcés found the Beñemé again on Mohave River[10] and in the western part of Mohave Desert.[11] Hodge misidentified Garcés' Beñemé as Panamint. It should be Chemeweve, for we now know that the Panamint territory comprises Death Valley and adjacent torrid valleys and ranges from Owens Lake on the west to the Amargosa Desert on the east—an area wholly north of the Chemeweve, whose territory consists of the Mohave Desert from the Colorado River west to Mohave River—perhaps even farther.

---

[7] *Ibid.*, p. 244.
[8] *Ibid.*, p. 269.
[9] *Ibid.*, p. 240. The San Joseph here mentioned was at, or near, present San Bernardino.
[10] *Ibid.*, p. 243.
[11] *Ibid.*, p. 269.

PLATES 1-24

EXPLANATION OF PLATES

PLATES 1–8

A Western Wintoon Ceremony: The Big Head Dance at Grindstone Creek, May, 1923

PLATE 1

a. Indian house with roundhouse in the background.

b, c. Roundhouse, in which major part of the ceremony was performed.

PLATE 2

a, b. Michopdo Midoo Indian from Chico wearing flat headpiece with long upstanding single feather.

c. Performer wearing skirt of frayed willow bark, flicker-feather headbands, and headdress of wands tipped with California poppies.

PLATE 3

a. Bark-skirted performers with poppy and feather-tipped headdresses at entrance to roundhouse. Attendants arranging costumes.

b. Three performers, two with red caps and cloth skirts, one with bark skirt and flicker-feather headbands.

PLATE 4

a. Performer wearing skirt of frayed willow bark, flicker-feather headbands, headdress of wands tipped with California poppies, and carrying elder music sticks, approaching roundhouse.

b. Performer with big feather headdress and split willowbark skirt backing into roundhouse. Man behind him guides him to protect the large head plumes from injury.

c. Performer wearing red-cap headdress, flicker-feather bands, cloth skirt, white feather collar, and broad feather belt.

PLATE 5

a. Two performers wearing frayed willowbark skirts, white feather headdresses, and carrying music sticks.

b. Athletic performer (under flag), carrying quiver in right hand, bow in left; faced by semisquatting dancer.

PLATE 6

a. Three performers wearing feather headdresses, flicker-feather bands, and broad feather belts.

99

b. Two performers wearing bark skirts, poppy-tipped headdresses, and broad feather belts; one at left carrying split elder music sticks. Near entrance to roundhouse.

c. Dancer with bark skirt and poppy-tipped feather headdress (right), facing two cloth-skirted performers with red caps.

PLATE 7

a. Five performers in ceremonial costumes approaching roundhouse.

b. Left: two performers with feather headdresses, kneeling. Right: flagpole group.

c. Three costumed performers squatting.

PLATE 8

a. Spectators in front of roundhouse. None in costume.

b. Single performer with frayed bark skirt, white headpiece, white feather-tipped headdress, and flicker-feather headbands, carrying a sacred music stick in each hand and running toward the flagpole.

PLATES 9–16

The Expulsion of Sahte: A Stony Ford Pomo Ceremony

PLATE 9

Roundhouse or dance house of the Shoteah Pomo, Stony Creek, Colusa County.

PLATE 10

The head dancer.

PLATE 11

The head dancer, with red foxskin quiver and bow and arrows.

PLATE 12

From left to right: head dancer, dancer with maple-fiber skirt, and Sahte.

PLATE 13

From left to right: Sahte (rear view), head dancer, and dancer with maple-bark fiber skirt.

PLATE 14

Dancer with feather headdress and elderberry clappers.

PLATE 15

a. The flag dancer.

b. The head chief.

PLATE 16

Sahte.

PLATE 17

The Mourning Ceremony or "Cry" of the Mewuk

PLATE 17

a–c. Acorn cooking at Hachanah.

PLATES 18–23

The Mono Paiute

PLATE 18
  a. Mono Lake.
  b. Mono Craters.
PLATE 19
  a. Temporary hut used while gathering fly larvae.
  b. Summer house on desert east of Mono Lake.
PLATE 20
  a. Large thatched winter house west of Mono Lake. September 8, 1900.
  b. Pumice stone used for shaping arrows.
PLATE 21
  a. Temporary brush hut on east shore of Mono Lake.
  b. Windrows of *Ephydra* fly larvae (kutsavi) on shore of Mono Lake.
PLATE 22
  a. Nut pine near Mono Lake.
  b. Top of nut pine showing unripe cones full of pine nuts.
  c. Buffalo berry bushes near shore of Mono Lake. September, 1900.
PLATE 23
  a. Paiute water bottles.
  b. Parching basket.
  c. Winnowing basket.

PLATE 24

The Ko-too-mut Ceremony

PLATE 24
  a, b. Baskets set on top of Ko-too-mut pole.

PLATE 1

a

b

c

PLATE 2

a

b

c

PLATE 3

a

b

PLATE 4

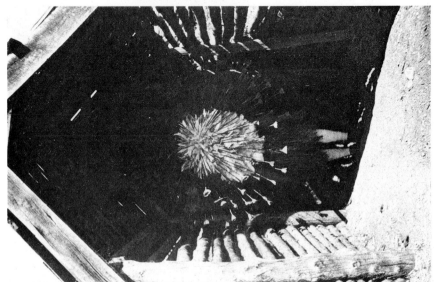

a

b

c

PLATE 5

b

a

PLATE 6

a

b

c

PLATE 7

a

b

c

PLATE 8

a

b

PLATE 9

PLATE 10

PLATE 11

Plate 12

PLATE 13

PLATE 14

PLATE 15

a

b

PLATE 16

PLATE 17

a

b

c

PLATE 18

a

b

PLATE 19

a

b

PLATE 20

a

b

PLATE 21

a

b

PLATE 22

a

b

c

PLATE 23

a

b

c

PLATE 24

a

b

NOTES ON MATERIAL CULTURE

Native Dwellings and Ceremonial Structures

[Plates 25–46]

The published accounts of California and Nevada Indians are generally deficient in illustrations of buildings. The photographs taken by Dr. Merriam therefore constitute an important contribution to our knowledge of aboriginal dwellings and ceremonial structures. The unique quality of these pictures, many of them a half-century old, makes them a record of particular value to the student of California Indian culture.

A number of these photographs are presented in plates 25 to 46, reproduced from prints in the Merriam Collection. Thorough search has failed to discover the negatives from which the prints were made and it is possible that they were deposited in the Library of Congress.

Figuring prominently in the Merriam photographs are large, round semisubterranean structures typical of California Indian culture. Commonly referred to as roundhouses or dance houses, these served for ceremonial performances.[1] The one shown in plate 40, *b* belonged to the Tuleyome, a group whose habitat is discussed in a separate article in this book.

The photographs of houses of Pyramid Lake Paviotso from the Great Basin form a welcome addition to our meager knowledge of this group, as do the illustrations of structures of the Mono Lake Paiute (pls. 29, *b*, 30). The photograph of the Esselen house (pl. 35, *a*) is in all probability the only one existing of the dwellings of these little known and now extinct people. The plate of the Tachi Yokuts' mat-covered house (pl. 37) likewise presents the only known photograph of such a dwelling.

The explanation of the plates (pp. 127–129) gives all the information available concerning the illustrations.—Ed.

---

[1] These structures have been discussed by J. Haeckel, "Das Männerhaus im nördlichen Kalifornien," *Mitt. d. Anthrop. Gesell.*, 70:144–258 (Vienna), 1940.—Ed.

105

Indians as Basket Collectors

In most homes of basketmaking Indians certain baskets may be found that have been obtained from other tribes as presents, in payment of debts, or by purchase or exchange. Such baskets ("intrusive baskets") are so common that collectors unfamiliar with the languages and types of work of the different tribes often make appalling mistakes as to the real source of their purchases. A short time ago I saw in an illustrated paper a picture of a Pomo feather basket discovered by the author among a widely different tribe, which he solemnly described as a characteristic home-made article. Errors of this kind are so common that the great majority of articles on basketry contain one or more faulty identifications.

The hop-pickings are great places for basket-bartering. A few summers ago a number of Piute were brought from Nevada to help pick hops near Ukiah, in the valley of the Russian River, California, where they came in contact with the Pomo tribe and for the first time in their lives saw the delicate, finely woven, feather-decorated baskets for which these Indians are famous. They had never seen such exquisite work and their admiration knew no bounds. When paid off, they promptly spent most of their earnings in purchasing these wonderful baskets, which they took home to astonish their own people in Nevada.

For many years the hop fields near Puyallup, in the Puget Sound region, have brought together annually a motley assemblage of Indians from across the mountains and from points along the coast of Washington and British Columbia and, in some instances, even from Alaska. About the first of September, 1897, I chanced to be on the wharf at Seattle when a shipload of Indians arrived from the north, bound for the adjacent hop yards. Their personal belongings were packed in hundreds of splendid baskets—worth at usual prices many thousands of dollars—which were pitched over the side of the vessel and stacked up in a great pile on the wharf. As soon as the shower had stopped, they were sorted and carried away by the indignant owners.

Indians love fine baskets and, where so many are gathered from different tribes, the opportunity for trading and purchasing those that take their fancy is unrivaled. And many change hands as a result of gambling.

Another source of intrusive basketry may be found in the practice of stealing wives, which until recently prevailed in many tribes. The women thus introduced into other tribes naturally continued to make the baskets characteristic of their own people. Still another source is illustrated by a handsome "Tulare" basket I recently saw in Owens Valley. It was made by a Shoshone woman who had been stolen by the Tulare when a little child and had lived with them until grown up. She then crossed the mountains and joined her own people, where she continued to make the elegant baskets she had learned to weave while among the Tulare.

The Navaho of northern Arizona use many baskets, but we are informed by the late Dr. Washington Matthews, the highest authority on this tribe, that the Navaho themselves make only two types, the others being purchased, mostly from the Ute. Similarly, the Hope' of Arizona, living in villages on the high mesas adjoining the Navaho country, who make many baskets of their own, also use those of other tribes—as I can testify from personal observation. These intrusive baskets are mainly Apache and Havasupai.

In California, Pit River baskets, particularly the burden baskets, are frequently found in the camps of adjacent tribes; I have several such. Professor Roland B. Dixon, in a publication of the American Museum of Natural History, has illustrated several that he obtained from the Midu of the northern Sierra, and among the Indians of Yosemite Valley—a branch of the Me'-wok of the middle Sierra—I have myself found baskets made by no less than six different tribes.

When I was at work on the upper Tuolumne in 1901, my nearest base of supplies was the Yosemite. On one of my trips thither for provisions I found a cache in a hollow tree, which contained among other things two rather small cooking baskets of the "Fresno" type. Going to the nearest Indian camp in search of the owner, I was told that she had gone down the Merced River to visit another Indian settlement. On my next trip she had returned and was living at the camp near Yosemite Creek, from which the Indians have since been cruelly driven out by the authorities. She refused a liberal offer for the baskets and, in reply to my inquiry whether I had not offered more than they were worth, nodded assent. To my further question why she would not sell, she said, "Me like him," and I had to pay about double their value before she consented to part with them. Wishing to test her truthfulness, I asked if she had made the baskets. Receiving a negative reply, I inquired if her mother had made them. Again she shook her head, saying that they were not made by her tribe at all but came from the Fresno country—which agreed with my original diagnosis and also with my previous experience with Indians, for I have found the various tribes uniformly truthful as to the sources of their baskets.

The Piute of eastern California and western Nevada are famous basket-makers and have in daily use no less than fourteen or fifteen kinds (pl. 29, *b*). Nevertheless, foreign or intrusive baskets are common among them. At Mono Lake one summer I heard that a valuable ceremonial basket, locally known as the "tribal" basket, was kept at the headquarters of the chief, six or seven miles from the lake. Finding the chief's wife, Bu-se-una, at a neighboring camp one evening, I told her I wanted to see her baskets, and arranged to meet her at her home soon after daylight the following morning.

I set out bright and early, crossed the sagebrush plain to Rush Creek, and followed the creek up to the Indian camp. All was plain sailing until the neighborhood of the camp was reached. Here the river bottom, choked with tall willows and other brush, was down in an open canyon far below the mesa level, and a side canyon which came in at this point left a bare hill between the forks. On the mesa on both sides, and on the hill between, I could see brush huts, some dome-shaped, others conical or teepee-shaped, but no Indians and no signs of life could be discerned. Not knowing which way to go but hoping to strike a trail, I pushed my horse down into the thick bushy bottom and came suddenly upon a small garden patch from which a trail led up the hill. It was a foot trail, but by walking ahead and parting the thick brush, I was able to lead my horse through, and finally came out on top, where I found two old men, scantily clad and living entirely alone. From their home in this remote and elevated spot they commanded an inspiring view over the surrounding country.

One was the former chief, a tall, sturdy, splendidly built man with a fine head, kindly features, and dignified presence. He could speak no English, but I made him understand that I was in search of the lodge of his daughter, Bu-se-una, and that she had agreed to meet me there. He shook his head and pointed away toward the camp at Williams Butte, where she had gone the day before. On looking about the place—a circular brush enclosure with a willow hut on one side and a brush shelter near by in which articles could be hung up out of the sun—I found a few water bottles, an ornamental burden basket which he told me had been made by Bu-se-una, a fine old Yokuts cooking basket that belonged to his wife, long since dead, and a pair of openwork snowshoes or tule shoes. For all of these I offered a fair price in silver, which he promptly accepted. He then led me down a zigzag trail through the brush to Bu-se-una's cabin, the most substantial Piute house I had seen. All the other huts were on top of the mesa, but this was hidden among the willows in the bottom. Close by was a small opening carpeted with grass, part of which had been cut and spread out to dry for winter use. While waiting, the old man took a large knife, got down on his knees, and resumed his task of cutting the grass.

Finally Bu-se-una came. She had left her horse some distance below and walked up. After greeting her father she opened the door of her cabin and showed me her baskets, which, to my surprise, were locked in a large wooden chest. At first she brought out only common ones, but I insisted on seeing the "tribal" basket. "How you know?" she asked impatiently, and it took a good deal of coaxing to induce her to bring it to light. In reply to my inquiry as to price, she shook her head and said emphatically, "No sell *him*"—with the emphasis on the "him." She explained that the basket was used for cooking acorn mush on ceremonial occasions in the fall or early winter, at which season the scattered bands gather here for the acorn feast. Acorns do not grow on the east side of the mountains and have to be brought from the Yosemite and other points far away across the High Sierra. Again and again I offered Bu-se-una a liberal price for the basket, but her answer was always the same, "No sell *him*." To make a long story short, after much persuasion, reinforced by tempting gold pieces dropped into the palm of her hand, I finally overcame her scruples and rode away with the prize, together with a ribbed trinket basket and a small bowl used for dipping the mush out of the large ceremonial basket. These, with the baskets and tule shoes I had secured from her father, made such a large and unwieldy load that she kindly offered to help carry them, and rode back with me to the other camp.

Bu-se-una's ceremonial basket, like many others in use among the California Piute, proved to be not Piute at all but a fine example of the so-called "Fresno" type. It is a beautiful specimen of the style of finely woven coiled baskets on a thin grass-splint foundation, with flat bottom and straight flaring sides. In color it is a rich yellow, and the design, wrought in the jet-black root of the brake fern, consists of two horizontal zigzag bands broken on each side by three vertical zigzags, below which is a signature mark, followed by five small double rectangular symbols arranged in a horizontal row. This type of design, with minor variants, is common among the ceremonial baskets of the upper Fresno Creek region on the west side of the Sierra.

Tulare Basketry

The coiled basketry of the tribes inhabiting the foothills and lower slopes of the southern Sierra region, from San Joaquin River south to the South Fork of Tule, differs materially from that of all other regions and is commonly spoken of as "Tulare," or of the "Tulare type." Its distinctive features are: (1) foundation, grass coil; (2) body, cladium root; (3) design, bold and rather large, in black and red—the black, the root of the brake fern (*Pteridium*), the red, the terminal branches or sprouts of the redbud (*Cercis*).

The Indians making these baskets belong to two widely different linguistic stocks—the Yokuts and the Shoshonean. The tribes are the Yowelmanne, Wiktchumne, Wuksache, Emtimbitch, Chokimina, Choenimne, Gosh-sho-o, Kokoheba, and Holkoma. Closely similar baskets are sometimes made by neighboring tribes on the north—the Pitkahte, Chuckchancy and Nim tribes, and even by the southern members of the Chowchilla Muwa—but the typical basketry of these last tribes differs essentially.

Coiled baskets resembling those of the Tulare type are made also by certain unrelated tribes farther south, notably by the Tubotelobela of the valley of the South Fork of the Kern, the New-oo-a (or Kah-wis-sa) of Piute Mountain, and various tribes of the Tehachapi-Tejon region. The southern tribes, however, normally use different materials. While the coil is grass, as in Tulare basketry, the body material is split willow strands instead of cladium root, the black is Devil's Horn (*Martynia*) instead of fern root, and the red is the root of the tree yucca (*Yucca arborescens*) instead of branches of redbud.

Furthermore, each tribe, and to a certain extent each family, has its favorite designs. Formerly these were distinctive, but now they are so much imitated and copied that most of them no longer serve to identify their makers.

BASKETS OF THE CHOWCHILLA AND MARIPOSA MUWA[1]

In the pine woods northeast of Mariposa I found two or three small camps of Muwa Indians. They were shy at first, but soon talked freely and gave me a lot of information about their food, baskets, and basket materials. They opened several large sacks and threw down on the ground for me to see coils of split willow strands and bundles of rods for baskets. They had been most industrious and had a large stock on hand. They also took me into the bushes and showed me the kinds the rods came from, so I could make sure of the species.

In making the three kinds of coarse openwork baskets known as che-kah-lah (burden basket), cham'-ah (broad shallow scoop), and ching-go (deep spoon-shaped scoop with handle), the rods used may be either *Ceanothus integerrimus* (oh-hoo-ne) or *C. cuneatus* (pi'-wa or pi'-wah'). The split strands for twining the rods together are black oak, *Quercus californica* (te-lay-ly), mostly young shoots which have great strength. The rods used in the fine coiled baskets may be either syringa, *Philadelphus Lewisii* (pull-le), or sour squaw bush, *Rhus trilobata* (tum-mah), or *Ceanothus integerrimus*.

The outside strands in their coiled baskets they call "willow" of two kinds, sak-kal (or suk-kal) and tap-pa-tap-pah. The former surely is a willow; the latter I believe to be the redbud (*Cercis occidentalis*). The black used for the design is the split root of the brake fern (*Pteris aqualina*) which they call lu-na la. They had one small basket made of the Tulare marsh root, which they call pa-wee-sah.

In making manzanita cider (made from the berries of *Arctostaphylos mariposa*), the berries are merely broken or mashed a little, not ground fine at all, sprinkled with water, and then placed in an openwork bowl basket called too-poo-lah (sometimes the ordinary broad scoop, cham-ah, is used). Then the squaw, after washing her hands, sprinkles water with her hand over the crushed berries and keeps on doing this until all the good has leached out.

The too-poo-lah meanwhile rests on two sticks placed across the basket or other vessel, which receives the delicious juice as it filters through. The cham-ah baskets are used regularly for this purpose—for holding split

---

[1] "Notes on the Chowchilla and Mariposa Mu'wa (Miwok) Indians," California Journal for 1902 (Sept. 17-20), pp. 206-225.

acorns—and also for split peaches and figs and other fruit laid out to dry. The most usual material for the rods of the cham-ah is the smoke brush, *Ceanothus cuneatus.*

They have large numbers of the Fresno acorn-cooling bowls of medium and rather large size, all of which they call oh-hah. They would not sell these since they were saving them, and collecting acorns and pinole seeds, for the great acorn feast to be held in the Kolorow or Bear Creek country in about two weeks. One old squaw, who had about a dozen of these baskets varying in size from a capacity of two quarts up to nearly two bushels, told me she hadn't half baskets enough for the Indians to use at the feast to eat na-pah-dy, acorn mush. This was also true of some of the camps I visited near Mariposa yesterday.

I found a woman just finishing a neat coiled bowl with strong spider-web design in black fern root (lu-na!), and waited till she finished it, when I bought it. She called the bowl the usual name pul-luck-ka (pul-luck-hah or pul-luk-ah). She showed me the materials and called the rods pul-le (syringa) and the split strands of the outside tap-pa tap-pa. She spends summers in Yosemite and lives at Bear Creek.

One of the squaws showed me a lot of rolls of broad willowlike split strands which she said she bought of the Mono Paiute "to make Paiute basket."

When the Indians near Mariposa make cider of manzanita berries, they use the Chowchilla openwork bowls, too-poo-lah, to filter the juice through, the basket retaining the broken berries.

They now make few if any good coiled baskets, but have many (several dozen) Fresnos, and some made by the northern Muwa of the Sonora region. The best they refused to sell at any price, but I got a set of their work baskets and a superb old het-tal' made by the oldest woman long, long ago. They make many straw baskets of the ribbed trinket basket style, with string ribs, ornamented with wool or frayed red flannel or flannel and quail plumes, like some I got at Sonora, only more decorated.

The wife of the chief of the Mariposa Muwa has a superb large semi-globular narrow-mouthed basket, with bold design in black, made by her grandmother, who lived on Bull Creek but is now dead. The name of this basket is toy-you. I offered her thirty dollars for it, but she positively declined to sell it, because it was given her by her grandmother. It is a very choice basket and should be secured later.

They have many grass-splint baskets with vertical stitches of thread or twine and with design in red flannel (frayed) and plumes of valley quail. Some are small bowls (5–8 in. in diam.), and some are small-mouthed and depressed. Both forms are called koh-tee.

The following baskets are made by the Mariposa and Bear Creek (or Kalarow) Muwah.

che-kah-lah	burden basket
cham-ah	broad shallow scoop
ching-go	deep spoon scoup (with handle)
hick-eh	papoose basket
pul-luck-kah and al-loo-wah	coiled mush bowl[2]
hoo-ma-ah	dipper
het-al	circular winnower
chat-tat-toom-he	big circular gambling tray
koh-tee	grass-splint bowls[3]

Besides the names for these baskets that they themselves make they have the following for baskets constantly in use among them but made by other tribes or other bands or camps of Muwa.

hoo-le......big deep bowl for cooking acorns, made by the Sonora and Angels Camp Muwa.

oh-hah......acorn-cooking bowl made by Fresno Indians.

toy-you......large subglobular (guara-shaped) decorated basket with narrow mouth, made by Bull Creek Muwa. Possibly these were once made here also.

het-al......circular winnower. Nine out of ten of those in use—and they have many—are made, they say, by Fresno Indians.

ta-ma......closely woven snowshoe-shaped, scooped winnowing baskets made by the Mono Paiute. They have many of these.

ke-wo-na......closely woven Paiute burden baskets. They have some of these in each camp but, instead of calling them by the Paiute name, they call them che-ka-la, the same as the openwork ones of their own make.

wa-woi......thin deep bowls of diagonal twined weave, made by the Mono Paiute.

I saw only two of these last, and the Indian owning them did not know their name. The husband of the squaw who has them asked me if I could tell where they were made. When I told him Mono Lake, he said yes, that was right and added that I knew more about baskets than anyone, white or Indian, he had ever seen. I identified a lot of northern Muwa and Ne-ce-non baskets for him also.

Some of them have also a very pretty and nicely made broad scoop or cham-ah which they say they get from the Chuckchancy Indians; they call it kum-ty-se. The cross strands are closed up (brought together) in bands of three to five, forming compact belts alternating with belts (usually narrower) of the open rods. They are nice baskets.

---

[2] Both medium-large and small sizes, the small one used as dippers.

[3] With vertical stitches of thread or twine and ornamented with flannel or feathers. Sometimes drawn in at the mouth and flattened.

The following materials are used in making baskets.

Species	Indian Name
Ceanothus cuneatus	pi-wah
Ceanothus integerrimus	o-hoo-ne
Rhus trilobata	tum-mah
Philadelphus Lewisii	pul-le
Cercis occidentalis	tap-pa tap-pa
Salix	suk-kal
Quercus californica	te-lay-ye
Pteris aqualina	lu-nah (loo-nah)

The first four of these species are used for rods; the last four for split strands.

On September 19, 1902, I left Mariposa and, reaching Chowchilla Hill, walked one and a half miles along the north side of Chowchilla Canyon to an Indian camp. One of the women in the camp was making several baskets, none of which was finished. By this I mean that she, like many Indian women, keeps several different kinds of baskets going at once; if she tires of one, she goes on with another.

One was a circular winnower (hettal) of the usual type found among the Muwa. I have been purchasing these for years, from Yosemite Indians and Indians as far north as Sonora and Murphys, and all told me they were made farther south, by the Mariposa or Chowchilla or Fresno. At Mariposa camps, however, where I saw many, they told me they made none but bought them from the Chowchilla and Fresno. Here I found several recently made and one about three-fourths done, in process of construction, so at last I have run the hettal down. The yellow grass used for the foundation of the hettal is *Epicampes rigens*; it is called ho-loop.

This woman told me that she and her sister make many of these and sell to Indians farther north—the ordinary ones for three dollars each, which is what I paid her for one; this is much less than I have paid for many purchased farther north and in Yosemite. This same woman and her sister have nearly finished two beautiful bowl baskets of the so-called "Tulare" type, made of the Tulare root.

This Chowchilla camp is headquarters for the round deep scoop of openwork called too-poo-lah, used for filtering manzanita cider, and for other purposes. I got several of different sizes. They had one "Fresno" bowl and two Paiute bowls, one of which I got, and one deep Sonora bowl of the coarse kind.

Mrs. William M. Sell, wife of the proprietor of the Ahwahnee Hotel, has a collection of the "Tulare" root baskets purchased from Muwa, Chuckchancy, and "Fresno" women in this region. It contains some fine baskets and many good ones, but for most of them the actual tribe of the maker is not known.

The Indians in Chowchilla Canyon have a lot of baskets, mostly coarse, but some good. Among them are some from Sonora, some from Mono Lake (Paiute), and two or three handsome large bowls of the Tulare root made by Chuckchancy. These they would not sell at any price. They have a type of basket I have never seen except at Mariposa and Chowchilla. It is of twined weave, with a curious double-woven bottom, and a handle which may be either fixed or hinged. It is a coarse basket with simple design made by leaving on the red bark of the willow or redbud on certain strands. They call it pum-pum-mist and cham-my'-ah.

Another new type which I bought (new here, though near Murphys I got one like it, only deeper) is a pocket of openwork rods. It is called hoop-pah-lo. The one I got is a very old one with a cloth patch on the bottom. A very small and plain and rather coarsely made, subglobular coiled basket, which I also got from the old woman in Chowchilla Canyon, she calls so-tan-o.

They had a lot of cham-ah baskets of different sizes and too-poo-lahs and che'-ka-las and het-als, of their own make, and several Paiute te'-mas and one small good Paiute bowl which I bought.

On September 6, 1901,[4] I visited the Mew-wa Indian camps in Yosemite, and got a few more old baskets.

Most of the burden baskets made here (called che-ka-la) are of two kinds of material. The cylindrical vertical rods are *Ceanothus integerrimus*, which they call o-hu-nee. The distant horizontal split strands are split willow and are called wo-tok. The willow itself (untreated) they call sok-kal or sok-al. Some baskets are ornamented with red horizontal strands, which they say are maple. Sometimes some of the vertical rods are unpeeled and look red, but are simply willow with the bark left on—or possibly maple. Most of the compactly woven baskets are of willow, but some are of the root of a kind of grass. The black split root of the brake fern (*Pteris*) which they use for the designs is called lu-na, but some of them call it tu-hu-hee.

All of the fine old baskets I have found, the Digger squaws who own them bought, so they say, long years ago from the Fresno Diggers.

The circular winnowing baskets used for sifting acorn meal and called het-al are made of grass, either not ornamented at all or with a light design of fern root. They say they buy them of the Mariposa Indians.

On August 8, 1901,[5] I visited the three Digger Indian camps and bought a couple of baskets—one a circular shallow winnowing basket which they

---

[4] California Journal for 1901 (Sept. 6), pp. 116–117.
[5] *Ibid.* (Aug. 8), p. 51.

call het-al', and sometimes pe-ka'-eh (the last syllable aspirated). The burden basket (open weave) which the Paiute call wo-na the Yosemite Diggers call che-ka-la. The large bowl-shaped baskets eighteen to twenty inches in diameter and nearly as deep they call a-la-mok. I am not sure that they cook acorns in these baskets but think they do. Those I saw are thinner than those used by the Paiute for boiling acorns.

The Basketry of the Mono

The Mono Paiute near the ranches now do most of their cooking in frying-pans and tin or iron pails and kettles. At the same time they cook certain things, particularly acorn mush and pine-nut soup, in baskets, and those living farther away appear to do most of their cooking in this aboriginal fashion.

Near the northwest corner of Mono Lake I once watched two squaws cook acorn mush for a band of about twenty Indians. The acorns had been first reduced to meal by hammering with stone pestles in deeply worn mortar pits dug out of the solid rock and had been sifted in the winnowing baskets by an adroit motion which separates the fine from the coarse—a motion the novice can never get. It was then "leached" to take away the bitter taste. This was done by allowing water to filter through it in a primitive but ingenious way. The place selected was a dry sandy knoll. Here a shallow hole a foot deep and four or five feet in diameter was dug and lined with two pieces of cloth, laid over one another at right angles. The meal was placed on the cloth and large basketfuls of water were laboriously brought from a neighboring stream, carried up the hill, and poured over the meal, which was patted by the hands until thoroughly wet. The water sank through into the porous sand and was replaced by fresh basketfuls until, after repeated tastings, the women found the bitterness sufficiently washed out. The meal was then scraped together by the hands and heaped up in irregular masses; part was at once put into a large basket to cook; the remainder was afterwards made into cakes for future use and laid in the sun to dry.

The cooking basket was filled a little more than half full of water and placed near the fire. Then four hot stones, six or eight inches in diameter, were taken out of the fire by means of two sticks and dropped into the

117

basket. Almost immediately the water began to boil and the mush to thicken. During the twenty minutes or half-hour required for the cooking one of the squaws stirred it slowly with a stick, apparently to prevent the stones from resting on one spot long enough to burn the basket. The stuff boiled exactly like porridge, throwing up multitudes of miniature volcanoes and spluttering as if over hot coals. When it was done, the second squaw filled two small bowl-shaped baskets with water to receive and rinse the hot stones, which the first squaw fished out with a flat stick. Quickly and dexterously the old squaw washed off the adhering mush before the water got too hot for her hands and tossed the stones back into the fire. The contents of the small baskets, which had now become thin porridge, were then poured into the thicker mush in the big basket and stirred, giving the whole the desired consistency. This completed the operation.

On cooling, the acorn mush jellies; and if put in a moderately cool place, it keeps for some days. Its color is drab or drab pink, and it has no particular taste when fresh. It always seemed to me that a little salt and a good deal of cream and sugar would improve it mightily. Still, it is eaten without seasoning or sweetening and with evident relish. In summer, if kept too long, it ferments and gives off a sour liquid of a disagreeable odor. Among the Mono Paiute it is not an everyday food but a luxury, for the reason that they have to go so far to obtain the acorns; but it is today the staple food of numerous tribes in northwestern California, of Indians of the west flank of the Sierra, and of many of the Luiseño and other "Mission" tribes in the southern part of the state.

Most of the utensils of the Mono Paiute, including dishes, water bottles, and vessels for cooking, are baskets made by their own hands, as of old. (Cf. pls. 28, *a*, 29, *b*.) These baskets may be classed by forms or uses into a dozen categories: cradles or papoose baskets, large cornucopia-shaped burden baskets, snowshoe-shaped winnowing baskets, scoop-shaped winnowing baskets, spoon-shaped baskets with handles for collecting pine nuts, deep bowl-shaped baskets for cooking; individual mush bowls; ribbed trinket baskets; jugs and bottles for holding and carrying water, deep cylindrical baskets for collecting worms; small flat, oval seed paddles, with a handle, for knocking seeds off standing plants; and small conical baskets worn by the squaws as hats (cf. pl. 47, *e*), and also used for gathering berries and fruit.

Some of the baskets are plain; others ornamented with intricate, striking, and beautiful designs, woven in black and red. The black is the split root of the brake-fern (*Pteris*), the red the inner bark of the redbud (*Cercis*). Besides these, some of the coarser baskets, particularly the large conical ones for carrying burdens, are ornamented by simply leaving the bark on some of the willow strands of which they are composed.

The best and finest of the Mono Paiute baskets are those made for cooking. They may be large or small, with straight-flaring or rounded sides, but all have flat bottoms and all are of what Professor Mason calls the "three-rod foundation" type. This class includes the ceremonial baskets—the most sacred and precious possessions of the tribe. The designs on these are symbolic, but their meaning is exceedingly difficult to ascertain. At one time I thought the ceremonial baskets should be put in a class by themselves, but the difficulty of discriminating between some of them and some of the ordinary cooking baskets is so great that no hard and fast line can be drawn. The ceremonial baskets are used for cooking acorn meal at certain ceremonial feasts, and are now sometimes used also for cooking the ordinary pine-nut soup—a sign of the waning respect for aboriginal rites.

These water bottles (o-sa, o-sa-ha) are of various shapes and sizes; they hold from half a gallon to twelve or fifteen gallons each. The larger ones are for camp use only, being much too heavy, when full of water, to be carried on horseback. They are always broad and spindle-shaped, a form beautifully adapted for use when lying on the ground. The lower or bottom part is much longer than the upper, which is given off at such an angle that, when one side rests flat on the ground, the mouth is thrown upward so far that the bottle can be filled nearly full without spilling. If the point of the bottom is sunk just a little in the sand, it will lie on its side quite full without letting any water escape. But this is by no means the only advantage of the spindle shape, for when the basket is full, the weight is so delicately adjusted (the broad middle part acting as a fulcrum) that the slightest pressure on the mouth is sufficient to tilt it down enough to let the water flow out—a most convenient arrangement for filling other receptacles and also for drinking when one is reclining on the ground. On the desert at the east end of Mono Lake I have seen a baby crawl to one of these bottles, take the mouth in its mouth, tilt it down and drink its fill, without touching a hand to the bottle. When let go, the bottle immediately tipped back to its former position without the loss of a drop. A more simple, efficient, and ingenious device would be hard to find.

Other kinds of bottles, convenient for use on horseback or for other purposes, are of relatively small size, rarely holding more than two or three gallons. All Paiute water bottles are woven of split willow strands in a thin sheet of diagonal twined weave; they are light, strong, and elastic but will not hold water until coated with the resin or pitch of the piñon pine put on hot, which sinks into the innumerable interspaces and thus adheres on the inside, rendering the bottles continuously waterproof, even in the arid atmosphere of the desert. They are provided with two small loops or ears of horsehair or plant fiber, firmly woven in on one side, to which the carrying rope is attached. This point of attachment is selected with reference to the center of gravity when the bottle is full and also to the way they are to be supported. In the spindle-shaped bottles they are woven into the swollen middle part; in the tall, jug-shaped bottles they are placed above the middle.

The big camp bottles, when full, are exceedingly heavy. In carrying them the body is inclined forward so as to distribute the weight over the back, and they are kept from slipping down by a broad band which passes over the forehead. I have seen a squaw, who had taken one to a small stream to fill, find herself unable to lift it in position alone; but when assisted, and once the heavy burden was in place, she walked slowly off with it and climbed the hill to her camp, perhaps an eighth of a mile distant. In summer they are usually tucked into the brush at one corner of the wickiup, sheltered from the direct rays of the sun.

The burden baskets (wo-na and ka-wona) are huge conical baskets or cornucopias, three or four feet in length and one and a half or two feet in diameter. Like the papoose baskets, they are carried on the back by means of a band which passes over the forehead. They vary in size, diameter, and fineness of weave according to the uses for which they are intended. Those made for carrying fuel, roots, and other light articles are large, coarsely and openly woven, and have broadly open mouths. They are called wo-na. Those intended for grass seeds and other seeds of small size, called ka-wona, are smaller and narrower, are woven closely of fine materials, and are usually somewhat ornamented.

The papoose baskets are of the usual Paiute pattern, of openwork, with flat backs and with arched tops to shade the baby's head. When traveling, the squaws carry them on their backs; when at rest, they stand them up in their wickiups or lean them against a sagebrush bush.

Winnowing baskets (te'-ma) are large, flat, broadly subtriangular or showshoe-shaped baskets, more or less concave or scooped and nearly always ornamented by one or more bands, sometimes with rather elaborate designs. They are of two principal types: slightly concave, deepest in the middle or deeply concave, deeply scooped at or near the big end. They have many uses, such as winnowing grain and seeds, sifting meal made from acorns and nuts of the nut pine, separating the fine meal from the coarse, winnowing fly larvae so that the skins are blown away leaving the meat or kernels, and so on. The women become exceedingly skillful in their use and it is interesting to watch them work. The large te'-mas, deeply scooped near the broad end, are used for winnowing grain and other heavy seeds, which are tossed up to allow the wind to carry off the chaff.

The shallow winnowing baskets are of two kinds, compactly woven and openly woven. The openly woven ones are used for roasting pine nuts. Coals from the fire and a quantity of the nuts are thrown into the basket, and it is adroitly agitated, something after the manner of a popcorn shaker, until the nuts are sufficiently roasted. This blackens the interior but does not seem to burn it injuriously. The compactly woven ones are used for separating the fine meal from the coarse after the acorns or pine nuts have been pounded in stone mortars. The movement is graceful and very skillful.

Scoop-shaped baskets, used as piñon scoops, resemble the winnowing baskets but are coarser, deeper, and usually much narrower.

The cooking baskets (opa, opa-che-da) are bowl-shaped coiled baskets of the 3-rod foundation type, with relatively small flat bottoms. Most of them are beautifully made, and many are handsomely decorated. The ceremonial baskets are usually of this order and their designs are sacred and symbolic. They are the finest baskets made by the Paiute. In the older ones the designs are usually simple, but strong and highly effective. In some of the modern ones they are more diffuse and much less artistic. Some of the small ones, now made to sell, are overloaded with design and the design is brought down over the bottom—a thing I have never seen in an old Paiute basket. They are examples of modern degenerate work, which is common among tribes which make baskets for the trade instead of for their own use. Nevertheless, such baskets find a ready market and bring good prices, so that there is very little incentive for continuing the old styles.

Small, compactly woven coiled baskets are used as individual mush bowls; they have a single-rod foundation and smooth, flat, even surface. Each of the vertical stitches embraces two of the horizontal rods in alternating couplets in such a manner that the coils do not project, either inside or out, but leave a continuously flat surface; the baskets thus differ widely from the coiled baskets of the 3-rod foundation type. Some are perfectly plain; others are ornamented with more or less complicated designs. Some have the rim finished by winding two or three split strands round and round in a continuous spiral.

Fruit baskets (wa-woi), medium or small deeply bowl-shaped baskets, are compactly woven of split willow in a single thin sheet of diagonal twined weave. The rim is strengthened by a bundle of strands often reinforced by a stout willow hoop. They are usually ornamented by one or more reddish bands of the same material as the rest of the basket but with the bark left on.

Deeply bowl-shaped, somewhat flexible baskets with rounded bottoms and unfinished (or un-reinforced) rims are used as hats. They are of diagonal twined weave like the wa-woi. I took one from the head of a very old Paiute squaw near Bishop at the head of Owens Valley, in August, 1901. They are sometimes used as dishes as well as hats and are very similar to baskets made by the Washo in Steamboat Valley, Nevada, except that the latter are more closely and finely woven.

The ribbed trinket baskets are small coiled baskets of single-rod foundation, with the vertical strands widely spaced so as to appear like ribs on the surface, leaving the horizontal rods broadly exposed between. They are light, simple, easily made baskets, with contracted mouths, which give them a pleasing form; they are usually ornamented with simple harmonious designs in purple or black.

Subcylindrical or pocket-shaped openwork baskets (car-ru-sa), a foot or more deep and coarsely woven of willow, are used for collecting the large worms or larvae that sometimes infest the nut pine. The body of the basket is of vertical rods held in place by widely spaced horizontal split strands which embrace the rods in alternating couplets by simple twining, as in the coarser burden baskets. At the top, which is slightly contracted, the vertical rods are carried around in a thick bundle (as in the burden baskets made by the Mariposa Indians). The worms do not come every year. Mrs. Adam Farrington, who has lived near the Mono Paiute for many years, tells me that when the worms are plentiful, trenches are dug around the trees into which the worms fall, to remain until collected by the Indians. The worm baskets are light and handy and are doubtless used for other purposes also.

Spoon-shaped openwork baskets about a foot long with a handle five or six inches long are used to gather the nuts of the nut pine and for other purposes. They are made of parallel willow rods, held in place by twined strands, and brought together at one end to form the handle. They are called che-go and yad-da.

Indian Hats

[Plates 47–48]

Did the Indians wear hats before the white man came? To be sure they did, at least in many tribes; and in some they wear them still. The wearers, except in the coast region of British Columbia, are mainly if not exclusively the women, and the hats are not bought at the milliner's at prices to bankrupt the husbands but are made by the women themselves—woven with infinite patience from finely split roots and stems of plants and decorated with delicate and beautiful designs wrought in red, black, and other colors. The black is sometimes the stem of the maidenhair fern, sometimes the split root of the brake fern, sometimes the split pod of the desert *Martynia*, sometimes the split body of a rush, dyed black by being buried in mud in an iron spring. Hats to be worn at dances and other festive occasions are sometimes ornamented by pendants of white and red wampum, each ending in a rectangular piece of the iridescent shell of the abalone, like the top one shown in plate 48, *a*.

In Alaska the chiefs and medicine men of the Tlinkit tribe wear large hats with high cylindrical tops made of separate disks like guava-jelly boxes, fastened one on top of another and capped by a plume of feathers and ermine skins (pl. 47, *c*). These hats have a flange or rim on the inside to fit the head, and on the outside are usually ornamented with conventional designs representing the animal which is the emblem of the particular cult or clan to which the wearer belongs.

Among the Haida of the Queen Charlotte Islands, the natives of Vancouver Island, and some other British Columbia Indians both sexes wear hats. These are neatly woven of cedar bark, in the form of an inverted bowl, and are made double with an inside rim to hold them in place (pl. 47, *b*). They are large enough to protect the hair from rain—an obvious advantage in the rainy region in which these people live.

123

In the deserts of southern Utah the Paiute women wear rude hats of willow, usually without ornamentation but sometimes decorated with one or more black bands. Their relatives, the Paiute of western Nevada and eastern California, wear much better ones (pl. 47, e).

Among the Modoc and Klamath of the Klamath Lake region in southern Oregon, and the Pit River Indians of northeastern California, the women make neat, flexible, flat-topped skullcaps, decorated with large symbolic designs in black or dark brown on a whitish ground (pl. 47, a). Their neighbors, the Shasta, now nearly extinct, wear round-topped hats made mainly of roots of spruce, ornamented with rather intricate patterns (pl. 47, d). Still farther west in northern California, in a deep valley surrounded by mountains, dwell the most famous hatmakers of the present day—the Hoopa Indians. Their hats resemble those of the Shasta but as a rule are flatter and more finely woven, and consist mainly of the whitish blades of the bear grass, split into fine strands and ornamented in black and red (pl. 48, a).

The hats and caps thus far mentioned are thin and flexible and are woven in what is known as twined weave. There are others of a widely different type: these are relatively thick and rigid and are made in coiled work. They are now exceedingly rare but were formerly worn by the women of a number of tribes, among which were the Fresno branch of the Yokut nation (pl. 48, b), the practically extinct Santa Clara (pl. 48, b), and many bands of so-called Mission Indians in southern California (pl. 48, d, e). They have a use additional to that of the ordinary hat. The California Indians carry their burdens on their backs in large nets and baskets supported by a band which passes over the forehead; this band rests against the hat, which thus distributes the weight over the head.

The Mission Indian hats are said to be no longer made, and I have been repeatedly told that none could be found. Nevertheless, during a recent visit to certain bands of these Indians I secured three. Two of them I got one evening from women who had them on their heads as they sat around a camp fire in the settlement of Saboba (pl. 48, e).

The most beautiful hat in my collection is the one shown in plate 48, c. It is finely woven of split strands of the aromatic sumac over a kind of coil known as "grass-splint foundation," and is elegantly decorated in black and red. The principal design consists of four oblique bands of overlapping rectangles in red, bordered with black, the border extended at the projecting angles to form long black points. In the interspaces are clusters of symbolic designs. I did not obtain this hat direct from the Indians but it was evidently made by the Panamint—a small tribe of desert Indians living in canyons in the desolate sun-baked Panamint Mountains, which rise precipitously on the west side of Death Valley in southeastern California.

PLATES 25-48

EXPLANATION OF PLATES

PLATES 25–46

Native Dwellings and Ceremonial Structures

PLATE 25
   Winter house frame, later to be covered with tule thatch. Northern Paiute. Pyramid Lake, Nevada, July, 1903.

PLATE 26
   a. Winter hut. Northern Paiute. Truckee River bottom near Pyramid Lake, Nevada. July, 1903.
   b. Summer houses. Northern Paiute. Pyramid Lake, Nevada. July, 1903.

PLATE 27
   a. Brush wikiup, unroofed. Note conical twined burden baskets and twined winnowing trays. Northern Paiute. Pyramid Lake, Nevada. July, 1903.
   b. Summer camp of unroofed brush wikiup and open roofed summer shade. Northern Paiute. Pyramid Lake, Nevada. July, 1903.

PLATE 28
   a. Summer camp. Note water jug, woman in rabbitskin blanket, and girl with burden basket. Northern Paiute. Pyramid Lake, Nevada. July, 1903.
   b. Summer camp. Northern Paiute. Pyramid Lake, Nevada. July, 1903.

PLATE 29
   a. Bark lean-to house. Washo. Tallac, Lake Tahoe, Nevada. July, 1903.
   b. Sagebrush hut camp. Note baskets in foreground. Northern Paiute. East end of Mono Lake, August, 1901.

PLATE 30
   a. Sagebrush hut. Note pile of firewood. Northern Paiute. East end of Mono Lake, California. August, 1901.
   b. Brush shelter used while gathering kutsavi (larvae of *Ephydra* fly). Northern Paiute. South end, Mono Lake, California. August, 1901.

PLATE 31
   a. Tule-covered house. Kabel village, Pomo or Dan-no'-kah tribe. West side of Upper Lake Narrows, Clear Lake, Lake County. 1918.
   b. Rear of same house showing pole framework of adjoining structure.

PLATE 32
   a, b. Tule-thatched house. Pomo. East side of Clear Lake at Highland Lodge on northeast side of Lower Lake, Lake County. July, 1927.

127

PLATE 33

a. Conical bark slab dwelling. Nisenan (Southern Maidu). Near Nevada City, Nevada County. September, 1902.

b. Bark and lumber conical dwelling. Nisenan (Southern Maidu). Near Hanks Exchange, Eldorado County.

PLATE 34

a. Tule house (cf. pl. 32). Kabel village, Pomo or Dan-no'-kah tribe. West side of Upper Lake, Clear Lake, Lake County. September, 1924.

b, c. Pole-frame houses. Northern Paiute. Walker Lake, Nevada. October, 1902.

PLATE 35

a. Pole and brush shelter. En-ne-sen (Esselen) tribe. Milpitas Valley at western base of Santa Lucia Peak, Monterey County, August, 1902.

b. Acorn caches and earth-covered dwellings. Note duck decoys attached to pole. From an original drawing by H. B. Brown. Maidu tribe. Near Colusa on Sacramento River, Colusa County. 1852.

PLATE 36

a. Conical slab dwelling. Note cradle, baskets. Nim (Monache) tribe. At North Fork on North Fork of San Joaquin River, Madera County. October, 1902.

b. Pole and brush shelter. Wiktchumne (Yokuts) tribe. Kaweah River near Lemon Cove, Tulare County. August, 1902.

PLATE 37

a, b. Pole-frame, mat-covered house. Tah'-che (Yokuts) tribe. On Tulare Lake about six miles southeast of Lemoore, Kings County. June, 1903.

PLATE 38

a. Semisubterranean roundhouse. Western Wintoon. Grindstone Creek rancheria, Glenn County. May, 1923.

b. Brush-covered roundhouse. Shoteah. Stony Ford, Colusa County. August, 1928.

PLATE 39

a. Roundhouse, abandoned and in disrepair. Kab-al-mem village, Wintoon tribe. Just east of Cook Springs, Colusa County. June, 1903.

b. Earth-covered roundhouse. Choo-hel'-mem-sel group of Wintoon tribe. On road between Bear Valley and Stony Ford, Colusa County. June, 1903.

PLATE 40

a. Earth-covered roundhouse. Kletwin group of Patwin tribe. Cortena rancheria, Colusa County. June, 1903.

b. Semisubterranean dance house. Tuleyome. St. Helena Creek near Middletown, Lake County. November, 1928.

PLATE 41

a. Roundhouse. Nisenan (Maidu). Auburn rancheria, Placer County. July, 1936.

b. Roundhouse. Nisenan (Maidu). Auburn rancheria, Placer County. July, 1936.

PLATE 42

   a. Kootbah village showing roundhouse. Nisenan (Maidu). Between North and Middle Fork of Cosumnes River, Eldorado County. December, 1904.

   b. Chief Hunchup and family beside his roundhouse. Note coiled baskets. Nisenan (Maidu). Between North and Middle Fork of Cosumnes River, Eldorado County. December, 1904.

PLATE 43

   a. Earth-covered roundhouse belonging to Casus Oliver. Mokelumne tribe. Near Ione, Amador County. October, 1905.

   b. Interior of roundhouse showing excavation of sides, center posts notched at top, and rectangular footdrum. Mokelumne tribe. Near Ione, Amador County. October, 1905.

PLATE 44

   a–f. Interior views of roundhouse shown in plate 43. October, 1905.

PLATE 45

   a. Roundhouse. Kum-mo'-win village, Maidu tribe. Bald Rock rancheria, near Mooretown, Butte County. September, 1924.

   b. Roundhouse. Nisenan (Southern Maidu). Four miles north of Colfax, Placer County. September, 1902.

PLATE 46

   a. Roundhouse. Mewah (Miwok). At Big Creek rancheria near Groveland, Tuolumne County. July, 1903.

   b. Village area showing two roundhouses. Mewah (Miwok). Near Murphys, Calaveras County. August, 1900.

PLATES 47–48

Indian Hats

PLATE 47

   a. Modoc and Pit River.
   b. Haida. Queen Charlotte Island.
   c. Tlinkit Shaman's hat.
   d. Shasta.
   e. Southern Paiute.

PLATE 48

   a. Hoopa.
   b. Fresno and Santa Clara.
   c. Panamint.
   d. Luiseño Mission.
   e. Saboba Mission.

PLATE 25

PLATE 26

a

b

PLATE 27

a

b

PLATE 28

a

b

PLATE 29

a

b

PLATE 30

a

b

PLATE 31

a

b

Plate 32

a

b

PLATE 33

a

b

PLATE 34

a

b

c

PLATE 35

a

b

PLATE 36

a

b

PLATE 37

a

b

PLATE 38

a

b

PLATE 39

a

b

PLATE 40

a

b

PLATE 41

a

b

PLATE 42

a

b

PLATE 43

a

b

a

b

c

d

e

f

PLATE 45

a

b

PLATE 46

a

b

PLATE 47

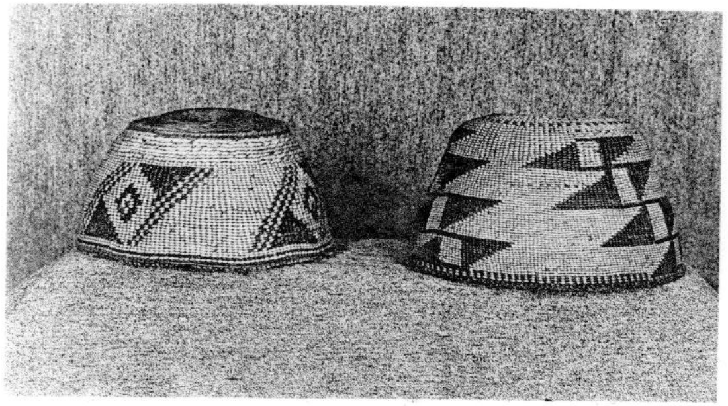

a

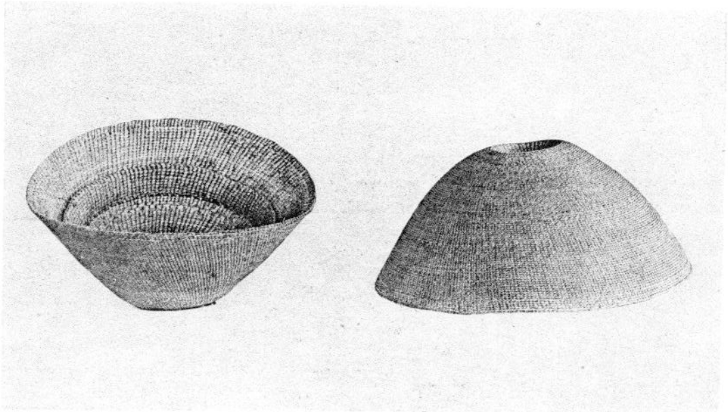

b

c

d

e

PLATE 48

a

b

c

d

e

COMPARATIVE
RECORDS

Pinart's Tcholovone Vocabulary

In 1907 Dr. Merriam published information which he had collected on the distribution of the Mewko (Plains Miwok) dialects.[1] *His informants claimed the Miwok occupied both sides of the San Joaquin River near its mouth. In 1908, Dr. Barrett presented statements by other informants to the effect that the Yokuts occupied the east bank of the San Joaquin at Stockton*[2] *and that possibly the Costanoans held the western bank. In the same year Dr. Kroeber published additional information supporting the Yokuts' occupation of the whole south Delta up to the junction of the San Joaquin and Sacramento rivers.*[3] *Part of this last evidence was a reference*[4] *to an obscure publication by A. Pinart,*[5] *in which a group of rancherias was listed with a vocabulary of their common language. Dr. Kroeber, from an abstract of the original article, identified this vocabulary as a Yokuts dialect.*

Dr. Merriam was able to locate the original article, published in a French journal, and had it translated into English. Because of the importance of this vocabulary in the study of linguistic boundaries in Central California, the entire translation is presented here.

Dr. Kroeber notes that a non-Yokuts and non-Californian vocabulary was

[1] "Distribution and Classification of the Mewan Stock of California," AA, n.s., 9:338–357, 1907; this reference, p. 348.

[2] S. A. Barrett, *The Geography and Dialects of the Miwok Indians,* UC–PAAE, 6:333–368, 1908; this reference, pp. 348–350.

[3] A. L. Kroeber, *On the Evidences of the Occupation of Certain Regions by the Miwok Indians,* UC–PAAE, 6:369–380, 1908.

[4] *Ibid.,* p. 370.

[5] Alphonse Pinart, "Etudes sur les Indiens Californiens," *Revue de linguistique et de philologie comparée,* 27:79–87, 1894.

133

appended by mistake to the Yokuts list. All words on pages 86 and 87 of the original article, and at least the last four words on page 85, probably belong to some Central American language, another area in which Pinart was interested.

In addition to this regrettable error, other problems are contained in the Pinart document. Only the Tcholovones, Jačikamnes, Pasasamnes, Nututamnes, Xosmitamnes, and Lakkisamnes are readily recognizable in the mission records, each representing a distinct "rancheria." The -amne ending is a Plains Miwok suffix, and has no meaning in Yokuts. It is associated in the mission documents with all the rancherias listed above except Xosmitamnes and Tcholovones. The consistent mission form for these two groups is, respectively, Josemit(e) and Cholvon. These two rancherias are the southernmost of the given settlements. All Jačikamnes and Cholvones had been drawn into Mission San Jose by 1819 and 1821 respectively; thus by the time of Pinart's observations at least sixty years had elapsed during which the linguistic affiliations of peripheral rancherias could have become confused in the memory of the few survivors. The conflicting information presented in the three ethnographic sources cited indicates that there was no agreement among these survivors on the aboriginal occupation of the Delta. Additional information from contemporary sources could be presented on both sides, but it is sufficient here to say that the following article does not settle the problem of Miwok-Yokuts boundaries but contains important data for future study.—Ed.

ON THE TCHOLOVONES OF CHORIS

The Tcholovones, or better Čolovomnes, were included [79] in the group of the family of the Tulareños Indians of the San Joaquin and of Tulare Lake. These Indians inhabited a "rancheria" or village situated nearly where the little town of Bantas is today. The other rancherias related to the Čolovomnes and speaking the same dialect were the following: Jačikamne, beside the town of Stockton, Pašašamne, Nututamne, Tammukamne, Helutamne, Taniamne, Sanaiamne, Xosmitamne.

All these rancherias were within the limits of San Joaquin County. A little farther up on the San Joaquin River and on its branches were the Lakkisamnes, the Notunamnes, the Tuolumnes who spoke dialects very close to that of the Jačikamne.

It is not strange that Choris should have seen [80] these Čolovomnes in the Bay of San Francisco. Indeed the missionaries had brought a number of these Indians to the missions of San Jose, Santa Clara, and even San Francisco. In examining the ancient books of these missions, I have many times found mention of baptisms administered to individuals from that rancheria. But the description and especially the types of these

Indians given by Choris[6] could be only absolute fantasies. These Tcholovones (Čolovomnes) are probably nothing but Kanakes from the Hawaiian Islands brought to California by the Russians. The California Indian type is very variable, their color especially, which, it is true, varies from a clear lustrous yellow to a very dark brown. But I have never seen, among all the California Indians that I have examined, a single one bearing a resemblance to the types given by the French artist of the Kotzebüe expedition.

In 1880, while at the little Indian rancheria situated a few miles from the town of Plaranton [Pleasanton][7] in the Contra-Corta [Contra-Costa], I had the fortune to find there a woman named Maria, of Jačikamne origin, and it was from her that I obtained the information given above. She claimed to be the last survivor of her rancheria. She told me that she had also lived in the rancheria of the Tcholovones (Čolovomnes) but that that rancheria had long since disappeared. Maria's husband, Philippe de Jesus, is a Lakkisamne Indian, that is, from a rancheria friendly and related to the Sačikamne [typographical error for Jačikamne]. He corroborated his wife's statements, adding that he also had lived in the rancheria of Čolovomne and that the Indians of that rancheria differed in no respect from the other Trilareños [Tulareños] Indians.

LIST OF JAČIKAMNE WORDS FURNISHED BY MARIA

mountain	hatle [85]	eclipse of the moon	peihehen hopē
sky	tipxne	rain	šeel
fog	kohomol	it rains	šeeleu
cloud	thro	doesn't it rain?	han šeeheleu
sun	suyō	the rain has begun	uittihinin šeele
moon	hopēm	storm	šeeleu mateni
sunrise	tissen suyō	wind	iuma
forenoon	alalšuka	south wind	x'omox'o
day	lake eĭe	north wind	tox'x'oi
evening	kexili	west wind	x'osin nitiuno
sunset	suyō kopnen	southwest wind	nutotiatiuno
the sun has set	suyō kopinin	lightning	ppalmosa
night	to-i-o	thunder	čat-čače
during the night	to-i-ne	snow	hai-iao
full moon	cheneen hopē	hail	pxoueč

[6] August C. Mahr, *The Visit of the "Rurik" to San Francisco in 1816*, Stanford Univ. Publs. in History, Economics, and Political Science, 2:267–460, 1932.

[7] Throughout this translation the bracketed comments in text are interpolations of the translator; numbers in brackets are page numbers of the original article.—Ed.

LIST OF JAČIKAMNE WORDS FURNISHED BY MARIA—*Continued*

cold	čičik	beaver	kot čata [83]
it is very cold	namik čičik	otter	iokač
I am cold	kxeč keneuna	badger,"mapache"	saunaka
hot	taakkă	to fish	vilo
water	ilikie [82]	to fish with nets	ioxxo
bay, *estero*	uakatat	fishhook	ts'oiek
tide	uollexe	net to catch ducks	šaami
bank of river	tuku-čolloče	wild hemp	poxuč
river	čolloče	bird	oiol-oiol
lake	teik	duck	laala
embarcadero	akaies	duck, a species	uskai
tule raft	šua	duck, a second	
poles used for the		species	uoi-ui
raft	kaapa	crane	totoko
large poles used to		thick-necked swan	šoxoloič
direct the raft	euokos	little swan of the	
rock	selel'	*tular*	uaaša
cliff	matesilet	crow	aluts
sand	soxusot	large crow	x'otoi
gravel	xole	*chañate*	hakalo
mud	čupot	hawk	iemilits
slough	čupokaal	hawk, one kind	uakuak [Wek
tular	uitik		wek]
tule (kind of reed)	loope	hawk, another kind	suppux'
tule flower	tikle	owl	soots'
tule root	pileis	*tecolote*	eheme
dry tule root	katsats	*tecolote*-tokok	uetsitsa
hill	wan	quail	umulu
forest, underbrush	ts'ammax'al	little birds (generic	
thick forest	činik	term)	tsipiax'
	ts'ammax'al	hummingbird	tinei-ie
island	komelomit	gull	uiali
sea	čox'oē	large black gull	kokčo
fish	lopič	beak	čiutit ta
salmon	koosi	feathers	pielli
white fish	pulmus	wings	x'aapač
perch	iuaš	tail	koot
barbel	polux'u	eggs	hon
tule mussels	x'epič	nest	x'apiš
river mussels	kehue	bear	ullui

LIST OF JAČIKAMNE WORDS FURNISHED BY MARIA—*Continued*

wolf	eue	wood in general,	
lion	tammala	tree	ites [85]
wildcat	čollomma [84]	bark	čxatip
fox	iu-uel	leaf	kappaš
coyote	če-ia	dry leaf	čaxait kappaš
badger	čxanu	acorn	uokiš
squirrel	šitki	oak	itsetsi
flying squirrel	meue	live oak	šaša
shrew	čaluikse	alder	male
hare	homix	willow	poko
rabbit	tehū	*sauz chino*, Chinese	
bat	tekkiš	willow	matepoko
mole (one kind)	atauaua	*torote*	hauoš
stag	sox'oko	laurel	sokkote
deer	talaxe	madrone	halats'
antelope	kanaiut	poplar	taapič
dog	čukko	elder	tx'oi
cat	tonjē	toyon	suxul-li
turtle	saux'it	mulberry	iukku
toad	pōtpōto	datura	amonoi
frog	uatakša	*estafiata*	ts'aitš'aiš
lizard	tappena	poison oak	suoš
ant	kxai-amaš	herbs	šukoi
grasshopper	ts-anauiš	pinole	touč
pinacate [ill-smell-		grains	xennik
ing black beetle]	tšišešampo	mortar	kxolup
worm	tšete	pestle	xumuč
snake	iax	to crush, to pound	laku
mosquito	kašup	to cut	čišet
fly	mouo	to pull	koottok
to smoke	paamo	arrow	šai-ie
wild tobacco	kaje	arrow point	lai-ie
smoked	mučok	bow	tamikka
ashes	itexl	cedar	oco
fire	pooto	avocado	beu
live coals	saalo	seyba	buri
to light the fire	hootelka	jobo	aiña
extinguish	šaapka	guava	henoso
the fire is out	šaapinnin	pawpaw	papanaxo [86]
firewood	ites	pineapple	činxō

LIST OF JAČIKAMNE WORDS FURNISHED BY MARIA—*Concluded*

plantain, green	pata	stag	bigi
plantain, ripe	patakora	wild hog	pido
brown sugar	nekua	monkey	xidoi
sweet	xuambui	rat	paodo
corn	pe	*tigrillo*	uriuri
ear of green corn	pe-biri	sloth	busia
poivrelon, aji	pida	*guagua*	penora
caimito	tuxō	tortoise	sibi
bejuquillo (*liane*)	hinxero	iguana	opoa
bamboo	sioro	alligator	ori
herbs	sirua	snake	tama
crab	ixarre	centipede	heto
sardine	auarra	tarantula	torema
barbel	pau	mosquito	lampara
"fish (?)"	kidačiraua	scorpion	uritoro
partridge	čokoro	ant	meče
owl	bibira	bowstring	sests'e
hawk	nexopui	quiver	iu-el'
eagle	nexoku	to beat	loouse
crane	toa	to kill	hahašit
crow	toxe	he has killed him	hašin
parrot	xamiso	he is dead	hašinhin
parrot ♀	kaiu	dead	hahanihik
ara	para	enemy	tauca
hummingbird	impisu	friend	čometemluš
peahen	tusi	chief	ottie
peacock	paui	chief (woman)	xanuat
vulture	ankoso	house	exe
turtle dove	huma	roof	innihi
hen	terre	wall, side	inu
eggs	neumu	rush mat	čini
dog	husa	to spread the rush	
armadillo	ečurru	mat	činiak
l'once	imama	to sleep	uo-oiak
lion	imamapuru [87]		
fox	pesai	[Signed] Alphonse Pinart	

Words for Tobacco and Pipe

Tribe	Tobacco	Pipe
ATCHOMAWAN		
Mo-des'-se...............	oop'	skōt'
	ōp'	
	is'-soo ōp (Indian tobacco)	
A-choo'-mah'-we..........	oop	skot'
	ō'p	it-spoo'-e' (straight)
		ah-poots-put chăs-waj-je (with mouth straight up)
At-wum'-we..............	oop'	skōt'
		skot'
As'-tah-ke-wi'-che.........	ōp'	skawt'
		te'-lah (long straight pipe)
At-soo-kā'-e..............	ow'-tem	skot'
	o'-pe	
	o-pe'	
Ap-woo'-ro-kā'e..........	o-pe'	skŏt
Ham-mah'-we.............	oop'	skŏt
		skawt'
		te'-lah (long straight pipe)

Tribe	Tobacco	Pipe
ATHAPASKAN		
Northwestern California		
Hah'-wun-kwut (Smith River)	hus'-sa^ch yah'-we	ā'' chah
	sĕ^ch-yu	
	sā^ch-yu	
	yahn-se^ch-yah'-we	
and/or		
Tol'-lo-wah (Crescent City) (Hus)	sĕ^ch-te-ju	ā''-chah
Trinity and Redwood Region		
Tin'-nung hen-nā'-o (Hoopa)	min'-tā-itch'-wah	king-i'-he-ahng
'Hwil'-kut (Redwood Creek)	min-del'ch-wah (?)	king-i'-k'yang
	min-tā'-chwah	king-ah'-ke-ang'
	mit-tā'-tchwah	
	ho'-chim min'-tā-tchwah	
Eel River Region		
Nek'-an-ni'	yo'-bah-chung	sā-tel'-le-yo'
Mat-tōl' (Bet-tol')		sĕ'-tel-yo (straight, of wood)
Lo'-lahn'-kok	sē'n-yo'	be'-si-til-yo'
		si'-til-yo
Ket-tel	———	———
To-kub'-be ke'-ah	sēn'-yo	sēn-yo-tsi (tobacco stick)
	sin'-yo'	
Ken-nes'-te Wi-lak-ke	sig-ñyo	
To-cho'-be ke'-ah	sēn-yo	se'-ñyo-tsi
	sig-ñyo	
Set'-ten-bi'-den ke'ah	sĕ'-tcho	sĕ-cho'-tsoi
	set'-yo	
	sit'-yo	
Tsen'-nah ken-nes'	sā'-yo	bē'-sā-tel'-yo
		sā-yo'-tse
Cahto Valley Region		
To-chil'-pe ke'-ah-hahng (Kahto)	klit-tan'-nung	be-klah-tan'-nah

Tribe	Tobacco	Pipe
CHEMAREKAN		
Che-mar'-re-ko . . . . oo'-wah		o'-ne-pah (no pipes in early days)
	che-mar'-roo (che'-mar, man; oo'-wah, tobacco)	
CHUMASHAN		
Kahs'-swah . . . . sho		oo-ash
Kal'-ă-wah-sah' (Santa Ynez) sho'		ahks pah'-mo
Kah-sah'-kom-pă'-ah . . . . ———		———
Chu'-mahs (Ventura) . . . . saw'-oo		tip-haw'-pe
Hool'-koo-koo (San Emigdio) shaw'-hoo-wah		koo-koo
ENNESEN		
En'-ne-sen' (San Antonio) . . . tah-lahm'		tah-oon
	tel-lam	tro'-win
	trah'-lam	trah'-hahl
		tră'-hon
ESSELENEAN		
Es-se-len . . . . k'a'-ah (Henshaw)		suk-nas enne (Pinart)
KAROKAN		
Kah'-rok . . . . e-hā'-dah		oo'-her-rahm'
Kah-rah'-ko'-hah . . . . e-hā'ram		o-wher-rahm'
LUTUAMIAN		
Klamath-Modok . . . . sook'-kul[s] "katckal"		pah'-k's (Pox)
MEWAN		
Mewuk		
Me'-wuk (Northern) . . . . . . kah'-su		pah-oo-mah
	kah'-sah	pah'-o-mah
Tuolumne Me'-wa (Middle) . . . . kah'-sŭ		pah-oo-mah' kah'-wah'-chě (of ash, straight) pah-o-mi
Chow-chil'-lah Mew'-wah (Southern) . . . . kah'-hŭ		pah-oo'-mah
Mewko		
Mokal'umne . . . . kah'-sŭ		tă-bo'-kel-lah
Wi'-pā . . . . kah'-sŭ		to-rā'-pah

Tribe	Tobacco	Pipe

Tuleamne
  O-lā'-yo'-me (Coyote
    Valley) . . . .
	ki'-ow
	hin'-til ki'-ow
		soom-ge-too-mi
		  (straight, of wood
		  smoking stick)

Hookooeko
  Hoo'-koo-e'-ko (Tomales
    Bay) . . . .
	o'-yen ki'-ah (grows
	  on river land)
	ki'-ow (ki'-yow)
		soom'-ke (straight,
		  of wood)

O'-la-ment'-ko
    (Bodega Bay) . . . .
	ki'-ow	soo'-koo
		soo-koo loo'-poo
		  (new stone, mod-
		  ern)

MIDUAN Kum-mo'-win	pan'-ne	kool-koo'-le
Nis'-se-nan	pan pahn	koo-lah'
No-to'-mus-se	pan'	koo-lah'
Mitch-ō'p'-do	pahn'-ne	pan-pen koo'-lah (?) pah'-ning koo'-lah (smoking-pipe)
No-to-koi'-yo (Big Meadows band)	pah'-nim pan'-neem	pan-neem'-lo-lo

O-so'-ko (American Valley
    band) . . . .
	pan'-nim	pan'-nim-no-lo (of
		  straight stone, 5–
		  6 in. long)

No-to-koi'-yo	———	———
Nis'-sim pā'-we-nan'	pahn'	wahd'-di'
Kow'-wahk	pahn'	koo'-lah'

Tahn'-kum	pah'-ne'	pan'-ning go'-lah (of
		  stone, 8 in. long or
		  longer)

	pahn'-nim pan'-ne	koo-lahm'
MOHINEAN (MO-HIN'-E-AN) Mo-hinean	pē'vt	ah-we'-kah

Tribe	Tobacco	Pipe
Mah'-re-am	pē'vt	ah-we'-kah
	pŭ-pe-vab	
Tuvah (Mahl'-ke)	pe'-wah	
Kah'-we-sik'-tem (Palm Springs)	pe'-vaht	yu'-le
		yu-lil^ch
Pow'-we-am (Cahuilla Valley)	pe'-vaht	
Koo'-pah	pe'-v̌aht	ē'-chit
	pe'-e-vaht	e'sh
	pĕ-pe'-bah	
Piyumkan		
Pi-yum'-ko (Luiseño)	pe'-vaht	no-nah'-hah
So-vo'-va (So-bo'-bah)	———	———
Kitanamwits		
Ke'-tan-a-moo'-kum	che'-woot	we'-ke-hwaht
Cahuenga (Mohave Desert)	tse'-woot	nĕ-we'-ko

OLHONEAN

Tribe	Tobacco	Pipe
Kah'-koon (Room'-se-en)	sow-wans	hoo'-rup (straight, of cane)
Hoo'-mon-twash' (Moot'-soon)	mat'-tret	soo'-koom'
(Santa Clara)	mah'-tār	

POLIKLAN

Tribe	Tobacco	Pipe
Po-lik'-lah	wah'-koom	raw'-ah'-wus
	hah'-koom'	
	haw'^ch-koom	
Ner-er'-ner	hah'-koom'	rah'-wah'

SHASTAN

Tribe	Tobacco	Pipe
Shas'-te	o-wah	ahp'-soo
	oo'-ah	
Ko'-no-me'-hoo	oo'-wah	ahp'-soo
	o'-bah	
Hah-to-ke'-he-wuk	o-wah	up-soo
Tlo-hōm-tah'-hoi	koo'-mah-tsā'-wah	ah'-nah-pah

POMOAN

Northern Division

Tribe	Tobacco	Pipe
Mah'-to-po'-mah	suk-kah'	
Me-tum-ki po-mah	suk-kah'	hi-shut-tōl

Tribe	Tobacco	Pipe
Po-mo'-ke-chah' (Potter Valley)	sah-hah'	sah-hah'-kah'-be
Ki-yow'-bah^{ch}	sah-hah'	sah-hah' hah'-bĕ
Stony Creek Division		
Sho-te'-ah	shah'-ko	sak'-kah boo'-te
	sah-kah	kol'-lon
	shah-kah	
Yokiah-Boyah Division		
Bo'-yah	sah-kah'	pe'-pah (Spanish)
Tah'-bah-tā	sah-kah'	sah'-kah kah'-be
Yo-ki'-ah	sah-kah'	sah-kah'-kah'-be
Sho'-ko'-ah	sak-kah'	sak-kah' kah'-be
Hah-nah'-bah^{ch} or Clear Lake Division		
Dan-no'-kah	sah-hah'	sah-hah'-hah'-be
Ho-al'-lek	sah-kah'	sah-kah'-hah'-be
She'-kum	sah-kah'	sah-kah'-hah'-be
Ku-lan-nă'-po	sah-hah'	sah'-hah hah'-be
Lower Lake Division		
Ham'-fo	to'm-ko-ah	'hi'-ko
		ko-ah' kah'-be
		'hri'-ko
Mah'-kah-mo-chum'-mi		
Mah'-kah-mo-chum'-mi . . .	kah'-wah	loo-chah' kab-bĕ (stone)
We'-shah-chum'-mi	kah'-wah	loo-chah' kă-bĕ
We-shum'-tat-tah		
Kah'-tah-we chum'-mi	kah'-wah	kah-wahk'-bĕ (long and straight, of ash wood)
		loo-chah'-kă-bĕ
Me'-dah-kah' tum'-mi	kah'-wah	
Coast Division		
Kah-chi'-ah	kah'-wah	loo-chuk'-ă-be
		loo'-wĕ-chok kă-be

SHOSHONEAN

Monache Piute

Neum' or Nim'	saw'-gō	to-ēs
Woponutch	hōm	to-ēs'
	so'-go (when pounded)	
Hoo'-doo-ge'-dah	so'-go	to-o'-she
		to-oish

Tribe	Tobacco	Pipe
Em'-tim-bitch..........saw'-gǒ		tǎ-doo-esh
		to-ēsh'
		tas-soo'-kah-mi'
Towinchebah or Holkoma . hō'm		so'-go (?)
	ho'-ōm	
	so'-go	
Ko-ko-he'-ba...........at-to'-ish		
Wuksache.............saw'k		pe-che'-mǎ
	saw'-go	pe'-chum
Northern Piute		
Burns and Malheur Lake . . pah'-moo		to-ish'-a
Bannok (Ft. Hall).......pah-mo		to'-ish
	tǔ-mi'-yu-ah	
Ft. Bidwell Piute........pah'-mo		to-is'
Koo-yu'-e-wits' (Pyramid		
Lake)...............poo-e-bah'-mo		to-is'
		nu-er-ro-is
Walker Lake...........pah'-mo		to-e'-sah
Bridgeport.............poo-e-bǎ'-mo		to-e'-shah
Koo-tsah'-be-dik'-kah		
(Mono Lake)..........poo'-e-bah'-mo		to-e'-sah
Owens Valley Piute		
Bishop................pah-tum'-be pah		to-ish'-she
	mo	
	bah'-mo	
Big Pine..............pah'-mo		to-ish'-she
Lone Pine.............pah'-mo		pitch-chim'-mah
	saw'-go	to-ish'-she
Southern Piute		
Siv'-vits...............ko-ahp'		choong
Kiv-vǎ'-vits ....sah-wo'-wahb		tsoong
Ute of Utah............pow-rah		tsong
Ute...................ko-ep' (kvap)		t'choots'
Chem'-e-we'-ve.........ko-ahp'b		choong'-o
		choo-mo'-pe
New-oo'-ah and		
Tol'-chin-ne...........ko-o'-pe		ko-et'-tik
	sah-o'-dah	pah-um'-bah
	pish-pǎ-vah'-te	
Pah-ran'-e-get-seu.......sah-wahk'-wah-be		cho-noo'-pe
Moǎ'pa...............sah-wah'-wahp		cho-noo'-pe

Tribe	*Tobacco*	*Pipe*
Nu-vah'-ahn-dits........sah-wahk'-wah-be		choo-moo'-pe chung'
Shoshone		
Shoshone, Ft. Hall, Idaho	pah'-mo	taw'-ĕ
Shoshone (centr. Nevada)	bah'-ho	bah'-ho do'-e
So'-so'-ne (NE Nevada)...pah'-ho		to'-e
		do'-e
Goseute...............too'-pah		to'-ă
	pah'-mo	taw'-e
Pak'-wah-zid'-je		
(Panamint)..........bah-hō'm-be		pah-hum-do'-e
Panamint.............pah-hum-be		pah-hoon'-too-e
SULAHTELUKAN		
Soo-lah'-te-luk...........kwahs'-wuk		kŭ-ŭ'-paw
Pah'-te-waht............. ———		———
We'-yot................ă-kwahs'-wuk		mah-ses'[1]
		kŭ-ŭ'-paw
		kas'-wah-kil
TONGVAN		
Tong'-vā................pā-es'-pe-vot		
	pās-pe-baht	wee'k-chot (straight)
	pish'-pă-vah-te	ko-et'-tik
TU'-BOT-TE-LOB'-E-LAN		
Tu'-bot-te-lob'-e-lā........sho-kont		oo-gaht' (10–12 in. long)[2]
	so-gunt	o-got'
Pahn'-ka-lă'-che..........so-kunt'		o'-kut
WASHUAN		
Wah'-shoo...............ban-kōs; ban-koos		ban-koosh tă-ak (tobacco stone)
	pan-kush	
	bahng'-kus (dried and smoked)	"bahn'-kus dă-ek" (smoke rock)
	wah-shoo bahn-kus (Indian tobacco)	
WINTUNAN		
Win-toon' (McCloud R.)....lŏl'		hol'-lah
	lawl'	haw'-lah

[1] Three names; mah-ses' best.
[2] Of cane; mouthpiece, small stick.

Tribe	Tobacco	Pipe
Win-tu' (Trinity R.)	lawl'	haw'-li
Nor'relmuk	lawl'	haw'-lah
Ono-Wintu	lawl'	hŏl'-lah
Chen'-po-sel	lŏl	bo-te'
		but'-te
'Ket' Win	lŏl	bō'-te
	lawl	bot'-te
Ko-pĕh Win	lŏl	bo-tel
		bot-te
Ko'-roo (Pah'-tin)	lawl	bot'-te
Choo-hel'-mem sel	lawl'	bo-mit'
Pat'-win	lol	toh'-bo
		to'-po (Spanish)
Poo'-e-win	lol	to'-poo (Spanish)
Nōm-lik-kah	lawl'	lōl-kok
Noi-muk	lol	lol-kok

YAHNAN

Yah'-nah or No'-se	mo'-yu	chan-nah'-mo-nah (stone)

YOKUTAN

Cho-e-nim'-ne	sho'-kin	sho'-kŭt
	shaw'-kin	shā'-kil
Cho-ki'-min-nah	sho'-kin	shā'-kil
Wik-tchum'-ne	sho'-kon	
Too-lol'-min	so'-kon	pow'
Yow'-el-man'-ne	sŏ-k'l	pah-oom'
	so'-kon	
Yow-lan'-che	so'-kon	pah-mo'-e
Tā-dum'-ne	sho'-kon	sook-mi
Ketch'-ā'-ye	———	———
Tin'-lin-ne	saw'-kon	pow'-ŏ
	saw'-kah	
Chūnut	saw'-kom	pis-sā-e
		sook'-mi (of wood)
Tah'-che	po'-net	pe-ish
	po'-neet	pe-shā-he
		pe-sā-he (of stone)
		sook'-mi (of wood)
Gosh-sho'-o	pah'-um	soo'-kut
Chuk-chan-sy	pah-ō'm	soo'-kut
	pah'-um	

Tribe	Tobacco	Pipe
Ko-yet'-te	so'-kon	
Yo'-kotch (Fresno R.) (or Choi-yo-choi-ye)	san-nis'	sŭ-koot'
No-tu'-no-to	sō'-kon	sook'-mi (wood, 3 or 4 in. long)
	kā'-pish (for eating)	
Pal-low' yam'-me	so'-ken-ne	pah'-mung-ti

YUKEAN

Tribe	Tobacco	Pipe
Mi-yahk'-mah	loo'-chă	loo'-chā-lel
	loo'-chĕ	loo'-chĕ lel' (stone)
Hootch'-nom	———	———
Oo'-kum'-nom	woi-muk	woi-o-al
	woi-ŏh	
Oo'-ko-ton-til'-kah	woi'-mil	woi'-me-lil'
	wi-mā'-ă	

YUMAN

Tribe	Tobacco	Pipe
A-wah'-kah-wahk' (Campo and Mexico)	oop'	mo'-kwin'
Kam'-me-i' ('Diegueno')	oop'	am-mo-kwin'
Kam-m'yi (Imperial Valley and Colorado Desert)	oop'	mo-kwin'
Mohave	a-ō'v	mal'-ho
	ah-oov'	
Yuma	o-vah	mel'-yah-hŏ'
	ah-ō'v	
	mil-yah-oov'	

Shoshonean Tribal Names

Since early historic times in the Southwest, the name Piute in one or more of its various forms has been used for a Shoshonean tribe or group of tribes occupying a considerable extent of country north of the Big Bend of the Colorado River; and in more recent times the same name has been, and still is, applied to a widely different group of Shoshonean tribes inhabiting eastern California, northwestern Nevada, and eastern Oregon—thereby giving rise to endless confusion.

As early as 1776 the Spanish *padre* and explorer, Garcés, looking toward the Colorado from the south, saw smoke rising on the north side; this, he was told by his companions, apparently Yavapi Indians, came from the fires of the Payuchas. In the course of his travels, he mentions the Payuchas at different times and places; thus apparently a century and a half ago the name was in common use among the Yavapi and other tribes of the Colorado River region.

In enumerating the sequence of tribes from the south northward Garcés gives the following tribes as living above the Mohave, and in the order mentioned: the Chemeguaba [Chemeweve], Yabipai, Payuchas, and Yutas.[1]

The name Payucha appears also on Font's map of 1777, and was used by Don José Cortez in 1799. In recent years also it has been learned that the Hope call the Piute Pai-yu'-chimŭ and that the Navaho call them Pai-yu'-tsĭ.[2]

It is obvious therefore that for a long period—doubtless many centuries—the southern Piute or Pahute tribes have been known to the desert

---

[1] *On the Trail of a Spanish Pioneer: the Diary of Francisco Garcés, 1775–1776*, trans. and ed. by Elliott Coues, p. 434, 1900.

[2] James T. Mooney, *The Ghost-Dance Religion*, BAE–R (1892–1893), p. 1048, 1806.

149

tribes farther south by some form of the name; but so far as known only a single tribe used the name for themselves. This tribe lived on Muddy River and Meadow Valley Wash in eastern Nevada. It was visited by Jedediah Smith in the fall of 1826 and by Major Powell in 1873. Smith states: "Passing down this river some distance, I fell in with a nation of Indians who call themselves Pa Utches."[3] And Major Powell, commenting on the widespread use of the terms "Piute" and "Pahute," observes, "but the Indians know only those on the Muddy by that name."[4]

It is a curious fact that the adjacent Utah or Ute tribe—written also Eutaw, Yutah, Iutas and so on—although in geographic contact with the Pahute of southern Utah and speaking a closely allied language, has been known from earliest historic times by its own distinctive name. Thus Garcés in 1776 and Font in his map of 1777 mention the Yutas as next beyond the Payuches (from the south).

It is now of interest to examine the interrelationships and boundaries of the tribes to which the names Piute and Pahute are commonly applied. Roughly speaking, it may be said that the names cover three quite distinct divisions of Shoshonean stock, namely: (1) the Northern Piute, inhabiting northwestern Nevada, eastern California, eastern Oregon, and southwestern Idaho; (2) the Southern Piute or Ute-Chemeweve, inhabiting parts of southeastern California, southern Nevada, southern Utah, and northwestern Arizona; (3) the Monache, inhabiting Owens Valley east of the Sierra Nevada and also generally isolated valleys on the west slope of the Sierra. Because of its geographic and linguistic isolation this group will be considered separately (see pp. 168–174).

The earliest published references to Piute (regardless of spelling) relate to tribes of the southern or southeastern division, and the first syllable of the name (Payucha, Payuchas, Payuches, Payuchis) as written nearly one hundred and fifty years ago by La Fora, Garcés, Font, Escalante, and Cortez, has the "pi" sound; but many later authors in referring to the same tribes, changed the Spanish "pay" ("pi") to "pah"—as in Pa-uches, Pa-Uta, Pah-utes, Pah-Utas.

On the other hand, the majority of modern authors have adopted the "pi" sound—as in Piute, Paiute, Pi-Utas, Py-Utes, Pyutt, Py-uta, Pi-utah, and so on—for the tribes of the northwestern division, tribes ranging from eastern Oregon south over northeastern California and northwestern

---

[3] So printed in the French version in *Les nouvelles annales des voyages*, ser. 2, 7:208–212 (not 308–312 as given by H. G. Dale), 1833; copy in Library of Congress. Misspelled "Pa-Ulches" in the *Missouri Republican* (Oct. 11, 1827), as reprinted in H. G. Dale, ed., *The Ashley-Smith Explorations* (*1822–1829*), p. 188, 1918; and in the copy of Smith's letter in the letterbook of the Supt. Ind. Affairs now in the Kansas State Historical Society at Topeka. But this letter is a copy, as I am informed by Miss Clara Francis, Librarian, and "is not in Jedediah Smith's own handwriting."

[4] J. W. Powell in *Rept. Commr. Ind. Affairs for 1873*, p. 45, 1874.

Nevada. Nevertheless, both spellings, *Pi-* and *Pah-*, are in common use for both sets of tribes.

In 1856 Dr. Garland Hurt attempted to discriminate by definitely adopting the form Py-Utes for the northern division, and Pah-utahs for the southern (including the tribes of Utah).[5] He was followed by Simpson, who states that the Py-utes are "frequently confounded with the Pah-utes, with which they show only a distant affinity"—the Py-utes (or Piutes) living in extreme eastern California and western Nevada, the Pah-utes in central Nevada (and Utah).[6]

Gatschet in 1876 took the same ground, stating: "Presumably there exists a difference between them [the Pah-Ute of Utah] and the Pi-Utes in northwestern Nevada."[7]

But Powell,[8] Waterman,[9] and Dixon,[10] reversed the usage recommended by Hurt, Simpson, and Gatschet, and designated the southern group "true Paiutes," thus following the earliest users of the name, the Spanish explorers La Fora, Font, Garcés, Escalante, and Cortez, who gave the "pi" sound (which they wrote "pay") to tribes of the southern division.

Waterman recognized the southern division as "true" Piute, and stated specifically that the Northern Piute do not admit this to be their name. He ascertained also that the term "Paviotso" applied to them by Powell, Kroeber, and others "is no more their own tribal name than the former [Piute] is."[11] He refers also to "what has been described as the Mono-Paviotso or Mono Bannock division," but like Kroeber fails apparently to recognize the dialectic and geographic distinctness of the Monache tribes of Owens Valley and the Sierra from the Northern Piute (including the Mono Lake band) to which the Shoshone term "Paviotso" has been applied.

It is obvious therefore that no form of the name has been used consistently for either of the two great divisions, that most of the spellings have been applied to both, that efforts to discriminate by the use of *Pi-* and *Pah-* have failed, both having been recommended for each division, and that, as the matter still stands (1920), the nomenclature of the two groups remains in utter confusion.

The principal difficulty arises from the unpleasant fact that the various tribes and bands have no collective name for themselves, using only the distinctive local names for each. Therefore, in order to discriminate the

---

[5] Garland Hurt, *Rept. Commr. Ind. Affairs*, H. R. Doc. 1, 34th Cong., 1st sess., p. 779, 1856.
[6] App. O, J. H. Simpson, *Rept. of the Exploration of the Great Basin of Utah*, pp. 37–38, 1876.
[7] A. S. Gatschet, *Zwölf Sprachen aus dem Südwesten Nordamerikas*, pp. 80–81, 1876.
[8] *Rept. Commr. Ind. Affairs for 1873*, pp. 41–53.
[9] T. T. Waterman, *The Phonetic Elements of the Northern Paiute Language*, UC–PAAE 10:14, 1911.
[10] R. B. Dixon, "Indian Population," *Census of 1910*, p. 98, 1915.
[11] Waterman, *Phonetic Elements of the Northern Paiute Language*, p. 14.

northern from the southern group of tribes, there appear to be four possible courses.

1. To restrict the name Piute to one division, Pahute to the other. This, as already stated, has been tried and has failed.

2. To restrict the term Piute or Pahute to one division and employ a wholly different term for the other, adopting one of the names applied to it by neighboring tribes. This was done by Powell in retaining Pi-Ute for the southern division and introducing the Shoshone name, Paviotso, for the northwestern division. He was followed by Kroeber, but this course has not met with general favor.

3. To invent new names for both—a procedure which was predestined to failure.

4. To employ the term Piute or Pahute as a blanket name for both groups, with a distinctive name for each separately.[12]

There are both advantages and disadvantages to the use of Piute as a blanket name. The name Piute (or Pahute) is so well known and so definitely applied that it would be difficult to displace it. At the same time it must be admitted that there are two weighty reasons against its retention: first, the wide linguistic separation of the two groups to which it is applied; second, the existence of other tribes, such as Bannok, Shoshone, and Ute, which are much more closely related to one or the other of the two divisions than are the two to one another.

It is a curious and regrettable circumstance that tribes so distantly related as the Northern and Southern Piute should be almost universally recognized by the same or closely similar names, while tribes closely allied to each of these groups—like the Bannok to Northern Piute, the Ute to Southern Piute—have been known since earliest historic times by wholly different names. Nevertheless, convenience, coupled with the difficulty of forcing a new name into the literature, may justify, for the present at least, the retention of the name in combination with a distinctive geographic prefix—Northern Piute, Southern Piute.

In order to gain a clearer conception of the problem it may be helpful, before going further, to glance at a classification of Shoshonean tribes. This classification is intended to show in a general way the relations of Northern and Southern Piute to one another and to related tribes, a knowledge of relationships being essential to a correct understanding of the group.

In this connection it is not necessary to include the Mohineam, Kahwesik, and Piyumko of Southern California—much less the Tongva and Tubotelobela, whose relationships to Shoshonean are exceedingly remote.

---

[12] Oscar Loew did this in 1876; but he did too much, making the name "Payutes" almost equivalent to Shoshonean stock. Wheeler Survey, *Report for 1875*, App. JJ, 1876.

Classification of Piute and Pahute Tribes

Northern Piute . . . . Walpape
                                              Yahooskin
                                              Kooyuewits
                                              Kootsabe-dikka
                                              Aggi-dikka
                                              Oroseam
                                              Bannok

Monache . . . . Monache
                                              Yianche
                                              Nim
                                              Holkoma
                                              Kokoheba
                                              Emtimbitch
                                              Woponutch
                                              Wuksache
                                              Toohook'mutch
                                              Padoosha (or Potwisha)

Southern Piute or Ute-Chemeweve . . Chemeweve
                                              Nuvahandit
                                              Pah-ran-ne-gets-seu
                                              Newooah
                                              Tolchinne
                                              Ute

Shoshone . . . . Pahkwasidje
                                              Panamint Shoshone
                                              Shoshone (proper)
                                              Comanche

The term "Paviotso" rests on a substantial footing, its origin being well known and its application reasonably definite. It is the name used by the Shoshone of central and southern Nevada for the Northwestern Piute, and was first introduced into literature by Powell in 1874. Powell believed these Indians to be "a branch of the Bannocks," and said: "They should be known as Pa-vi-o-tsoes, as this is the name by which they know themselves, and by which they are known throughout the surrounding tribes."[13]

In stating that the name is one "by which they know themselves," Powell was misinformed, as pointed out by Waterman in 1911,[14] and as I have repeatedly learned by personal inquiry among the Piute of Pyramid

---

[13] H. R. Misc. Doc. 86, 43d Cong., 1st sess., pp. 5, 6, 11 (Jan.), 1874; *Rept. Commr. Ind. Affairs for 1873*, p. 53, 1874.

[14] *Phonetic Elements of the Northern Paiute Language*, p. 14.

Lake, Wadsworth, and Walker River. For instead of accepting the name, they resent its being applied to them by the Shoshone. Powell therefore in giving the name "Pa-vi-o-tsoes"[15] to the Northern Piute introduced a term foreign to their language.

In 1907 Kroeber introduced the compound term "Mono-Paviotso," using it in a very broad sense as covering both the Monache and the Northern Piute—thus overlooking their linguistic distinctness. He gave their distribution as extending "from the 36th to the 46th degree of latitude," and included, according to his own statement:[16]

... the Shoshoneans on both sides of the Sierra Nevada north of Kern river, most of whom are generally known as Monachi or Mono; the people of Owens Valley, east of the Sierra Nevada, who have been called both Monachi and Paiute; the so-called Paiute, Powell's Paviotso, of Walker river and apparently all northwestern Nevada; the Shoshoneans of eastern Oregon, called both Snake and Paiute; and probably certain of the Bannock or other Indians of Idaho.

Essentially the same arrangement occurs in the *Handbook of American Indians* (Pt. I, p. 932, 1907); but Dixon, in the *Census of 1910*, gives Mono and Paviotso separately, misdefining Mono as elsewhere indicated in this article (p. 151) and restricting Paviotso to "the Snakes and so-called Paiutes of southeastern Oregon, western Nevada, and the easterly edge of California as far south as Lake Tahoe." His Paviotso therefore corresponds essentially with Northern Piute as used by Waterman and myself; but the selection of Lake Tahoe as their southern limit is unfortunate, inasmuch as they never inhabited the Lake Tahoe region, that being wholly within the territory of the Washoo.

THE NORTHERN PIUTE

The various versions of names used for the Northern Piute by earlier observers are given in the accompanying table.

---

[15] Other pronunciations of the name obtained by me from the Central Nevada Shoshone are Pav'-ve'o'zo, Bab'-be-yuz-zo, Bav'-ve-o-zo; from the Panamint and Pahk-wah-zid-je Shoshone, Pahb'-be-o'-zo; and from the So-so'-ne of Ruby Valley, Bab'-be-o'-so.

[16] A. L. Kroeber, *Shoshonean Dialects of California*, UC–PAAE 3:98, 114, 1907.

EARLY SPELLINGS OF THE NAME NORTHERN PIUTE

Name	Authority	Date of observation	Date of publication	Locality
Pah Utes..............	W. T. Hamilton	1844	1844	Pyramid L. to Carson R.
Piutes[a]................	John Dunn	Before 1844	1844	Colorado and Salt L.
Pahutes of the North.....	Don Pablo Belarde	1844	1922	N Nevada
Paiuches..............	T. J. Farnham	1845 (?)[b]	1845	N Nevada
Pyentes[c]..............	Joel Palmer	1845	1847	Ft. Bridger[d]
Paiuches..............	Farnham[e]	1844	....	......
Pah Utah..............	C. F. Hoffman[f]	1850	1867	Mono L.[g]
Pi-utah..............	Holman	....	1852	Carson R.
Pyanches..............	*Daily Alta California*	1851	4/23/1851	E of Sierra
Pintas'................	Holman	....	1853	Carson R.
Pah-Utah..............	Bonneville (?)	....	1853(?)[h]	
Pah-Utahs..............	E. G. Beckwith	....	1855	Upper Pit R.
Pah-Utah or Digger Indians..............	Beckwith	....	1855[i]	Between Carson and Walker lakes, Nevada
Pah-Utahs..............	Beckwith	1854	1855	Lower Humboldt Valley
Pah Utah or Digger Indians..............	W. H. Emory and A. A. Humphreys	....	1854–57	Carson R. and L.[j]
Pi-Utah..............	H. R. Schoolcraft	....	1855	Carson Valley
Py-utes, Py-ute........	Garland Hurt	1856	1856	Humboldt Sink
Pah Utah or Digger Indians ("Root Diggers or Pai-utes")............	Warren (map)	....	1857	NW Nevada
Pyutt................	J. M. Hutchings	....	1858	W Nevada
Pah Utes..............	T. H. Rolfe	Oct., 1857	1857	......
Pah-Utah..............	F. A. Bishop (map)	1857	1859	W Nevada
Piutah................	Spaulding	....	1859	NW Nevada
Pah-Utahs..............	C. M. Welles	....	1859	Carson Valley
Pah Utahs..............	*Placerville Observer* (Calif.)	1859	1859	NW Nevada
Pah-ute; Pah-Utes.......	Dodge	1859	1860	NW Nevada
Pah Utah..............	*San Joaquin Republican*	....	1859	Carson Valley
Pah Utahs; Pah-Utahs....	*San Francisco Weekly Herald*	1860	1860	Humboldt R., Nevada
Paiuli(s)..............	Jules Remy	1855	1860	NW Nevada
Paiulee................	Remy and Brenchly	1855	1861	NW Nevada
Pah-Ute................	A. S. Taylor	1860	1861	NW Nevada
Pa-Yuta (Pey Utes)......	R. F. Burton	....	1861	NW Nevada

[a] John Dunn's "Piutes" of 1844, if properly belonging here, is the earliest record I have thus far found of the use of the name for Northern Piute. But he had only hearsay information from trappers, and his locality, loosely stated as "within the Colorado and the Great Salt Lake," is by no means conclusive.
[b] In Dr. Merriam's typescript the date of observation (written in longhand) reads: "map 1845 ??".—Ed.
[c] Misprint for Pyeutes. By error of transcription the *u* is often made to read *n*.
[d] [Used by] wives of trappers temporarily at the fort.
[e] After Dr. Lyman.
[f] Information from Jos. Screech.
[g] Visitors from Mono Lake.
[h] Name on Colton's map.
[i] Map 3, Pacific R.R. Repts., Route of 41st parallel.
[j] Pacific R.R. Repts.

EARLY SPELLINGS OF THE NAME NORTHERN PIUTE—*Continued*

Name	Authority	Date of observation	Date of publication	Locality
Pah-Ute.................	W. P. Dole	....	1861	W Nevada
Pah-Ute; Pah-Utes......	James W. Nye	....	1861	W Nevada
Pah-Ute; Pah-Utes......	W. Wasson	....	1861	W Nevada
Pah Utahs..............	A. J. Simmons	1862	1862	NW Nevada
Piute..................	*Red Bluff Independent*	1862	1862	N Nevada
Pajutis.................	J. J. Benjamin	1859	1862	N Nevada
Pahutes................	W. P. Dole	1862	1863	Carson Valley
Pah Utes..............	W. Wasson	1861	1863	W Nevada
Pah Utah..............	J. T. Lockhart	....	1863	W Nevada
Pi-Utes................	A. S. Taylor	....	1863	W Nevada
Pah-Utes..............	W. H. Knight	....	1864	NW Nevada
Pah-Utahs..............	J. C. Burch	1864	1865	Lower Humboldt R.
Pah-Utahs..............	Lockhart	1864	1865	NW Nevada
Mono Pi-Utes..........	A. H. Campbell	....	1866	Mono L.
Walker R. Pi-Utes.......	Franklin Campbell	1866	1866	W Nevada
Pah-Utes..............	J. Q. A. Stanley	1866	1866	California; Nevada
Pah-Utes..............	Burch	....	1865	W Nevada
Pah-Utes..............	F. H. Head	1866	1866	SE Nevada; SW Utah
Pi-Utes................	F. Campbell	1866	1866	[N Nevada]
Pah-Ute...............	F. Campbell	1865	1867	Carson region
Pai-Utes[k].............	F. Campbell	1866	1866	SE Nevada
Pah-Ute...............	Wasson	1865	1867	Carson region
Pah-Utes..............	Justin Edwards	1865	1867	Carson region
Pi-Utes...............	F. Campbell	1866	1866	NW of "Upper Colorado"
Pi-Utes...............	Hermann Ehrenberg	1866	1866	Nevada
Pi-Utes; Pi-Ute..........	H. G. Parker	1866	1866	......
Pah-Utes..............	T. T. Dwight	1867	1868	NW Nevada
Pi-Utes...............	F. Campbell	1867	1868	NW Nevada
Pah-utes..............	Gen. H. W. Halleck	1868	....	NW Nevada[l]
Pah-Utahs..............	J. Ross Browne	....	1869	W Nevada
Pah Utahs of Mono L.....	C. L. Brace	....	1869	Mono L.
Pah-Utes..............	Sarah Winnemucca	....	1871	NW Nevada
Pah-utes..............	G. W. Perrie	1857–59	1873	Pyramid L.
Pah-Ute...............	C. A. Bateman	1873	1874	Pyramid L.
Pah-Utes; Pah-Utes or Pa-vio-tsos; Pa-vi-o-tsus.................	J. W. Powell	1873	1874	W Nevada; NE California
Pah-Utes..............	Commr. Ind. Affairs	1874	1874	W Nevada
Pi-Utes...............	Commr. Ind. Affairs	1874	1874	E Oregon
Pi-Utes...............	Commr. Ind. Affairs	1874	1874	S Oregon
Pai-Ute...............	Bd. Ind. Commrs.	1874	1875	W Nevada
Py-Utes...............	Hurt	1860	1876	E base Sierra Nevada
Pah-Ute...............	Powell	1876	1876	Pyramid L.
Pi-utes................	J. H. Simpson	1859–60	1876	W Nevada
Paviotso[m].............	Powell	....	....	NW Nevada; NE California

[k] Pai-Utes regarded as distinct from Pi-utes.
[l] MS, War Department.
[m] Shoshone name.

EARLY SPELLINGS OF THE NAME NORTHERN PIUTE—*Concluded*

Name	Authority	Date of observation	Date of publication	Locality
Pah-u-tes.............	L. H. Bunnell	1853 (?)	1880	NW Nevada
Pi Ute..............	H. L. Wells[n]	....	1882	NE California
Payute..............	A. S. Gatschet	....	1890	S Oregon
Pah Ute.............	John Muir	Various	1898	W Nevada; E California
Pah Utes............	Hamilton	1844[o]	1905	Pyramid L.; Carson R.
Mono-Paviotso.........	A. L. Kroeber	....	1907	NE California; NW Nevada
Paiute..............	A. E. Chamberlain	....	1910	Nevada
Mono-Bannock.........	T. T. Waterman	....	1911	NW Nevada
Northern Paiutes........	W. L. Marsden	....	1923	Harney region, Oregon
Northern Paiutes........	Kroeber	....	1923	......
Paviotso.............	Kroeber	....	1925	Central Nevada
Paviotso.............	W. D. Strong	....	1927	All N Nevada

[n] *History of Butte County, California,* p. 110, 1882.
[o] It is open to question whether Hamilton's use of Pah Utes dates from the time of observation (1844) or from subsequent information.

The Northern Piute use the following names for their own tribes and divisions.

Ag'-di dik'-kah kud-dy[17] (meaning "fish eaters")............................Walker L. Piute

Ar-rid'-de kud'-dy neu'-ma (meaning "fish-eating people")......................Name used by Pyramid L. Piute for Walker L. Piute

Kotso'-dik-kah'-ra (meaning "buffalo eaters")............................Northern Piute name for Bannok

Koo-tsă'-be dik'-ka kud'-dy (meaning "koo-tsă-be eaters").................Walker L. name for Mono L. Piute

Koo-yu'-e-wit kud'-dy or Kwe-yu'-de-kut (meaning "sucker eaters").............One of the names used for Pyramid L. Piute by themselves

Koo-yu'-e-dik-kah' (meaning "sucker eaters")............................Name used by Mono L. Piute for Pyramid L. Piute

O-ro-se-am.........................Winnemucca and Mason Valley Piute

Pan-nă-nud'-de Kwi-tă-hoo ("Pelican or west people")........................Pyramid L. Piute name for themselves

Pe-ton'-a-kwats (meaning "southerners")..Name used by several bands for tribe living farther south

---

[17] Spelled Agai'h-tika'-ra by Mooney.

Tă-bah-nah-gwă′-tĕ (meaning "east
   people")...........................Name used by Mono L. Piute for
                        Walker L. Piute
Tivatika (meaning "— eaters").........At Belmont, Nevada, and also Hot
                        Springs Canyon south of Mt.
                        MacGruder.[18] BAE–R 14
Tu-ba′-de kud′-dy (meaning "pine-nut
   eaters")...........................Name used by Pyramid L. Piute for
                        Walker R. Piute
Tu-ne-gă-bah′........................Name sometimes applied to them-
                        selves by the Mono L. Piute

The following names are applied to the Northern Piute by other tribes.[19]

Ah-poo′-e (Ă-poo′-e)...........Name used by Pit R. tribes
A-vi′ dik-kah..................One of the Monache names for Walker L.
                    Piute. See also Kween-ag′-gwe-tah
Bab′-be-yuz′-zo, Bab′-be-o′-so,
   and Bav′-ve-o′-zo..............Name used by Panamint Shoshone. See also
                    Pah′-be-o′-zo and Bŭ-ŭ
Baloh.........................Name used by the Washoo. Powers, MS, 1876.
                    See also Palŭ and Paleu
Bŭ-ŭ.........................One of the names used by Panamint Shoshone.
                    See also Pah′-be-o′-zo and Bab-be-o′-so
Bav′-ve-o-zo..................Another pronunciation of Bab′-be-o′-zo used
                    by Panamint Shoshone. See also Pah′-be-o′-zo
Hen′-nah......................Name used by the Ap-woo′-ro-kā′e and At-
                    soo-kā′-e
Hogăpä′ goni.................Name used by Wyoming Shoshone. Mooney,
                    1896
Kwe-nă′-gwe-tah or Kween-ag′-gwe-
   tah and A-vi′ dik-kah.........Bishop Cr. Monache names for the Walker L.
                    Piute
Koi′-yu-wak or Koi-aw′we-ek.....Name used by Northern Mewuk
Koo-yu′-e-dik-kah.............Mono L. Piute name for Pyramid L. Piute
Mo-nahk or Mo-nok............Name used by Middle Mewuk
Mo′-nah′.....................Name used by Southern Mewuk
Monozi or Mona..............Name used by Northwestern Maidu. Kroeber,
                    Handbook, p. 582, 1925
Paleu........................Name used by Washo. Kroeber, *Handbook*, p.
                    570, 1925
Palŭ.........................Name used by Washo. Henshaw, 1883. See
                    also Baloh and Paleu

---

[18] W. J. Hoffman, BAE–R 14 (1892–1893), p. 282, 1896.
[19] The data in this tabulation are Dr. Merriam's (initialed C.H.M.), except as otherwise noted.—Ed.

Pah'-be-o'-zo (Bab'-be-yuz'-zo, Bab-
    be-o'-so, Bav'-ve-o'-zo, Bŭ-ŭ)...Name used by Panamint Shoshone. (MS,
                      1902, 1909)
Paviotso.....................Name used by Shoshone. Powell, 1874.
Po-hă-vă-ră'-ze................Monache Piute name for Piute on mountains
                      N of Benton Valley
Saht'.......................Name used by Klamath tribe of Klamath L.
                      region
Tah-bah-nah gwă-tĕ (east people) . Mono L. Piute name for Walker L. Piute
Toloma.....................Name used by Northeastern "Maidu." Kroe-
                      ber, *Handbook*, p. 582, 1925
Tul-lo'-mah or Tul-lum'-mah.....Name used by No'-to-koi'-yo Midoo

THE SOUTHERN PIUTE

Of the Southern Piute tribes, the Chemeweve and Nuvahandit may be regarded as the most typical, with Ute standing somewhat to one side. The Newooah and Tolchinne tribes, while closely related to one another and belonging to the same group, are the most aberrant. Some of their words are common to Monache, others to Panamint and Pakwazidje Shoshone, and, strange as it may appear, some are common to Northern Piute. This is the more surprising because of the wide geographic separation of these tribes—a separation that must date back to a very remote period.

EARLY SPELLINGS OF THE NAME SOUTHERN PIUTE OR PAHUTE[a]

Name	Authority	Date[b]	Locality
Payuchis	La Fora (map)	1766–72	S Utah
Payuchas; Payuches	Garcés	1776[c]	S Utah
Payuches	Escalante	1776	N Arizona; S Utah
Utahs Payuches			
Yutas Payuchis			
Iutas Payuchis			
Payucha	Font (map)	1777	S Utah
Payuches	Cortez	1799	S Utah
Pa Ulches[d]	J. Smith (1826)	1827	Muddy R., Nevada
Payuches (Payoutches)	Armijo (1829)	1830	S Arizona; S Nevada
Pa Utches[e]	J. Smith (1826)	1833	Muddy R., Nevada
Piutes	T. J. Farnham	1843	Sevier R., Utah
Piutes	John Dunn	1844	Between the Colorado and Great Salt L.
Pah-Utah	J. Fremont (map)	1844	Muddy R. region N of Vegas
Piutes	Farnham	1844	S Utah
Paiuches	Farnham[f]	1844	S Utah
Piutes	Dunn	1844	"The Colorado and Great Salt Lake"
Pa-utah	Fremont (text)	1845	Mts. head R. Virgin
Paiuches Indians	Farnham (map)	1845	S Utah
Pa-Utah	Mitchell (map; text)	1846	S Nevada (N of Vegas)
Pa-utah	Rufus B. Sage (1843)	1846	S Utah
Paiuches	Simpson (map)	1848	S Nevada; S Utah
Pah Utah	C. E. Kells (?)	1848	S Utah
Pah-Utah	Bonneville[g]	1849	S Nevada[h]
Piyutah	G. F. Ruxton (1846)	1849	S Utah
Pah Utah Indians	John Disturnelli (map)	1849	S Nevada
Pah-Utah	Bryant (map)	1849	NW of Virgin R.
Pah-Utah	J. T. Brooks (map)	1849	S Nevada; Utah
Pah-Utah; Pah Utah	Colton (map)	1849	SE Nevada
Pah-utah	John Dower (map)	1850	S Nevada
Pahnutes (or Paynutes);			
Utahs	John Wilson (1849)	1850[i]	Colorado R. (S)
Pah Utah Indians	Thomas, Cowper, and Co.	1851	S Nevada
Pah-Utahs	Eastman	1852	S Nevada[j]
Piutes	Farnham[k]	1852	S Central Utah
Pah Utah	J. B. Tassin (map)	1851	S Nevada
Pah Utah Indians	R. M. Martin[l]	1851	S Utah
Pah Utahs, Pah Utes	Stansbury	1852	Utah Valley or S Nevada
Pah Utahs	C. D. Gibbs (map)	1852	S Nevada; Utah
Pah-utah	Bonneville	1853 (?)[m]	......

a Incomplete.
b Presumably date of publication.—Ed.
c Not published until 1854.
d Error for Pa Utches.
e In French translation.
f After Dr. Lyman.
g Washington Irving, *Adventures of Captain Bonneville*, 1849.
h Muddy origin. May go back to 1837 ed.
i Letter, H.R. Ex. Doc. 17, 31st Cong., 1st sess., p. 185, 1850.
j Map, Schoolcraft.
k T. J. Farnham, *Life, Adventures, and Travels in California*, pp. 375–380, 1852.
l Map, Tallie's Atlas.
m Map by Colton.

EARLY SPELLINGS OF THE NAME SOUTHERN PIUTE OR PAHUTE—*Continued*

Name	Authority	Date	Locality
Pah-Utahs...............	Geo. Schroeter (map)	1853	S Utah
Pah Utahs..............	Sitgreaves	1853	S Nevada
Pah-Utes...............	*Los Angeles Star*	1853	Mohave Desert
Pah-Utahs.............	G. H. Heap	1854	Santa Clara; Muddy R.
Payutas................	Henry Lange (map)	1854	S Utah
"Pah Utahs (Chem-e-hue-vis)"..................	Whipple and Ives (map)	1854	Colorado R. below Needles
Mountain Pai-Utes.......	A. W. Whipple	1854 (or 1856)	Mohave Desert
Pi-u-chas..............	J. A. Graves	1854	Southern
Pah-Utah..............	Beckwith[n]	1855	Sevier R., Utah
Pahutas................	Merriwether	1855	Arizona
Pah Utah..............	Beckwith (map)	1855	S central Nevada
Pah Utah; Pah-Utah......	Beckwith (text)	1855	W central Utah
"Paiutes or Chemehuevis"; Pai-Utes; Payuches.....	Whipple	1855	Colorado R.
Pah-Utahs..............	Whipple	1855	S Utah
Pah Utah Indians........	Black (map)	1856	S Nevada
Pah-utahs..............	Hurt	1856	S Utah
Pi-u-ches..............	J. P. Beckwourth	1856	S Utah
Pai-ute (Pah-Utah)....... Pai-utes, Pai-Ute Paiutes	Whipple	1856	S Utah
Piutes, Piuches, Pai-Utes, Pah-Yutes, Pā-Utes.....	Whipple; Ewbank and Turner	1856	Colorado R. region
Pahutes................	S. N. Carvalho (1854)	1857	Muddy and Virgin region
Pah Utes..............	Warren (map)	1857	W of Needles, California
Pah-Utes...............	*San Francisco Weekly Bulletin*	1857	E Mohave Desert
Pah Utahs..............	Ives (map)	1858	NW of Vegas, Nevada
Pah-Utahs.............	Mollhausen	1858	Southern
Pah-Utes...............	Lange (map)	1858	NW of Bend of Colorado R.
Pah-utes...............	J. H. Simpson (1858)	1859	W Utah
Pah-Ute................	J. H. Carleton[o]	1860	Mohave R., California (Camp Cady), and Santa Clara Run, Utah
Pai Utahs and Pai-Ute.....	E. H. D. Domenech	1860	New Mexico (?)
Pah-Ute................	*Los Angeles Star*	1860	Mohave Desert
Pi-ute.................	*Los Angeles Star*	1860	Mohave Desert
Payusitas...............	J. Remy (1855)	1860, 1861	SW Utah
Peyute and Pey-utes......	Forney	1860	Nevada and Utah
Pah Utahs..............	Capt. H. S. Burton	1860	N Colorado R.
Pah-Utes..............	Forney	1860	S Utah
Pah Utah..............	J. J. Benjamin	1862	SE Nevada
Payutas................	T. Ettling (map)	1863	S Utah
Pahutes................	Commr. Ind. Affairs	1863	......
Pah Utah Indians........	A. J. Johnson (map)	1864	S Nevada
Pah-Utah or Digger Indians	A. J. Johnson (map)	1864	S Nevada
Pai-Utes...............	T. C. W. Sale	1865	E Nevada; W Utah
Pah Utes...............	O. H. Irish	1865	SW Utah

[n] Text, 1853.
[o] "Old Files Division," Adj. Gen.'s Office, No. 215c, filed with 75c, 1860.

EARLY SPELLINGS OF THE NAME SOUTHERN PIUTE OR PAHUTE—*Concluded*

Name	Authority	Date	Locality
Pai-Utes[p]	Commr. Ind. Affairs	1866	SE Nevada
Pi-Utes	Commr. Ind. Affairs	1866	W and SW Nevada
Pah-Utes	T. T. Dwight	1868	......
Pah-Utes	F. H. Head	1868	S central Utah
Pah-Utes	Fenton	1870	Utah; Arizona
Pah Utes	Roger Jones	1870	Colorado R.
Pah Utes	Jones	1870	Bend of Colorado to Diamond R.
Pi-Ute	F. A. Walker	1872	SE Nevada; S Utah
Pi-Ute	G. W. Ingalls	1872	SE Nevada; S Utah
Paiute	Powell MS	1873	......
Pai-Utes	Commr. Ind. Affairs	1874	S Nevada; SE California
Pai-Utes	Powell (1871–73)	1874	SE Nevada, S Utah
Pi-Utes	Commr. Ind. Affairs	1874	SE Nevada
Pah-Utes	G. M. Wheeler	1875	E Nevada
Southern Payutes	Oscar Loew	1876	S Nevada, Colorado R.[q]
Pah-Utes	A. J. Barnes	1876	Moapa R. Reservation
Pah-Utes	A. Pinart	1877	Arizona
Pah-Utes	J. S. Campion	1878	Mohave Desert
Pahute	W. W. Elliott and Co.	1883	Mohave Desert
Pai-uta	Gatschet	1890	......
Pai-yu'-chimŭ	J. T. Mooney	1896	......
Pai-yu'-tsi	Mooney	1896	......
Paiute	Chamberlain	1910	Arizona
Paiute	Waterman	1911	......
Paiute	E. Sapir	1915	......
Southern Paiute	Kroeber	1923	......
Southern Paiute	W. D. Strong[r]	1927	S Nevada
Piute	*Hanford Sentinel* (Calif.)	3/21/1923	......
Piute	*Salt Lake Tribune*	3/21/1923	......
Piute	*San Francisco Chronicle*	3/22/1923	......
Piute	*Salt Lake Tribune*	3/23/1923	San Juan Co.
Piutes	*Salt Lake Tribune*	3/25/1923	San Juan Co.
Piutes	*Washington Star* (D.C.)	3/26/1923	......
Piutes	*Washington Post* (D.C.)	3/27/1923	Near Moab, Utah
Piute	*Salt Lake News*	4/5/1923	San Juan Co.
Piutes	*Salt Lake Tribune*	4/6/1923	......
Piutes	*Salt Lake Telegram*	4/6/1923	......
Piute	*Salt Lake Tribune*	4/9/1923	......
Piute	*Salt Lake Telegram*	4/14/1923	San Juan Co.
Piute	*Salt Lake Tribune*	4/17/1923	SE Utah
Piute	*Salt Lake Tribune*	4/18/1923	......
Piute	*Ogden City Standard* (Utah)	4/18/1923	SE Utah
Piute	*Sacramento Bee* (Calif.)	4/18/1923	San Juan Co.
Piute	*Salt Lake Tribune*	4/25/1923	......
Piutes	*Salt Lake Telegram*	4/30/1923	San Juan Co.

[p] "Different people from 'Pi-Utes.'"
[q] True Southern Piute. (C.H.M.)
[r] Map, AA.

The following names are applied to the Southern Piute by themselves and by other tribes.[20]

Name	Tribe	Authority	Date
Auölasu's	Pima	ten Kate	1885
Nüma[21]	S. Piute	......	....
Pa'gonotch	S. Ute	Gatschet (MS)	....
Pai-â'-ti	Panamint	Henshaw (MS)	....
Pi-yu'ch (Pi-ū'ch); Pah'-vo-wats	Ute	Merriam (MS)	1912
Pai-yu' chimŭ	Hope	Mooney	1896
Pai-yu' tsĭ	Navaho	Mooney	1896
Payuchis	......	La Fora	1766–72
Payuchas; Payuches	Mohave; Yavapi	Garcés, Font, et al.	1776–77
Neu-mǎ toi-ab-be-mah	Bishop Cr. Piute[22]	......	....
Nüwü	S. Piute	Kroeber[23]	1925

USE OF THE NAME PIUTE FOR THE CHEMEWEVE

The earliest known authors to use the name Piute did not apply it to the Chemeweve but to a tribe farther north. La Fora on his map of 1766–1772 gave Payuchis; Garcés and Font in 1776 and 1777 wrote it Payuchas and Payuches. But in the 'fifties (1853–1858) the name was definitely applied to the Chemeweve by Whipple and others of the Pacific Railway Surveys, also by Mollhausen, and was usually written Pah-Utahs (both with and without the hyphen); it was also spelled Pah-Yutes, Piutes, Pai-Yutes, and Piuches; while Padre Domenech in 1860 used the ancient spelling, Payuches.

The following tabulation (incomplete) of names definitely applied to the Chemeweve does not include the various spellings of the word "Chem-eweve," such as Chemebet, Chemeguaba, Chemehuevis, Shimawiva, and so on.

Name	Authority	Date
Chenegnadas	Colton (map)	1849
Chemeguebas	John Dower (map)	1850
Chameguabas	Thomas, Cowper and Co. (map)	1851
"Pah Utahs (Chem-e-hue-vis)"	Whipple and Ives[24]	1854
"Paiutes or Chemehuevis"	Whipple	1855
Pah-Utah and Pah-Utahs	Whipple	1855
Pah-Utahs	Mollhausen	1858

[20] Tabulation very incomplete.
[21] Also used by the Shoshone.
[22] Name for Piute Mountain tribe.
[23] A. L. Kroeber, *Handbook of the Indians of California*, BAE–B 78, p. 595, 1925.
[24] Map, Pacific R.R. Surveys.

Payuches......................Domenech   1860
Chi-mi-way-wahs................Capt. H. S. Burton   1860
Chemeguabas...................A. J. Johnson (map)   1864
Chimewawas....................G. W. Ingalls   1872

The following names are used for the Chemeweve by other tribes, as well as by themselves.

Name	Tribe	Authority	Date
Mat-hat-e-vatch................	......	Whipple	1856
Mat-jus.........................	......	Heintzelman	1857
Eche-mo-hua-vas................	......	Thomas	1868
Cheminaviel Pibutes.............	......	D. H. Smith[25]	1876
Tan'-ta-waits...................	......	Powell	1877
Tantawats......................	......	Gatschet	1879
Tontewaits.....................	......	ten Kate	1885
Tantawas......................	......	Commr. Ind. Affairs	1895
Tantüwach......................	......	Kroeber	1908
Tan'-tah-vāts or Tan'-tah-vi'ts....	......	Merriam (MS)	....
Ahalakat (meaning "small bows")...	Pima	Kroeber	1925[26]
Nüwü.........................	Chemeweve	Kroeber	1925
Mat-hatevach (meaning "northern-ers").........................	Yuma	Kroeber	1925
Tantawats or Tantüwach (kinsmen's name meaning "southerners")...	......	Kroeber	1925
Yuakayam (name given by "Serrano" groups)......................	......	Kroeber	1925

THE TERM "MONO"

Among the confusing tribal names used by ethnologists, the word "Mono" occupies a conspicuous place. It was early applied to the band or tribe of Northern Piute living in the Mono Lake desert in eastern California, but when or where it first appeared in print no one seems to know.

This much is certain: in 1851 it was published in the *Daily Alta California* as the name of the Mono Lake tribe; and the following year was used by Lt. Moore for the same Indians—the tribe for whom he named Mono Pass.[27] It was used in the same sense (for Mono Lake Piute) in 1858 by J. M. Hutchings; in 1859 by L. H. Bunnell; in 1864 by Alexander S. Taylor; in 1866 by Franklin Campbell (who called them Mono Pi-Utes); in 1869 by J. Ross Browne, who states that Mono Lake "derives its name from the tribe of Indians originally inhabiting the vicinity,"[28] and so on to the present day.

[25] Letter to A. Pinart.
[26] The references to Kroeber, 1925, are to p. 595 of the *Handbook.*—Ed.
[27] *Hutching's California Magazine*, 1:8, 1856.
[28] *Resources of the Pacific Slope*, p. 303, 1869.

The name, however, has been much abused and at the present time is often misapplied—even to the extent of including the Monache tribes of both sides of the High Sierra. Perhaps its most prevalent misuse, especially by basket collectors, is in the designation of the Nim tribe on the North Fork of the San Joaquin River. In a broader sense it is loosely applied to several related Monache tribes inhabiting isolated valleys in the great pine forest of the western slope of the Sierra Nevada from North Fork to Kings River. Among ethnologists—sad to relate—its application is even less definite, sometimes contradictory, and in certain cases geographically erroneous. Thus, in the official *Handbook of American Indians*, the word Mono is defined as "a general term applied to the Shoshonean tribes of southeastern California by their neighbors on the west."[29] This very loose statement involves at least two serious errors: a geographic error, the region meant being far north of the area commonly known as "southeastern" California; and an error of classification, the Shoshonean tribes of southeastern California belonging to several widely different divisions of the stock.

The further statement that "the origin and meaning of the term are obscure" is only in part true, for a glance at the appended table of names used by other tribes for the so-called Mono shows that Mo'-nah, Mo-noh, Mo-ni-ah, and Monă-musse are names by which the Northern Piute tribes to the east, including those of Mono Lake, and in some cases also the Monache Nim of North Fork, have been long known to some of the tribes of the west slope of the Sierra, notably the Mewuk and Nissenan.[30]

Kroeber (1907) applies the term "Mono" to Piute tribes on both sides of the Sierra, mentioning the "San Joaquin Mono" and "Mono west of the crest of the Sierra Nevada," and on the same page introducing the term "Inyo Mono," by which he means the Monache of Owens Valley (a brief vocabulary of whom he obtained from a Kern Valley woman of a different tribe).[31]

Dixon, possibly influenced by the implied association of the name of the lake and county, defines Mono as "a group of tribes occupying since the early 19th century a considerable area, mainly in Mono and Inyo counties, California, and the adjacent part of Esmeralda County, Nevada."[32] This conflicts fundamentally with Kroeber's definition and with the use of the word as ordinarily understood, for Dixon expands the Mono area to embrace parts of two or more quite distinct linguistic groups. For Mono County in California and the adjoining Esmeralda County in Ne-

---

[29] *Handbook of the American Indians*, Pt. I, p. 932, 1907.

[30] It may be noted also that the Northern Piute are called Monah by the Miduan Kow'wak of Nevada County, and Meh-nah'-tse by the Ap-woo're-kāe of northeastern California.

[31] Kroeber, *Shoshonean Dialects of California*, p. 114; vocabularies, pp. 71–89.

[32] "Indian Population," *Census of 1910*, p. 97, 1915.

vada are inhabited by bands of Northern Piute ("Paviotso" of Powell and Kroeber), while Inyo County is inhabited by the Panamint and Pahk-wahsitch (or Pah-kwah-zid-je) Shoshone and the Monache—the latter being one of the tribes comprised in Kroeber's Mono!

So far as I am aware, Kroeber makes no mention of the Mono Piute of the Mono Lake region of middle-eastern California, to whom the name was originally applied, nor does he include them in his use of the term Mono except under his hybrid group name "Mono-Paviotso." The term as used by him therefore (singly and in combination) covers two quite distinct divisions of Shoshonean stock. For the Mono of Mono Lake speak a very different dialect from that of the Owens Valley and Sierra tribes which he calls Mono, and belong to the Northern, not the Monache, division.

The term "Mono" therefore, is indefinite and confusing and should be dropped, for the following reasons: because of its use by other tribes and by numerous authors for the Piute of Mono Lake; because of its popular use for a different tribe or group of closely allied tribes on the west flank of the Sierra; and because of its unhappy use by ethnologists for two or more divisions of Shoshonean stock.

NAMES APPLIED TO MONO LAKE PIUTE IN PUBLICATIONS

Name	Authority	Date of observation	Date of publication
Monas......................	Major Savage [a]	1851	1851
Monos......................	Whitney	1852	1870
Mono.......................	Lt. Moore [b]	1852	1856
Mono.......................	Wessels	1853	1857
Monos......................	J. M. Hutchings	....	1858; 1871
Monos and Mono Indians.........	*Hutching's Magazine* [c]	....	1858
Mono(s)......................	L. H. Bunnell	1853	1859; 1861
Mono Indians...................	Britton and Rey (map)	....	1857; 1860 (3d ed.)
Monos.......................	A. S. Taylor	....	1860; 1863
Mono Indians...................	W Rebellion Records [?]	1862	1897
Monos or Monutes..............	A. S. Taylor	....	1864
Mono Pi-Utes..................	H. G. Parker	....	1866
Mono Pi-Utes..................	F. Campbell	1866	1866
Monos.......................	Taylor	....	1869
Mono tribe...................	Ross Browne	....	1869
Pah Utahs of Mono Lake.........	C. L. Brace	....	1869
Cozaby Pah-Utes................	F. Campbell	....	1870
Mono........................	A. W. von Schmidt	1856	1857
Monos, Mono tribe..............	Kneeland	....	1871
Monos.......................	H. H. Bancroft	....	1871
Monos.......................	J. E. Lester	....	1873
Mono Pi Utes..................	Bancroft [d]	....	1874
Mono Indians..................	Williams (map)	....	1876
Moan'-au-zi...................	S. Powers	....	1877
Mono Indians..................	C. F. Gordon-Cumming	1878	1884
Monos; Pai-utes................	Bunnell	1851	1880
Mono Lake band of Pah-Utes; Mono Lake Indians...........	Thompson and West	1862	1881
Mono (Pah-uta).................	Hutchings	....	1886
Mono Indians..................	John Muir	Various	1901
Monah; Monahk (Mewuk name)...	C. H. Merriam	1902; 1903	......
Mono Indians..................	Fiske (Le Conte)	188(?)	1918
Monos.......................	Gordon	....	1892
Mo'nah; Mo'namusse............	Passienan (C.H.M.)	1905	......
Mo'nos; Monos.................	Galen Clark	....	1904
Mono........................	R. B. Dixon	....	1915
Monos.......................	*San Francisco Chronicle*	....	8/4/1916
Monos; Mono Indians............	W. A. Chalfant	....	1922
Mono Indians..................	*Bishop Register* (Calif.)	1923	4/19/1923
Mono tribe [and Piute]..........	*San Francisco Daily News*	....	7/26/1924
Mono Indians..................	*San Francisco Call*	....	7/27/1924
Mono Indians [Lake].............	*Fresno Bee*	....	8/4/1924
Monos.......................	Ansell Hall [e]	....	12/11/1924
Mono........................	A. L. Kroeber	....	1925
Monos of Nevada [at Yosemite]....	*Mill Valley Record* *Yreka News*	....	7/24/1926; 7/22/1926
Mono Indians..................	*San Fernando Sun*	....	2/12/1932

[a] *Daily Alta California.*
[b] Mono Pass (leading to Mono L.) named after Indians of that name. *Hutching's California Magazine* (July), 1:8, 1856. Author of article not stated.
[c] Valley on branch of Walker R., W Nevada, named "Big Mono" from Mono Indians found there. *Ibid.* (June), 2:520 523, 1858.
[d] After Von Schmidt (after Campbell).
[e] *Merced Sun*, Dec. 11, 1924.

The following names are applied to the Mono Lake Piute by other tribes.[33]

Koo-chah'-be-ah-wah'-te neu-mă
(Kwe-chah dik-kah) . . . . By Bishop Cr. Piute
Koo-tsa'-be dik'-kah kud'-dy
neu'-mă . . . . By Pyramid L. and Truckee Piute
Kwe'-nă-gwet'-tah . . . . Bishop Cr. Monache name for Long Valley
                                       Piute (tribe same as at Mono L.)
Koo-zab'-be-te-kah'
(Poo-tsah'-be-te-kah') . . . . Monache name for Mono L. Piute
Moan'-au-zi . . . . By Nishinam[34]
Mo'-nah, Mo-ni'-ah . . . . By Yosemite Muwa; applied to both Mono L.
                                       Piute and Piute tribes of the Sierra
Mo'-nah and Mo'-nă-mus-se . . . . . By the Nis'-sim Pā'-we-nan of Poosoone
Mo-nahk or Mo-nok . . . . By Tuolumne Mew-wah
Pah'-be-o'-zo . . . . By Olancha Pak-wa-zid-je
Se'-be-doo-mah . . . . By Muwa (?)
Se-wan'-a-gwat . . . . By Muwa(?)
Too-ne-gă-bah . . . . One of their names for themselves
Tu'-in-de-sow'-wa (Tun'-de-sow'-
wa) . . . . Nuvahandit name

THE MONACHE

The Owens Valley Piute, together with the series of small isolated "Piute" tribes occupying certain mountain valleys on the west flank of the Sierra in the interior of California from the upper waters of the San Joaquin to those of the Kaweah, constitute the Monache group and, although presenting among themselves certain individual dialectic differences, are closely related. They include the Nim of the North Fork region, sometimes erroneously called Mono, their near neighbors the Yianche of Little Joaquin, the Holkoma of Pine Ridge north of Kings River, the Entimbitch[35] of Mill Creek near Dunlap, the Woponutch (or Wo-pung'-witch) a little higher up in the same region, the Wuksache of Eschom Valley, and the Padoosha (or Padwishe) of Three Rivers. The dialects spoken by these tribes are so close to that of the Owens Valley Monache as to leave no doubt of their origin from that tribe. But why and how long ago they mi-

---

[33] The data in this tabulation are Dr. Merriam's (initialed C.H.M.), except as otherwise noted.—Ed.
[34] S. Powers, *Tribes of California*, 1877. Doubtless the same as my Mo'-na-mus-se, and by inference applies to Piute from Mono Lake northward to Walker River region and may include Washoo.
[35] Kroeber in a note at the end of his *Shoshonean Dialects of California* (p. 165), states on the authority of S. A. Barrett, that the "Endimbitch" are "Yokuts, not Shoshonean Mono." This is a most unfortunate error, due doubtless to the circumstance that Barrett's informant spoke both languages. I obtained an excellent vocabulary from the Entimbitch in 1903, which I have since verified.

grated west over the lofty passes of the High Sierra to the remote and isolated valleys they now inhabit no man can say. In an air line the territory of the northernmost bands, the Nim and Yianche of the North Fork region, is less than forty miles distant from that of the Mono-Piute of Mono Lake (a Northern Piute tribe), but a barrier of lofty mountains intervenes and the languages are materially different.

Waterman recognizes "two 'Paiute' languages, both spoken in the Great Basin area"—the Southern and the Northern; but errs in classing the Sierra Monache (whom he unhappily calls "Mono") with the Northern, saying that their language "is very similar."[36]

The Monache are of mixed affinities, their interrelations with other Shoshonean tribes being intricate and complicated. Linguistically, the closest relationship appears to be with Panamint and Pakwazidje, more words being common to Monache and these tribes than to Monache and Northern Piute, although the preponderance is not great. Some words (as hŭ'-pe for "woman," and pi'-ah for "water") are distinctive, differing from those of all the surrounding tribes; yet a considerable number agree with Chemeweve, a typical Southern Piute tribe; others with Newooah and Tolchinne—the most aberrant of the Southern Piute series.

Exceptionally, Northern Piute and Monache agree and are arrayed against all the other tribes, as in no'-ve, the word for "house," whereas in Shoshone, Panamint, Pakwasitch, and Southern Piute (Chemeweve, Nuvahandit, and Newooah), "house" is gah'-ne or kah'-ne.

Hence, while in many respects Monache is intermediate between Northern Piute and Panamint Shoshone, it differs materially from both; and while in certain words it resembles Newooah on the south, in others it resembles Chemeweve on the east.[37] This quadruple relationship shows that Monache could not have been derived from any of these in their present forms, denoting a greater antiquity for the tribe than one would be led to suspect from its present geographic position. In other words it seems clear that the ancestry of the Monache dates back to a period antecedent to the complete differentiation of the surrounding tribes.

The accompanying table (incomplete) gives the names used for the Monache of Owens Valley in various accounts.

---

[36] Waterman, *Phonetic Elements of the Northern Paiute Language*, p. 14.

[37] My vocabularies show that a materially larger number of Monache words agree with the geographically remote Chemeweve than with the geographically nearer Huvahandit. This is suggestive, in view of the ancient origin of the group.

NAMES FOR MONACHE OF OWENS VALLEY

Name	Authority	Date of publication	Locality
Pyanches	*Daily Alta California*	4/23/1857	"Other side of Sierra"
Monoes[a]	E. F. Beale	1856	......
Mono	A. W. von Schmidt	1856	......
Pah-Utahs	Capt. H. S. Burton[b]	1856	Owens Lake
Mono	Henley (1856)	1857	Owens Valley
Pah-Utahs	Burton	1857	Owens Lake
Wokopee	Beale	1859	Owens Valley
Monatchee	Wm. H. Knight	1863	"In Tulare Valley"
"Monos or Monutes"[a]	A. S. Taylor	1864	......
Monache	Daley (1865)	1867	Owens Valley
Py-utes	Simpson	1869	Owens and other rivers of Great Basin
Monache	J. B. McIntosh and J. W. Miller	1870	Owens River
Monacha	B. C. Whiting	1872	East of Sierra
Monos[a]	J. E. Lester	1873	......
Western Payutes	Oscar Loew (1875)	1876	Inyo and S Mono counties
Monache	Belknap	1876, 1877+	Owens River
Monache	Commr. Ind. Affairs	1877+	Owens River
Manaches; Monachees	S. Powers	1877	Owens Valley; Sierra Nevada
Mono, Monos	Powers	1877	Owens Valley; Sierra Nevada
Pa-Uta	Gatschet	1879	......
Tohaktivi	J. W. Powell	1881	Owens River; White Mountains
Monache	Hoffman	1886	......
Monaches	War Rebellion Recs.	1897	......
Mono; Monachi	A. L. Kroeber	1907	......
Monache; Mo-nä′-che	C. H. Merriam (MS)	1909	......
Monos	*Fresno Herald*	1922 (Dec.)	Hills back of Fresno
Wakopee	W. A. Chalfant	1922	Owens River
Mono; Eastern Mono	Kroeber	1925	......
Eastern Mono	W. D. Strong	1927	......
Monachi (Yokut name)	Kroeber	1925	......

[a] Not certain whether the name related to Owens Valley or to Sierra Monache or both.
[b] MS, War Department.

The following names were applied to Owens Valley Monache and their several bands by themselves and neighboring tribes.[38]

Chak′-ke-sev′-uts..........Name used by Monache (of Lone Pine) for Monache band on first creek N of Independence Cr.

Horse-thief tribe..........Term used for Indians of Owens Valley and of W slope of Sierra. *San Francisco Daily Chronicle,* June 26, 1854

[38] The data in this tabulation are initialed C.H.M., except as otherwise noted.—Ed.

Kwe-am′-mit. . . . . .Olanche (Pahkwăsidje) name for Bishop Cr. In-
dians
Kwe′-nah-pat′-se. . . . . .Monache name for related band in Round Valley
Mo-nă′-che. . . . . .New-oo′-ah and Wiktchumne name for Owens Val-
ley Monache
Monache. . . . . .Yokut name for Owens Valley Monache
Monachi. . . . . .Yokut name for E and W "Monosh." Kroeber,
Handbook, p. 585, 1925
Nom-bi′-ie. . . . . .Olanche (Pahk′wasid′je) name for Owens Valley
Monache
No′-no-pi-nă-neum. . . . . .Name used by Monache of Independence Cr. for
Monache of Lone Pine
O′-kah-vi-da-kah. . . . . .Name used by Monache (of Lone Pine) for Bishop
Cr. Piute
Pah-ah′-go-hots (or
Pah-hah′-gah-hootch′). . . .Name used for themselves by Monache on Turtle
Cr. in Owens Valley
Pak-wă-zid-je. . . . . .Name given by Olancha Shoshone to Owens L.
tribe
Pe-ag′-gah-te-kah′. . . . . .Name used by Monache (of Lone Pine) for band
in Long Valley
Pe′-sah-poo′-at′-te-neu′-ma. .Bishop Cr. Piute name for themselves
Pe-tah′-nă-gwaht′-tă. . . . . . . .Name used by Bishop Cr. Monache for related
bands at Big Pine, Lone Pine, and Independence
Pe-ton-ă-kwaht (or
Pe-tah′-nă-gwat). . . . . .Mono L. Piute name for Monache band at Bishop
Cr.
Pitanakwat. . . . ."Mono" of Owens Valley name for themselves; also
used by their kinsmen for them. Kroeber, *Hand-
book*, p. 585, 1925
Se′-ve-nă-gwet′-tah. . . . . . . .Bishop Cr. Monache name for related band in Fish
L. Valley
Tak′-ke-sev′-vuts. . . . . .Monache band on Oak Cr., N of Independence
Ut′-tă-oo′-le gwet′-tah. . . . . . .Bishop Cr. Monache name for Monache band at
Benton
Wo′-ko-rōb′. . . . . .Monache band on Independence Cr.
Yiwinanghal. . . . . .Tubotelobelā name for Monache Piute of Inyo Co.
Kroeber, *Shoshonean Dialects*, 1907; *Handbook*,
1925

The names given in the accompanying table (incomplete) are used, in-
dividually or collectively, for the Monache of the west slope of the Sierra
Nevada.

NAMES USED FOR THE MONACHE OF THE WEST SLOPE OF THE SIERRA NEVADA

Name	Authority	Date of publication
Monas	McKee, Barbour, and Wozencraft	1851; 1853
Monoes	Johnston	1851
Monas	Ryer	1852
Monoes	Johnston (1851)	1853
Monas-Indians	Meyer (1850)	1855
Monoes [a]	E. F. Beale	1856
Monos [b]	Lewis (1856; 1857)	1856; 1857
Mono	Wessells (1853)	1857
Noo-tah-ah	Wessells (1853)	1857
Monos	Lewis	1856; 1857; 1858
Monos	A. S. Taylor	1860
Mo-nos	Lewis (1859)	1860
Ho-na-che	Hutchings	1861
Monos	Taylor (after Beale)	1860; 1863
"Monos or Monutes" [a]	Taylor	1864
Monos	Commr. Ind. Affairs	1862
Monatchee	Knight	1864
Monos [a]	Purcell	1870
Monos	H. H. Bancroft	1871
Ho-na-chee	Lester	1873
Monos [a]	Lester	1873
Manaches; Manachees	S. Powers	1877
Mono, Monos	Powers	1877
Nut-ha	Powers	1877
Pa-Uta	Gatschet	1879
Ho-nah-chee	L. H. Bunnell	1880
Ho-na-chee	*History of Fresno County*	1882
Monos	Gen. E. D. Keyes (1851)	1885
Pai-ute; Paiute	C. H. Merriam	1904
Ho-na'-ches	Galen Clark	1904
Mono-Paviotso	A. L. Kroeber	1907
Monachi; Monadji; Mono	Kroeber	1907
Mono	T. T. Waterman	1911
Monos	*Fresno Herald*	1922
Mono; Western Mono	Kroeber [c]	1925
Mono Indians [d]	*Fresno Republican*	1/1/1926
Mono [e]	*San Francisco Examiner*	1/6/1926
Monos [f]	*Fresno Republican*	4/24/1927
Western Mono	W. D. Strong	1927
North Fork Mono	Strong	1927

[a] Not certain whether the name relates to the Owens Valley or the Sierra Monache or both.
[b] Headwaters of the San Joaquin River.
[c] *Handbook*, pp. 584–585.
[d] Auberry region, Fresno Co.
[e] Sycamore Cr. Holkoma.
[f] Dunlap, Mill Cr. Valley Emtimbitch (T. T. Waterman).

The following names are applied to Sierra tribes of the Monache Piute by themselves and by other tribes.[40]

Balwisha.................Yokut name for "Monachi" on the Kaweah, especially on its S side. (Kroeber, 1925)

Emtimbitch..............Tribe on Mill Cr. near Dunlap, Fresno Co. Name
for themselves and also used by neighboring
tribes. (Merriam, 1904)

Hol'koma (Hol-o'-kom-mah
and To'winch-e'ba) ......Tribe on Pine Ridge N of Kings R. Names used by
themselves. (Merriam, 1904)

Holkoma.................Kroeber, 1925

Horse-thief tribe...........Term used for Indians of Owens Valley and on W
slopes of Sierra. *San Francisco Daily Chronicle*,
June 26, 1854

Kash-ă-woo-shah..........Wuksache name for Nim at North Fork San Joaquin

Ko-ko-he'-bah.............Tribe in Burr Valley and on W side of Pine Ridge,
Fresno Co. Name for themselves; also applied to
them by the Holkoma. (Merriam, 1904)

Monachi.................Yokut name for "eastern and western Monos."
(Kroeber, 1925)

Mo'-nah, Mo-ni'-ah ....Name applied by Yosemite Muwa to North Fork
Nim and other Sierra bands, and also to Mono L.
Piute. (C.H.M.)

Mo'no...................Name in common popular use for North Fork Nim,
and also for other Monache bands in the Sierra.
(C.H.M.)

Nim.....................Tribe on North Fork San Joaquin. Name for themselves. (Merriam, 1904)

Nuta'a (plur. Nuchawayi)....Yokut name for "western Mono." (Kroeber, 1925)

Pad'-doo-sha or Pad-wish-
shă...................Wuksache name for tribe at Three Rivers on Kaweah R. (C.H.M.)

"Posgisa or Poshgisha"......Yokuts name for band or tribe on Big Sandy and
heads of Little and Big Dry creeks. (Kroeber,
1925)

Pas'-se-watch.............Emtimbitch name for Wuksă'che. (C.H.M.)

Pă-zo-ō'ds...............Name used by Holkoma for Nim of North Fork
San Joaquin. (Merriam, 1904)

Pi'-yu-mi................Holkoma name for one of their villages on Pine
Ridge—not a distinct tribe. (C.H.M.)

Posgisa or Poshgisha........Yokut name for "Monos" S of San Joaquin R. on

[40] In the tabulation the various references to Kroeber, 1925, are to pp. 584, 585, and 586 of the *Handbook*; those to Merriam refer to his article "Distribution of Indian Tribes in the Southern Sierra and Adjacent Parts of the San Joaquin Valley, California," *Science*, n.s., 19:912–917, 1904. Comments initialed C.H.M. are so given in the original.—Ed.

	Big Sandy Cr. and toward heads of Little and Big Dry creeks. (Kroeber, 1925)
Toi'-nitch	Choenimne and Chokimina name for tribe at Trimmer Springs. (C.H.M.)
Too-hook'-mutch	Emtimbitch name for related tribe at Trimmer Springs, Kings R. (C.H.M.)
Towinche'ba	Same as Holkoma. (One of their names for themselves.) (C.H.M.)
Waksachi	Kroeber, 1925. (See Wuksă'che.)
Wă-pon-nutch (or Wo-pung'-witch)	Wuksăche and Wiktchum'ne name for tribe next above Emtimbitch, at Millwood Flume.
Winanghatal	Kern R., Tübatulabal name for "western Mono." (Kroeber, 1925)
Wobonuch	Yokut name for Monachi at head of Mill Cr. and in the pine ridges to the N. (Kroeber, 1925.) (See Wă-pon-nutch or Wo-pung'-witch)
Wuksă'che	Tribe in Eschom Valley; name for themselves. (C.H.M.) (Plur. Wakesdachi) [41]
Yi'-an-che	Muwa name for Monache tribe on Little Joaquin adjoining Nim, just E of North Fork. (C.H.M.)

A COLLECTIVE NAME FOR "SERRANO" AND "CAHUILLA"

Of the Shoshonean tribes of California the so-called "Serrano" and "Cahuilla" groups are well known to be much more closely related to one another than to any other tribes. Nevertheless they have no collective name for themselves, and so far as I am aware no collective name has been proposed by anthropologists. The need for such a term is obvious, not alone for purposes of classification but also for clear understanding.

Among other stocks the words for "people" and "man" have afforded convenient handles, but in this case they differ in the two series and are therefore not available.

After searching my vocabularies of the two dialects at intervals for some years I have arrived at the conclusion that, since both groups call the sun Tahm-yat and since the people, while not actual sun worshippers, hold the sun in great reverence, therefore the term "Sun People" would be appropriate—for Sun and Moon created the world and are its most sacred deities. And since in both series the stem of the word for "people" is tahk (plur. in Maream series tahk-tem),[42] I propose Tahm-yat-tahk-tem—Tamyattaktem, as it would be written by most anthropologists—as a collective or family name for the two groups.

---

[41] Kroeber, *Shoshonean Dialects of California*, p. 121.

[42] The vowel in the last syllable, as pronounced by different individuals, varies from *e* to *a* or *u*.

Tribal Names of the Tuleyome

The Tuleyome (Tu'-le-yo'-me) are the northernmost of the Mewan tribes. They are completely isolated, being surrounded by peoples of other linguistic stocks. Their territory extends from Mt. St. Helena northward to Lower Lake and from the Miyahkma Mountains on the west to Jerusalem and Pope valleys on the east. The following names are those used in a tribal sense and are names applied to the Tuleyome tribe as a whole.

Kel-lew'-win-fo and
    Te'-om-fo..............Names used by Pomoan Hamfo ('Ham'-fo) of Lower Lake for Olayome band of Coyote Valley and in general sense for Tuleyome tribe. Kel-lew'-win-fo means "coyote people." (C. H. Merriam, "Distribution and Classification of the Mewan Stock of California," AA 9:353, 1907.)

        Kliwin-hoi as Pomo name for Coyote Valley region. (A. L. Kroeber, *Handbook of the Indians of California*, BAE-B 78, p. 273, 1925.)

Ko-tsah'-to yo'-me or
    Yo'-me ko'-tsah.........Name used by the inhabitants of Hoo-koo'-yo-me rancheria for themselves; said also to be inclusive name for all the Olayome bands. See Hoo-koo'-yo-me po-koot.

Lake Miwok..............Name used by Kroeber for "Miwok," "in the basin of Clear Lake." (Kroeber, *Handbook*, map [pl. 27] facing pp. 172, 272–273, 883.)

        Name used by Loeb, after Kroeber. (E. M. Loeb, *Pomo Folkways*, UC–PAAE 19:399, 1926.)

175

Mo-ā'-yō'me . . . . Name sometimes applied to "all our tribes or rancherias," stated by several members of tribe.

Northern Coast or Lake area . Term used by Barrett for Tuleyome tribe. (S. A.
Barrett, *Geography and Dialects of the Miwok
Indians*, UC–PAAE 6:333, 1908.) An unhappy
misuse of terms, inasmuch as the "Northern
Coast" and the "Lake area" divisions are sepa-
rate tribes, clearly recognized by Barrett in his
vocabularies as "Marin (S. Coast)" and "Lake
(N. Coast)" (*ibid.*, col. headings, pp. 362–367).

Northern or Lake
Moquelumnan . . . . (S. A. Barrett, *Ethno-Geography of the Pomo and
Neighboring Indians*, UC–PAAE 6:314–315,
1905.)

Te'-ōm-fo and
Kel-lew'-win-fo . . . . Names used by the Pomoan Hamfo for the Tuleyome. See Kel-lew'-win-fo in this synonymy.

Tu'-le-yo'-me . . . . Territory extending from Mt. St. Helena N to
Lower Lake, and from the Miyahkma Moun-
tains on the W to Jerusalem and Pope valleys on
the E. The ancestral rancheria was Tu'-le-yo'-me
po-koot on the creek on Wilson Ranch in Excelsior Valley about 4 mi. S of the S end of Lower
Lake (or 3 mi. S of Lower Lake village). This
was the center of creation and the original home
of Coyote-Man and Wekwek. (Merriam, "Mewan Stock," pp. 352–353; also Barrett, *Pomo*,
p. 318.)

TULEYOME TRIBE LIST AND SYNONYMY

Alacyome . . . . See synonymy of Al-lōk'-yō'-me po'-goot.

Al-lōk-ko-boo-je . . . . Village 2½ or 3 mi. E of Lower Lake town, situated at S base of hill of same name (hill called
Lā-lish by the Pomoan Hamfo).

Al-lok-woo-boo-te . . . . Village 3 mi. S of town of Lower Lake (near Tu-le-
yo-me po-goot ?)

Al-lōk'-yo'-me po'-goot . . . . . . Tuleyome name for their village in Pope Valley,
Napa Co.; about a mile E of Pope Valley post-
office. (Merriam, "Corrections concerning California Indians," AA, n.s., 10:356, 1908.)

Synonymy
Alacyomi . . . . Band mentioned in San Rafael Mission Book of
Baptisms, 1818–1839, MS copy by A. Pinart,
1878, Bancroft Library.

Aloquiomi.............Band furnishing converts to Sonoma Mission. H.
H. Bancroft, after MS registers of San Francisco
Solano Mission, 1824–1837, in Bancroft Library.
(H. H. Bancroft, *History of California*, 2:506, fn.,
1885.)

Other spellings: Aloquio, Aloq., Aloqui, Aloq.^{mi}
Aloquiom, Alocyomi. San Francisco Solano Mission Books, 1824–1839. Original MSS in Bancroft Library.

Aloquiomi, Alocyomi....See synonymy of Al-lōk'-yo'-me po'-goot.

Caüiyomi.................Mission Books, San Francisco Solano Mission,
1824–1837. Original MS, Bancroft Library. See
Kah'-we-yo-mĕ.

Cauyomi.................Book of Baptisms, San Rafael Mission, MS copy
by A. Pinart, 1878. May be Cō'yōme of Barrett
(1908), which see.

Coyayomi or Joyayomi.....Mentioned in Mission Books of San Francisco Solano, 1824–1837. Original MS in Bancroft Li-
brary. (Bancroft, *Hist. Calif.*, 2:506, fn.; also Z.
Engelhardt, *The Franciscans in California*, p.
451, 1897.) See Kah'-we-yo'-mĕ.

Cō'yōme.................(Barrett, *Pomo*, p. 316.) See Shoyome (Sho'-yo-mĕ)
Kroeber. Located by Barrett on Putah Creek,
3½ mi. S of Guenoc.

E-lōk-no'-mah (Lōk'-no-mah) Miyahkma name (for Tuleyome band and village
near Middletown, used in a general sense) for
Tuleyome tribe. (Merriam, "Mewan Stock," p.
353.) E-lōk-no'-mah means, "Yes, Lōk-no'-mah."

Guenocks.................Name applied by whites to Olāyōme band of Tuleyome Indians in Coyote and Wennok valleys on
Putah Creek in neighborhood of place called
Guenoc (or Guenock) 4 mi. NE of Middletown
(place formerly a river ford and ranch postoffice;
an iron bridge there now).

The term originated doubtless in the native Indian name Wen'nok, applied to a small lake and
valley 4 mi. SE of Guenock and 6 mi. E of Middletown. It was first used by Taylor in 1860, and
later by others, for a rancheria and band indefi-
nitely located between Clear Lake and Napa.
Palmer in 1881 correctly placed it in Guenock
Valley, Lake Co., while Barrett in 1908 thought
it probably applied to Indians in and about Coyote Valley in the neighborhood of a small postoffice of the same name.

See also Wen'-nok.

Guenocks............Rancheria between Clear Lake and Napa. (Taylor, "Indianology," *California Farmer* [March], 1860.)

Guenocks............The Guenocks and Locollomillos lived between Clear Lake and Napa. Bancroft, after Taylor. (H. H. Bancroft, *Native Races of California*, 1: 451, and map opp. p. 322, 1874.)

Guenocks............"The Guenocks had their home in the valley of that name in Lake Co." (L. L. Palmer, *History of Napa and Lake Counties, California*, p. 45, 1881.) Palmer says the Guenocks are the same as his Koo-noo-la-ka-koi, which see in main list.

Guenocks............These Indians probably lived in or about Coyote Valley where there is a small postoffice by that name. (Barrett [after Taylor and Bancroft], *Pomo*, pp. 273, 317, 1908.)

Guenoc............Unidentified. (Kroeber, *Handbook*, p. 895.)

Haw'-hawl-po-goot........Village on N bank of outlet of Wen'nok Lake, near the lake. Named from haw'-hawl, the long cylindrical basket trap set in water to catch fish. (Merriam, "Mewan Stock," p. 353.)

Holiyomi.............Given as one of the "tribes" or bands N of San Francisco Bay against whom an expedition under Salvador Vallejo was sent in March, 1843. (Bancroft [after Vallejo], *Hist. Calif.*, 4:362–363, fn.) May have been Olayome (O'-lā-yō'-me), which see.

Hol'-wah-poo-koot.........Village on W side of Putah Creek close by barn at Phelan ranchhouse. (Merriam, "Mewan Stock," p. 353.)

Hoo-koo'-hyoo-me.........Hūkū'hyūme or Sīwĭy'ōme. (Barrett, *Pomo*, p. 316.) See Hoo-koo'-yo-me po-koot.

Hoo-koo'-too-mi po-koot....Village on E side of Putah Creek less than ¼ mi. N of Phelan ranchhouse. (Merriam, "Mewan Stock," p. 353.)

Hoo-koo'-yo-me po-koot.....Tuleyome name for their village on knoll on SW bank of Putah Creek in N part of Phelan Ranch valley (2½ or 3 mi. S of Guenock). The people call themselves Yo'-me ko'-tsah. The last remnant of the tribe in 1907 was living at this rancheria (but was later transferred to a small reservation near Middletown). (Merriam, "Mewan Stock," p. 353.)

Hūkū'hyūme or Sīwĭy'ōme
(Barrett)............Two names. See Hoo-koo'-hyoo-me.

Hūkūh′yūme or

Sīwī′yōme..........Inhabited modern village about 1½ mi. down-
stream from Guenoc. (Barrett, *Pomo*, p. 316.)
See synonymy of Hoo-koo′-yo-me po-koot.

Hutznomanoc (Book of Deaths,

Sonoma Mission)........See Utsnomanoc.

In-ne′ko Family...........Name proposed by Merriam for a family of Mewan
stock, comprising 2 subfamilies: Tu′-le-yo-me
and Hoo′-koo-e′-ko. (Merriam, "Mewan Stock,"
p. 341.)

Joyayomi or Coyayomi......Mentioned in Mission Books of San Francisco Solano, 1824–1837. Barrett refers it questionably
to his Cō′yōme, but it may have been Kah′-we-
yo′mĕ.

Ka-bool po-goot...........Tuleyome name for their old village on low point
E of N end of Wennok Lake behind rocky part
of point. (Merriam, "Mewan Stock," p. 353.)

Synonymy

kebū′lpūkūt

(Kĕ-bool′-poo-koot)...Barrett says village 2½ mi. SE of Guenoc (which
distance is far too short). (Barrett, *Pomo*, p.
316.)

Kebul...............Kroeber, *Handbook*, map, pl. 27, opp. p. 172.

Kah′-choo-loo-loo-koo-wahn

(ka′tcūlūlūkūwan, Barrett) Given by Barrett as Lower Lake Pomo ('Ham′-fo)
name for Tuleyome village Tsī′-tsapōgūt. (But
the chief of the Ham-fo tribe gave me 'K′-tah′-
koi as their name.) See tsī′tsapōgūt Barrett in
synonymy of Tsit′-sah yo′me.

Kah-dah′-yo-me...........Old village at Dry Creek bridge on road a little N
of Middletown. Said to have been at "Koo′-koo-
min house."

Kah-low′-yo-me............Name used by Hamfo of Lower Lake for "Stone
House" rancheria (Too′-le-yo′-me). (Not to be
confused with the Habbe-nap-po "Stone House"
at Kelseyville.)

Kah′-we-yo-mĕ

(ka′wīyōme, Barrett) .....Old village on S bank of Cache Creek about 1½ mi.
from Lower Lake. (Barrett, *Pomo*, p. 317.)

Caüiyomi...............San Francisco Solano Mission Books, 1824–1837.
This and Cauyomi (?) (San Rafael Mission
Book) may be spellings for Kah′-we-yo-mĕ.

ka′tcūlūlūkūwan (Barrett,

1908)................."Southeastern Pomo" Hamfo name for Tsit′-sah
yo′me. See tsī′tsapōgūt Barrett in synonymy of
Tsit′-sah yo′-me.

Ka'wīyōme (Barrett, 1908)...See Kah'-we-yo-mĕ.

Kĕ-bool'-poo-koot.........See kebū'lpūkūt Barrett in synonymy of Ka-bool po-goot.

Kebū'lpūkūt (Barrett, 1908).See synonymy of Kā-bool' po-goot.

Kel-lew'-win-fo or Kel-lew'-
win-ă-koi'-im-fo.........Hamfo name for Tuleyome tribe. See tribal synonymy.

Kil'-le-yo'-ke po-koot.......Tuleyome name for their former village on Putah Creek at N end of Coyote or Guenoc Valley. (Merriam, "Mewan Stock," p. 353.)

Kliwin-hoi.................Pomo name for Coyote Valley region. (Kroeber, *Handbook*, p. 273.) See Kel-lew'-win-fo in tribal synonymy.

Koo-noo-la-ka-koi..........'Koo-lan-nap-po name for tribe in Coyote Valley. (L. L. Palmer, *Hist. Napa and Lake Cos.*, p. 36.) See O'-lā-yome po-koot.

Koo-pa'-choo
(kū-pē'tcū Barrett).......Old camp site at Harbin Springs about 4 mi. NW of Middletown. (Barrett, *Pomo*, p. 274.) Wrongly referred by Barrett to "Wappo" (Miyahkma).

Ko-tsah'-to yo'me or Yo'-me
ko'-tsah (spoken both ways).Name used by people of Hoo-koo'-yo-me for themselves. See Hoo-koo'-yo-me po-koot. Also said to be inclusive name for all Tuleyome bands.

K'tah'-koi................Hamfo name for Tuleyome village Tsit'-sa-yo'me.

kūpe'tcū (Barrett, 1908).....See Koo-pa'-choo.

Lah-kah'-hyo-me..........See Laka'hyōme Barrett in synonymy of Lah-ki'-yo-me po-koot.

Lah-ki'-yo'me po-koot......Tuleyome name for their old village at N edge of present town of Middletown (called Lōk-no'-mah by the Yukean Miyahkma). (Merriam, "Mewan Stock," p. 353.) Both names mean the same—Goose Valley.

Synonymy
laka'hyōme (Lah-kah'-
hyo-me) (Barrett,
1908)...............(Tuleyome) name for "lōknōma." See Lō'knōma Barrett this synonymy.

Lal-nap-o-een.........'Ku-lan-nap-po name for tribe on St. Helena Creek, just W of Middletown in Loknomah Valley. (L. L. Palmer, *Hist. Napa and Lake Cos.*, p. 36.) Barrett (*Pomo*, p. 273) says this name probably refers to lōknō'ma, which he regarded as "Wappo" (Miyahkma) but which is here shown to be Tuleyome.

Lal-nap-o-een.........(Barrett [after Palmer], *Pomo*, p. 273.)

Loaquiomi............Tribe mentioned many times in San Francisco
Solano Mission Books, 1824–1837. Original MSS
in Bancroft Library.

 Evidently a spelling for Lah-ki'-yo-me; other
spellings in Mission Books are Loaquio, Loaquiom, Loaquio^mi, Loaq. Yomi.

Loaquiomi............(Bancroft [after Sonoma Mission Books], *Hist.
Calif.*, 2:506, fn.)

Loaquiomi ....(Engelhardt [after Bancroft], *The Franciscans in
California*, p. 451.)

Locollomillos.........Between Clear Lake and Napa, in neighborhood
of rancheria called Guenocks. (Taylor, "Indian-
ology.") Barrett (*Pomo*, p. 273), says it is possible these people lived in Pope Valley, but it is
more probable they lived near Middletown.
Name used by Bancroft for Indians in Loconoma
Valley on St. Helena Creek, near Middletown,
Lake Co. (Bancroft, *Native Races*, 1:451, based
on Taylor, "Indianology.")

Locollomillos..........(Bancroft [after Taylor], *Native Races*, 1:451.) Slocum, Bowen and Co. say the Locollomillos of
Bancroft's list are their Lal-nap-o-een. See Lal-
nap-o-een Palmer this synonymy. (Spelled Socollomillos, Bancroft, *Native Races* 1:363.)

Locollomillos..........(Barrett [after Taylor and Bancroft], *Pomo*, p.
273.)

Socollomillos..........Typographic error for Locollomillos. (Bancroft
[after Taylor], *Native Races*, 1:363).

Lok-no-mah..........Miyahkma name, adopted by Tuleyome, for Tuleyome band in Middletown Valley and for old
village which they called Lah-ki'-yo-me po-goot
on site of present town of Middletown. Means
"Goose Valley." (Merriam, "Mewan Stock," p.
353.) Barrett (*Pomo*, p. 273) wrongly refers to
"Wappo" (Miyahkma).

Lahl'-mōk po-goot..........Tuleyome name for their village on creek ½ mi. W
of Middletown. (Merriam, "Corrections con-
cerning California Indians," AA 10:357, 1908.)

Laka'hyōme (or lo'knōma)
 (Barrett, 1908)...........''Northern Moquelumnan'' (Tuleyome) name for
village NE of Middletown. See lō'knōma Barrett
in synonymy of Lah-ki'-yo-me po-koot.

Lal-nap-o-een (Palmer, 1881).Kulanapo name for tribe in Loknomah Valley. See
synonymy of Lah-ki'yo-me po-koot. "Tribe"
(village?) on St. Helena Creek W of present
Middletown. (Palmer, *Hist. Napa and Lake Cos.*,
pp. 36–37.)

Lake Miwok............Name used by Kroeber for Tuleyome tribe. See
      synonymy of Tuleyome at head of this tribe list.

Loaquiomi, Loaquio., Loaquiom.,
  Loaquio^{mi}, Loak. Yomi....(San Francisco Solano Mission Books, 1824–1837);
      Loaquiomi (Bancroft, *Hist. Calif.*, 2:506 fn.,
      1885); Engelhardt, *The Franciscans in California*,
      p. 451, 1897; see synonymy of Lah-ki'-yo-me
      po-koot.

Lōk-no'-mah............Yukean Miyahkma name, adopted by the Tule-
      yome for the old Middletown village which they
      called Lah-ki'-yo-me po'-goot on site of present
      town of Middletown. See Lah-ki'-yo-me po-koot.
      Both Loknoma and Lahkiyome mean "Goose
      Valley." (Merriam, "Mewan Stock," p. 353.)
      Barrett (*Pomo*, p. 273) wrongly refers Lok-
      noma to "Wappo" (Miyahkma).

Synonymy
  Locnoma............Mentioned in San Francisco Solano Mission Books,
      1824–1837, original MSS, Bancroft Library.
  Locnoma............(Bancroft [after Sonoma Mission records], *Hist.*
      Calif., 2:506, fn.)
  Locnoma............(Engelhardt [after Bancroft], *The Franciscans in*
      California, p. 451.)
  Locnoma............(Barrett [after Engelhardt], *Pomo*, p. 44, fn.)
  Lō'knōma or
    laka'hyōme.........(Barrett, *Pomo*, p. 273) and Loknoma (Kroeber,
      Handbook, p. 219; map, pl. 27.) Village NE of
      Middletown, wrongly referred to "Wappo" (Mi-
      yahkma).
  Lu'-pu-yo'-me............Former small "Hamfo" village on Rocky Islet in
      Siegler Creek N of Lower Lake village and S of
      Cache Creek. (Not to be confused with the Po-
      moan village of same name near Kelseyville.)

Mā-hwah-lĕ'-lĕ-no-mah
  (mēhwale' lenōma, Barrett) Old camp site near W bank of Putah Creek about
      3½ mi. SSE of Middletown. (Barrett, *Pomo*,
      p. 274.) Barrett's location seems erroneous.
      Wrongly referred by Barrett to "Wappo."

mēhwale' lenoma (Barrett,
  1908)................See Mā-hwah-lĕ'-lĕ-no-mah.
Mo-ā'-yo'me............"All our tribes or rancherias," said by several mem-
      bers of tribe.

Northern Coast or Lake Moquelumnan or Miwok (Bar-
  rett, 1908)............Name used by Barrett for Tuleyome. See synony-
      my of Tu'-le-yo'-me.

Northern or Lake Moquelu-
mnan (Barrett, 1908)......Name used by Barrett for Tuleyome. See synonymy of Tu'-le-yo'-me.

Oi'-ā-yum'-me-ko and
O'-ye-yo'-me-ko..........Hoo'-koo-e'-ko and Olamentko, name for Olayome
tribe on Putah Creek. Given me by both tribes in
1905. See the synonymy of O'-lā-yo'-me po-koot
below.

O'-lā-yo'-me (Merriam, 1907) Name of Coyote Valley band or division of Tuleyome. Sometimes used in tribal sense. (Merriam,
"Mewan Stock," p. 353.)

O'-lā-yo'-me po-koot........Village in N part of Coyote Valley ½ mi. S of Kil'-
le-yo'-ke but N of Guenock. (Merriam, "Mewan
Stock," p. 353.) Head village of Coyote Valley
band.

Synonymy
Holiyomi..............Given by Bancroft as "tribe" N of San Francisco
Bay (Bancroft, *Hist. Calif.*, 4:362–363, fn.).
May have been Olayome. See Holiyomi in main
list.

Oi'-ā-yum'-me and
O'-ye-yo'-me........Bodega Bay Hoo'-koo-e'-ko name for Olayome of
Putah Creek.

Oleomi, Oleyomi.......Mentioned as furnishing converts to mission at
Sonoma. (San Francisco Solano Mission Books,
1824–1837, original MSS, Bancroft Library.) No
information.

Oleomi...............(Bancroft [after Sonoma Mission Books], 1824–
1837, *Hist. Calif.*, 2:506, fn.)

Oleomi...............(Engelhardt [after Bancroft], *The Franciscans in
California*, p. 451.)

Oleomi...............(Barrett [after Engelhardt], *Pomo*, p. 317.)

ōlē'yōme [O-lā'-yo-me]..(Barrett, *Pomo*, p. 317.) See also Koo-noo-la-ka-koi
Palmer in main list.

Oleyome..............(Kroeber, *Handbook*, map, pl. 27, facing p. 173;
also p. 272).

Oleyomi, Oleomi.......Mentioned as furnishing four neophytes to the mission at Sonoma. (San Francisco Solano Mission
Books, 1824–1837, original MSS, Bancroft Library.)

Oleyomi..............Rancheria visited by Arguello in 1821. (Fr. Blas
Ordaz "Diario de la Expedición del Sr. Don Luis
Arguello," Archives Santa Barbara Mission
[1806–1821], 4:161–190.) Also referred to by
Bancroft, after Ordaz MS diary (*Hist. Calif.*,
2:448).

O'-ye-yo'-me and
    Oi'-ā-yum'-me . . . . Name used by Bodega Bay Olamentko for Olāyo'-me of Putah Creek. Same name pronounced Oi-ye'-yum-me is used by Tuleyome for Miyahkma tribe at Calistoga and in Alexander Valley on Russian River. Barrett (*Pomo*, p. 317) gives ōyē'yōmi (O-yā'-yo-mĕ) as name of village of "Southern Moquelumnan" (Hoo-koo-e-ko) at Freestone.

Oleomi . . . . (Mission Books, 1824–1837; Bancroft, *Hist. Calif.*, Vol. 2; Engelhardt, *The Franciscans in California*; Barrett, *Pomo*.) See synonymy of O'-lā-yo'-me po-koot.

ōlē'yōme (Barrett, 1908) . Village 1¾ mi. above Guenoc. See synonymy of O'-lā-yo'-me po-koot.

Oleyome (Kroeber, 1925) Principal village in Coyote Valley. See synonymy of O'-lā-yo'-me po-koot.

Oots-no-mah-nok . . . . See Utsnomanoc.

Oo-yoo'hah-no-mah
    (ūyū'hanōma Barrett) . . . . . Village on E bank of Putah Creek about 1½ mi. nearly due E of Middletown. (Barrett, *Pomo*, p. 273.) Erroneously referred by Barrett to "Wappo" (Miyahkma).

O'-ye-yo'-me or
    Oi'-ā-yum'-me . . . . Name used by Hoo-koo-e'-ko of Bodega Bay for Olayome. See synonymy of O'-lā-yo'-me po-koot.

Pagüenjelayomi . . . . Unidentified band at Mission at Sonoma. May not have been Tuleyome. (Bancroft [after Vallejo], *Hist. Calif.*, 4:363, fn.)

Pĕ'-te-no-mah (pe'tīnōma
    Barrett) . . . . Old village W of Putah Creek about 1 mi. NNW of Middletown. Site short distance N of cemetery at Middletown. (Barrett, *Pomo*, p. 273.) Referred by Barrett to "Wappo" (Miyahkma), but is Tuleyome.

pe'tīnōma (Barrett, 1908) . . . . See Pĕ'-te-no-mah.

Re'-ho . . . . Powers gave Re'-ho as "one name of the tribe in Pope Valley, derived from a chief. They early became extinct." (Powers, *Tribes of California*, p. 228, 1877.) Little is known of the Pope Valley tribes. "Re'-ho" may have been a nickname for a Win (Ko'peh) band, which was located in the east part of the valley. It is certainly not Tuleyome but the entry is included here for information.

Sahl'-sahl-po-goot.........Tuleyome name for their village in Wennok (Wen'-
nok) Valley on flat at base of Cone Pk. (Loo-
peek' po-we) at SE corner of Wennok Lake, S of
Phelan Ranch. (Merriam, "Mewan Stock," p.
353.)

Sah'-ti-yo-me po-koot.......Tuleyome name for their village in a rocky place at
S end of Coyote Valley about 2 mi. S of Guenoc.
(Merriam, "Mewan Stock," p. 353.) Not to be
confused with Sotoyome at Healdsburg.

Se-we'-yo-me (sĭwĭ'yōme
Barrett)................Another name for Hoo-koo'-yo-me. See Hūkū'-
hyūme Barrett in synonymy of Hoo-koo'-yo-me
po-koot.

Sĭwĭ'yōme................Given by Barrett (*Pomo*, p. 316) as another name
for Hūkūhyūme.

Shoyome.................Kroeber, *Handbook*, map, pl. 27, facing p. 172.
Based on Barrett's Cō'yōme, located "on S bank
Putah Creek about 3½ mi. below Guenoc."
(Barrett, *Pomo*, p. 316.) I failed to get this vil-
lage from the Indians.

Synonymy
Cō'yōme Barrett........*Pomo*, p. 316.
Socollomillos..............Typographic error for Locollomillos. (Bancroft
[after Taylor], *Native Races*, 1:363.) See synony-
my of Lah-ki'-yo-me po-koot.

"Stone House"............Well known place name near Tu'-le-yo'-me (in
Excelsior Valley). Not to be confused with an-
other of same name at Kelseyville in Habbe-
nap-po territory.

Te'-om-fo and
Kel-lew'-win-fo..........Names used by the Hamfo for the Tuleyome. See
Kel-lew'-win-fo Merriam in synonymy of Tule-
yome.

Toleomi (?)...............Rancheria. San Francisco Solano Mission Books,
1824–1837. See synonymy of Tu'-le-yo'-me po-
koot.

Tse'-tsah po-goot..........See tsĭ'tsapōgūt Barrett in synonymy of Tsit'-sah
yo'me.

Tsit'-sah yo'me (Tsit'-sah po-
goot and Tsit'-sah)......Village immediately N of Lower Lake village. The
Hamfo call it K'tah'-koi. (Salvador Chapo's
mother born and raised there.)

Synonymy
ka'tcūlūlūkūwan (Bar-
rett, 1908)..........See tsĭ'sapōgūt Barrett, this synonymy.
K'tah'-koi............Hamfo name for Tsit'-sah-yo'me.

Tsitsa................Kroeber, *Handbook*, map, pl. 27, facing p. 172.
tsī-tsapōgūt [prounounced
  tsē'-tsah-po-goot] or
ka'tcūlūlūkūwan (pronounced
  kah'-choo-loo-loo-koo-
  wahn..............."Southeastern Pomo" (Lower Lake or Hamfo)
                name for Tsit'-sah yo'me. Barrett says it is in
                NW part of town of Lower Lake. Site near Scott-
                man residence just N of the wagon bridge at
                Lower Lake. (Barrett, *Pomo*, p. 318.)
Tso'-kew po-goot..........Village in Pope Valley. (Merriam, "Mewan Stock,"
                p. 353.) Slurred form of Tso'-ke-yo-me po-goot
                Merriam, which see.
Tso'-ke-yo'-me po'-goot.....Principal village in Pope Valley, S of postoffice and
                close to creek. Slurred Tso'-kewme po-goot (Mer-
                riam,"Mewan Stock"; also "Corrections concern-
                ing California Indians," AA, n.s., 10:356, 1908.)
                This village was on Pope Creek at the first
                crossing of the main road coming S from Butts
                Canyon (on the Bank Ranch).
Tu'-le-am'-me or Tu'-le-yo'-me
  (Merriam 1907).........Used in tribal sense. See synonymy of Tuleyome.
Tuleomi (Mission Books,
  1797–1830)..............Rancheria. See synonymy of Tu'-le-yo'-me po-
                koot.
Tu'-le-yo'-me po-koot.......Old village 3 mi. S of Lower Lake. The most an-
                cient settlement of the tribe. Name used also for
                subfamily. (Merriam, "Mewan Stock," p. 353.)

Synonymy
  Te'-om-fo and
    Kel-lew'-win-fo.......Hamfo names for Tuleyome. See Kel-lew'-win-fo.
  Toleomi...............Rancheria. San Francisco Solano Mission Register,
                1824–1837, original MSS, Bancroft Library. (No
                information.)
  Tu'leamne (Tuleyome)
    or Olayome.........Slurred pronunciation for Tuleyome tribe. (Mer-
                riam, "Mewan Stock," p. 353.)
  Tuleomi...............Rancheria. San Jose Mission, Book of Baptisms,
                1797–1830, MS. (No information.)
  tū'lēyōme [Tu'-lā-yo-me] Village about 2 mi. S of the town of Lower Lake.
                Site is on E side of county road on what is called
                the Dock Murphy Ranch (Barrett, *Pomo*, p.
                318.)
  Tuleyome.............The metropolis of the settlements in the valley of
                town of Lower Lake. (Kroeber, *Handbook*, map,
                pl. 27, facing p. 172, and p. 272.)

Tulioni................Spelling in San Jose Mission Register. "Lista Alfa-
betica de Neofitos" [San Jose Mission, erro-
neously labeled Mission San Fernando], original
MS, Bancroft Library. No date.

Tuliyomi..............One of the tribes or bands N of San Francisco Bay
against whom an expedition under Salvador
Vallejo was sent in 1843. (Location indefinite.)
(Bancroft [after Vallejo], *Hist. Calif.*, 4:363, fn.)

Tulioni (Register San Jose
Mission)................See synonymy of Tu'-le-yo'-me po-koot.

Tuliyomi (Bancroft, 1886)...See synonymy of Tu'-le-yo'-me po-koot.

tūmi' stūmis (Tu-mis'-tu-
mis)....................Old village on small stream tributary of Putah
Creek about 2½ mi. NE of Guenoc. (Barrett,
Pomo, p. 316.)

Utsnomanoc..............Mentioned repeatedly in books of Sonoma Mission.
Spellings in Sonoma Mission Register (Padron
de la Misión de San Francisco Solano, 1824–
1833): Utsnomanoc 17 times; Utsnoma 6; Utsnoman 9; Utsnoman [*sic*] 6; Uatsnoma 2. (Libros de
Misión, San Francisco Solano, original MSS,
1824–1837, Bancroft Library.) See Oots-no-ma-
noc.

ūyū'hanōma (Barrett, 1908)..See Oo-yoo'-ha-no-mah.

Wen'-nok................Name of small valley and lake just S of Coyote
Valley on Putah Creek about 6 mi. E of Middle-
town. Valley contained 3 rancherias (one or more
may have been camps). See also Guenocks.

Wo-de'-di-tep'-pe po'-goot...Tuleyome name for their village in Jerusalem Valley; easternmost village. (Merriam, "Mewan
Stock," p. 353.)

Yo'-me-ko'-tsah or
Ko-tsah'-to yo'me........Name for themselves used by people of Hoo-koo'-
yo-me po-koot and other rancherias. Yo'-me is
the word for "home"; ko-tsah for "people," so
the name means "home people."

Yo'-tsah................Name used by Hamfo of Lower Lake for Tuleyome
rancheria on Putah Creek, 2 or 3 mi. E of "Stone
House" (Tu'-le-yo'-me).

California Mission
Baptismal Records

Between *1769* and *1823* the Franciscan Order established twenty-one missions along the coast of California, from San Diego north to Sonoma. The express purpose of these centers was the conversion of the Indians to Christianity, and in the sixty-five years of their operation the padres drew into the missions virtually all central and south coast Indians, as well as large numbers from the Great Valley. Records of individual baptisms, marriages, and deaths were kept at each mission from its founding until secularization in *1833*, with occasional entries up to *1837*.

In general, each baptismal entry records the native rancheria, personal name, sex, and age of the person baptized; occasionally, additional information concerning relatives or health is also given. These contemporary accounts are thus the best sources available for aboriginal demography in the mission area. Ethnographers of the present century found few survivors, and these were generations removed from aboriginal conditions, with memories blurred by time and acculturation. There are therefore many gaps in our knowledge of the Indians of the coastal strip of California which can be partly filled by data from the mission records.

In *1919* Dr. Merriam employed S. R. Clemence to compile from the original mission documents the native name of each recorded rancheria, its population statistics, and the dates of its contact with the mission. The resulting series of records from nineteen of the twenty-one missions is extremely useful in the study of the aboriginal population, native languages, and tribal distribution, and, in general, of the contact period in California. Five representative lists from Dr. Merriam's compilation have been selected for present publication—

the records from Santa Barbara, San Luis Obispo, San Miguel, Santa Clara, and San Jose.[1]

Students in various fields will find these records of value. Copies of these particular registers are either not readily available or contain too many errors to be reliable. Many of the rancherias associated with these missions are frequently mentioned in contemporary Spanish documents, hence the information contained in the registers is useful to historians as well as anthropologists. Detailed studies of Spanish explorations and military campaigns, as well as the ethnographic literature, often reflect the activity of the missions and have frequently made it possible to map the mission rancherias. Specific dates of baptism, such as are given in these records, may facilitate our understanding of documentary sources by clarifying the relationships between known and unplaced rancherias.

The minimal population figures available for each village can be used to approximate the total aboriginal population and thus to suggest indirectly the habitat. The figures showing the disparity in the sexes or the adult-child ratio, as well as the discrepancy between the figures for mission baptisms and those given in documentary sources for village populations, often indicate epidemics or the upset social conditions of the period of first contact with the whites. The terminal dates of baptisms may reflect the exhaustion of the rancherias or the depopulation of whole areas. In short, these copies of the mission records in the Merriam Collection provide in accessible form material which may shed new light on aboriginal California and the effect of European contact.

No essential changes have been made in Dr. Merriam's arrangement of the rancherias in alphabetical order. The names of some rancherias have as many as fifteen variants; different scribes heard and recorded different sounds and dialectic differences, while the lack of standardized spelling and purely mechanical errors account for many different versions. Many wrong variants in other copies of the mission records and in some published registers are due to the misreading of penmanship peculiarities, but the Merriam copies are exceptionally free from such errors and faithfully record the original variants. In general, the Merriam list uses the most frequent variant as the type name, all other variants being listed alphabetically below it. No changes have been made in this grouping, even though a detailed study using other sources might warrant such alterations.

The significance of these rancheria names is not always clear. "Rancheria," "familia," and "nación" are used synonymously at times, and it is therefore not always possible to distinguish between a village, tribelet, or dialect group. Repeated names of rancherias with a rather large population probably refer

---

[1] All records are available in the Department of Anthropology, University of California, Berkeley. —Ed.

to tribelets,[2] but the rare names, often with only one or two recorded baptisms, offer problems. Transcription errors are the most probable explanation for most of these infrequent occurrences, but specific villages within a tribelet may have been recorded occasionally. Then, too, visits from other groups or single excursions into new territory often resulted in a record of a distant tribelet never again represented at the same mission. Such unique records can often be distinguished by a comparison of the registers of adjacent missions.

In the following tabulations the native name of each group, as well as its variants, is listed under "Rancheria." Figures in parentheses after rancheria names indicate the number of times that that specific spelling occurs in the pertinent records. If no such figure appears, the name occurred only once. In the column headed "Year of baptisms" the number in parentheses following the date gives the number of individuals baptized in that year. Under the heading "Total no. of baptisms" is given the total number of recorded baptisms for each rancheria. These totals are not always accurate. Except in the Santa Barbara compilation the subtotals for the number of adult men, adult women, and children are also entered.—Ed.

---

[2] A tribelet is a group claiming a specific territory, containing one or more villages; the same dialect may be spoken by neighboring tribelets. A. L. Kroeber, *The Patwin and Their Neighbors*, UC–PAAE 29:258, 1932.—Ed.

SANTA BARBARA MISSION

The following list of rancherias was compiled from records obtained in 1919 from the Book of Baptisms of Santa Barbara Mission, with additions and corrections from the books of Deaths and Marriages and from the Register. All the original Santa Barbara records are at the Parochial Church in Santa Barbara. They include the "Libro de Bautismos de Misión de Santa Barbara, 1786–1825"; the "Libro de Matrimonios de Misión de Santa Barbara, 1786– "; the "Libro de Difuntos de Misión de Santa Barbara, 1786– "; and the "Padron de esta Misión de Santa Barbara" (begun in 1815 and continued to 1840). All of these records are beautifully kept. With the exception of the Book of Confirmations, the lists give rancheria names.—Ed.

SANTA BARBARA MISSION

Rancheria	Year of baptism	Total number of baptisms
Acqueschucmoc......................	1792 (1)	1
Acsu (Mat.).........................	1791 (1); 1798 (1)	1
Acsegu		
Aguasná............................	1787 (1); 1803 (1); 1804 (Dif.)	2
Aguasnon		
Aguamon (Dif.)		
Ajtanamú (Pad.).....................	1820 (2)	2
Actanamú		
Alcax (2)...........................	1787 (15); 1789 (6); 1791 (2); 1792 (1);	34
Alcáz (9)	1798 (1); 1800 (3); 1802 (1); 1803 (4)	
Alcas (9)		
Alcajch (6)		
Alcaza		
Alccaz (Mat.)		
Alcahj		
"Alcas or San Rafael"		
Sⁿ Francisco alias Alcajch		
Anagüe.............................	1788–1803 (9)	9
Anajue (8)		
Aquepe.............................	1804 (1)	1
Aquitsumu (10)......................	1788–1805 (16)	16
Acchumu		
Ausleyec............................	1787 (2); 1789 (1)	3
Ysluyc		
Caieguas............................	1803 (1)	1

NOTE.—Mat., "Libro de Matrimonios"; Dif., "Libro de Difuntos"; Pad., "Padron." Figures in parentheses following rancheria names in first column indicate number of occurrences of that variant; figures in parentheses following dates in second column indicate number of baptisms.—Ed.

SANTA BARBARA MISSION—*Continued*

Rancheria	Year of baptism	Total number of baptisms

"Cajats en la ysla" (20)...............
  "Cajats en la ysla de Enémess"
  "Cajátsa en las yslas (5)
  Cajatsa (2)
  Cajatssa en las yslas
  Cajachs
  Cajása
  Cajats (2)
  Cajátsa una de las rancherias colocadas
    en las yslas de la Canal
  Cagaz en la ysla
  "Jajas en la ysla"
	1787–1803 (15); 1814 (9); 1815 (10); 1816
	  (4); 1818 (1); 1819 (4); 1822 (3)
		46

Calaguasas (Dif.).......................
  Calahuasá (20)
  Calahuasac
  Calahuashá (2)
  Calahuacha
  Calabasa (2)
  Calabazá
  Calabazat
  Calabauaxa
  Calabasat
  Calauasa (2)
  Calauachá
  Calaguasá
  Qualaguasac
	1787–1798 (8); 1800 (8); 1802 (2); 1803
	  (8); 1804 (2); 1811 (1)
		29

Casil (23)..............................
  Casili
  Cassi (3)
  Cassil
	1787–1799 (13); 1800–1804 (14)	27

Castoi (2)..............................	1787 (4)	4

Castait (2) (Mat.).....................
  Castaita
  Catstaita (Dif.)
	1803 (1); 1801 (Mat.), 1802 (Dif.)	1

Caxtec................................	1820 (1)	1

"Cchiucchiuc (en las yslas)" (3)...........
  Chiuchiu (2)
  Chiucssiu
  Siucssihui en las yslas
  Siucsiu (3)
	1797 (1); 1798 (1); 1803 (1); 1816 (2);
	  1814 (3); 1815 (2)
		10

"Chahua on the island".................
  Chaua en las yslas
  Xaua
	1803 (1); 1822	1

Chailoú...............................
  Yxaulo
  Ysaulo
  Uaulo en el tular
  Xauloa (Pad.)
  Xolou (Pad.)
  Yxaulo (Pad.)
	1818 (1); 1825 (2)	3

SANTA BARBARA MISSION—*Continued*

Rancheria	Year of baptism	Total number of baptisms
Chniguas (11)........................ Chnihua Chnijuas Chniquaj (3) Esnigua Esniguaja Esniuaja Essnihuaj Inigua Nigua Niguaja Niguesa Niguaxa Snigua (2) Snihuas Sniguaj (2) Snihuaj (7) Sniguaxa Snihwiya Ssnihuaj Ysniguajuá Ysniguaga Ysniguaja (2) (Mat.) Ysnijuaja	1787–1798 (25); 1800–1805 (12); 1812 (5)	42
Cholossos en las yslas (5)................ Cholosos Choloxos Choloocoss en la ysla en frente de Mⁿ	1810 (3); 1814 (1); 1815 (5)	9
Cogoniup............................	1820 (1)	1
Coloc (18)........................ Coloco Coloc, alias El Paredon Holoc (2) Oloc (2)	1788–1799 (13); 1800–1804 (10)	23
Coochu.............................. Conocho Coochup (4) Couchu (Dif.)	1791 (1); 1795 (1); 1820 (4)	6
Cuyamu (10)........................ Cuyamu, llamada San Pedro y San Pablo Cuyamo (5) Cuyam Cuyas Cuiamu Cayamú Qujas	1787 (4); 1789 (1); 1800 (2); 1803 (7); 1812 (2); 1820 (1)	17

SANTA BARBARA MISSION—*Continued*

Rancheria	Year of baptism	Total number of baptisms
Eljman (10)............................ Elman Elgmána Gelmana (Mat.)	1797 (1); 1799 (1); 1800 (1); 1801 (1); 1803 (2); 1804 (1)	7
Elehuascui (8)........................ Eleuaxcuyu (2) Eluaxcù (yslas) (7) Elcuaxcuy (Dif.) Elehuascui (Mat.) Esnocyoā	1814 (3); 1815 (8); 1816 (3)	14
Geliec (20)............................ Gelioc (4) Geliet Geluec Geliegue Gelie Eliec Elihec Eliet "Geliec or las Llagas" (2) Rancheria de las Llagas ó Heliyic Geliuq (2) Geliuc	1787 (20); 1789 (5); 1791 (2); 1793 (1); 1796 (1); 1797 (3); 1798 (2); 1800 (1); 1803 (10)	45
Geliga.............................	1787 (1)	1
Gelmá (2)...........................	1788 (1); 1792 (1)	2
Geló (33)........................... Sⁿ Franᶜᵒ N. Padre (alias Gelo) Gelo or Sⁿ Miguel Gelui "de la ysla de Gelo" Sⁿ Francisco ó Gelo (Dif.) Geloo (Mat.) Gelho (Mat.)	1787 (25); 1789 (4); 1791–1800 (10); 1803 (29); 1804 (1)	69
Gelsege (2).........................	1800 (1); 1804 (1)	
Guainonase.........................	1786 (1)	1
Gucsapit...........................	1788 (1)	1
Guelegimena........................ Gelexmona Guelecme Huelecmen (Pad.) Velecmen (Pad.)	1789 (2); 1796 (1)	3
Rancheria Guima en las yslas...........	1814 (1)	1
Huisapa (7)......................... Huissapa Huichapa Huixapa Huixap Guiasap Guisapa (2) Guissapa Gisap (2)	1791 (2); 1800–1805 (10)	12

SANTA BARBARA MISSION—*Continued*

Rancheria	Year of baptism	Total number of baptisms
Huajulach..........................	1799 (1)	1
Huelequimé.........................	1793 (1); 1800 (1)	2
Huelequimit en la sierra		
Huelquimen (Dif.)		
Huililic (10).......................	1788 (6); 1791 (2); 1796–1799 (5); 1800	29
Huililicqui (3)	(3); 1801 (1); 1802 (2); 1803 (6); 1805	
Huililicque	(1); 1812 (3)	
Huililiqui		
Huililig		
Guililiqi		
Guililic		
Guiliqi (2)		
Guiligui		
Guililigue		
Guilelec		
Uililic (2)		
Yililic		
Achililiguo		
Jelelic "en una rancheria de la sierra lla-		
mada Huililicque" (Dif.)		
Humaligu.........................	1801 (2)	2
Jumaliguo del otro lado de Sⁿ Buenaven-		
tura		
Janaya (8).........................	1786 (2); 1787 (10); 1795 (3); 1788 (2)	17
Janayan (3)		
Janayan "alias el Pedregoso" (Dif.)		
Janajá		
Janagua		
Janayat		
Janagan (2)		
Janaian (4)		
Janayam		
Jonjonata.........................	1803 (1)	1
Lalale (2)...........................		
Lacayamu en las Yslas (6)...............	1802 (1); 1803 (2); 1814 (2); 1815 (3);	14
Lacayamú (2)	1816 (6)	
Lacaiamu (2)		
Lecayamu en las yslas (3)		
Liam (2)...........................	1787 (1); 1803 (1); 1811 (1); 1814 (7);	12
"Liam en las yslas"	1816 (1); 1817 (1)	
"Liam en las yslas en frente"		
Liama, de la ysla		
Yliama (Dif.)		
"Lupus en la ysla de Enemes"............	1791 (1)	1
Lùgups		
Malpuah cerca de los Tulares............	1798 (1); 1799 (1); 1804 (1); 1819 (1)	4
Malapuana		
Malapua		
Malapuama		

SANTA BARBARA MISSION—*Continued*

Rancheria	Year of baptism	Total number of baptisms
"Maschala en las yslas" (2)............... "Mascal (rancheria de la Ysla)" "Mastcháala (en las yslas)" "Maschala (yslas)" (2) "Maschal (en las yslas)" (12) Maschal (en la ysla en frente) Mascal, una de las rancherias de la Ysla Mascchaala en las ylas (Dif.) Masschal (Dif.)	1787 (1); 1791 (1); 1795 (1); 1803 (4); 1811 (3); 1814 (5); 1815 (11); 1816 (1); 1819 (1)	28
Matilxa.............................	1789 (1)	1
Matsnojotso........................ Macsnoctu (Pad.)*	1796 (1)	1
Miat..............................	1789 (1)	1
Miasap (6)........................... Miasapa Miasat (3) Mihausapip	1788 (1); 1791 (5); 1793 (1); 1799 (1); 1800 (2); 1805 (1)	11
Miguigui (50)....................... Miguijui (10) Miguihui (2) Miguihui ó Dos Pueblos Miguiul rancheria San Pedro y San Pablo, alias Miquigui [see also Cuyamu]	1787 (3); 1788–1799 (25); 1800 (21); 1802 (2); 1803 (66)	117
Milaluhûo en las yslas................. Milaluie en las yslas Miluluyo en las yslas	1795 (1); 1802 (1)	2
Milimelo...........................	1801 (1)	1
Mismatác (2; Dif., 1).................	1796 (1); 1800 (1)	2
Mitunami en los tulares............... Same in Pad.	1805 (1)	1
Misopsno (12) (Mat.)................. Misospno (4) Misospno (alias La Carpinteria) Misopsno alias La Carpinteria (Dif.) Misobs Michopsno (13) Mishopsno (alias Carpinteria) Pisospno	1788 (2); 1789 (5); 1791 (3); 1794 (1); 1796 (1); 1797 (7); 1799 (1); 1800 (4); 1803 (3); 1804 (4)	31
Mugu..............................	1796 (1)	1
Najalasegui.........................	1787 (1)	1
Nanagüani (yslas)....................	1815 (1)	1
Niacla en las yslas................... Niaccla en las yslas	1814 (1); 1816 (1)	2
Nimquelquel (en las yslas)............. Nunquelquel (2) (Mat.)	1814 (1); 1818 (2)	3
Onosyot........................... Onosio Onoxio (Mat.)	1787 (1); 1788 (2); 1789 (1); 1792 (1)	5

* In "Libro de Bautismos" this Indian was listed as from Siuicon.

SANTA BARBARA MISSION—*Continued*

Rancheria	Year of baptism	Total number of baptisms
Onomgio (6) .... Ononjio (2) Onogio Onopjio Onojio, alias La Gabiota Onumio Honomgio	1788 (2); 1789 (6); 1791 (2); 1796 (1)	11
Sajcaya (8) .... Sajcaia (2) Sajcay Saccaya (4) Sacaiya Sacaig (2) Saccaja	1788 (2); 1791 (1); 1800 (1); 1801 (2); 1803 (7); 1804 (3); 1805 (1); 1812 (1); 1819 (1)	19
Salagua (13) .... Salaguas (5) Salahuag (2) Salaguaj Salaguat Salahuaj Salagua ó El Montecito (3) Salagual ó de Montecito (2) Saloguat Salajuaj Sⁿ Bernardino, alias Salaguaj Salahuax Xalahuax Chalaguas Chalagua Chalaguaj alias San Bernardino (Mat.) Chalajuaj Chalajuaj alias Montecito Sulaguaj alias San Bernardino (Dif.) Xalauaj (Mat.)	1787 (10); 1791 (3); 1792 (1); 1795 (1); 1796 (2); 1798 (1); 1799 (2); 1800 (1); 1802 (3); 1803 (5)	29
Saspili (36) .... Saspilil (5) Saspil Saspili vulgo Mescaltitan Sajpili (7) Sajpilil (5) rancheria de San Miguel llamada Sajpili Sajpili, alias San Rafael San Miguel alias Sajpili (Dif.) Saxpilil (16) Saxpili (12) Sacpilil (2) Sacpili (2) Sacspili Sagxpilil Sagpilil Xajpili (5)	1787 (49); 1789 (15); 1791 (6); 1792 (2); 1793 (1); 1794 (3); 1795 (2); 1796 (6); 1797 (6); 1798 (1); 1799 (5); 1801 (1); 1802 (1); 1803 (30); 1804 (1); 1805 (1)	131

Rancheria	Year of baptism	Total number of baptisms
Sasguagel (4)........................... Sasguajel Sasuagel (2) Sashuaguel en las yslas Shuagil en las yslas Sashuegel Sasuaquel (1; Dif., 1) Sassguajel en las yslas el frente Sguagil en las yslas Yshuegel en las yslas (2)	1802 (1); 1803 (1); 1814 (2); 1815 (4); 1816 (1)	9
Sasuo............................ Sasguo	1788 (1); 1799 (1)	2
Siguaya (4).......................... Sihuaya (5) Sihuhaya (Mat.) Sigauia Siiguaya Siguaya en la sierra Siuhaya (3) Siiuaya Suiguia Yiguaya (2) Ciguaya	1787 (1); 1791 (1); 1795 (6); 1797 (3); 1799 (1); 1803 (2); 1800 (1); 1805 (5); 1812 (7); 1815 (4)	31
Siguicon (4)........................... Siguecom Sigueco Siguiccomo Sihuicon Siuicon (4) Siguijacono Siguecón Siuecóno Siguiecono	1789 (1); 1800 (1); 1803 (2); 1804 (1); 1805 (1); 1812 (1); 1815 (1); 1818 (6)	14
Sisabanonase.............................	1786 (1)	1
Sisuchi (29)............................. Sisuchy (2) Sesuchi Sisutxi Sisuchi ó alias la Quemada Susachie Sisuchy ó La Quemada (Dif.)	1787 (3); 1788 (1); 1789 (2); 1791 (1); 1795 (1); 1797 (3); 1798 (4); 1800 (16); 1801 (1); 1803 (25)	57
Siugtu (15)............................. Siuctu (10) Siujtu (21) Siugtu cerca del Presidio (2) Siugtu, proxima al Presidio (Dif.) Siucgtu Siutu (10) Sciuctu Siut (3) Siotu Siujtum Siujtu, alias Sⁿ Antonio (1; Dif., 1)	1787 (13); 1788 (8); 1789 (12); 1793 (1); 1796 (2); 1797 (31); 1798 (2); 1799 (1); 1800 (4); 1802 (3); 1803 (8); 1804 (3); 1808 (1)	89

SANTA BARBARA MISSION—*Continued*

Rancheria	Year of baptism	Total number of baptisms
Sitās.................................	1799 (1)	1
Sisolop.............................	1803 (3); 1804 (1); 1805 (1)	5
Chisolop		
Chicholops		
Chicholop (2)		
Chicholop, alias el Cojo		
Sisguasa.............................		
Snojoso (4).........................	1787 (1); 1789 (2); 1791 (1); 1796 (1);	13
Snojs (4)	1803 (1); 1804 (1); 1805 (2); 1812 (4)	
Sinoxo		
Sinojs		
Senojoch		
Scinogto		
Scinogso		
Snojotso		
Stnocoho		
Stnocotxo		
Tsnocotso (3)		
Tsnojotso (2)		
Ynoxo (2)		
Sinoxs (Mat.)		
Snajalayegua (14).....................	1787 (2); 1788 (1); 1791 (2); 1794 (1);	44
Snajalayehua (6)	1795 (2); 1796 (7); 1799 (1); 1800 (4);	
Snajalegue	1802 (1); 1803 (3); 1804 (5); 1805 (8);	
Snajalayeua	1811 (1); 1812 (3); 1814 (1); 1819 (1)	
Chnajalayegua (3)		
Chnayegua		
Esnajalayégua		
Esnajalegue (2)		
Esnajalayegue (2)		
Esnaxalayegua		
Esnajalayehua		
Ynajalayegua		
Najalayegua (4)		
Najalaiegua		
Naxjalajagua		
Najalasegui		
Najalayegue		
Naxalayegua		
Nisalayegua		
Jalayegue		
Soctono-cumu.......................	1791 (1); 1795 (1); 1804 (1)	3
Soctonocumu (2)		
Sotonocmo		
Soctonocmu		
Sotonocmu		
Somes (4)...........................	1789 (5)	5
Sonechi.............................	1791 (1)	1

SANTA BARBARA MISSION—*Concluded*

Rancheria	Year of baptism	Total number of baptisms
Succu, alias El Rincon................ Succu Sucu Chucu Chuccu Chuccu ó el Rincon	1791 (1); 1794 (1); 1803 (1); 1801 (1)	4
Stucu (11; Mat., 1)................... Stuc Stucu en la sierra rancheria de la sierra llamada Stucu Estucu (7; Mat., 1) Tucu (4; Mat., 1) Tucui	1787 (6); 1789 (8); 1791 (2); 1793 (1); 1796 (1); 1800 (1); 1801 (5); 1803 (1); 1804 (12); 1788 (4)	41
Taxlipu (10).......................... Taxlipo Taislipu	1818 (13); 1825 (1)	14
Taneexacxa.........................	1818	
Tequeps (57)......................... Tequebs (2) Tequepsch (2) Teqeps Teccex Tequepitz Teguepc (Mat.)	1788 (9); 1791 (8); 1793–1799 (11); 1800 (10); 1802 (2); 1803 (15); 1804 (15); 1811 (2)	72
Tigueco............................	1791 (1)	1
Tolocmoco.......................... Soltolmoco Tolomoco (Mat.)	1792 (2)	2
"Tucan en las yslas".................. "Tucamu en las yslas" Tucanu (Mat.) (Pad)	1803 (2)	1
Tuhacam (1; Mat., 1; Dif., 1)............ Tuac (3) Tuacam (Dif.)	1788 (43)	
Uchápa (8)........................... Uchap-pa Uisap (Dif.) Usap (Dif.) Usapa (1; Dif. 1) Ychjapa (Dif.)	1797 (1); 1800 (5); 1803 (2); 1804 (1)	9
Xilit................................	1787 (1)	1
Yalahuay............................	1805 (1)	1
Ychemèn (en las yslas)................. Ychueman	1803 (1); 1814 (1)	2
Youtu (2)........................... Yutu (2) Yuctu	1787 (5); 1791	5

SAN LUIS OBISPO MISSION

The following list of rancherias was compiled from material obtained in 1919 from the two Books of Baptism of San Luis Obispo Mission (1772–1823; 1823–1869). No rancherias are given in the Book of Deaths or Book of Marriages of this mission.

The San Luis Obispo Mission records are at the original mission.—Ed.

SAN LUIS OBISPO MISSION

Rancheria	Year of baptism	Baptisms*	Total number of baptisms
Asicto................	1803 (1)	1 F	1
Cahuiya (3).............	1835 (3)	3 M	3
Calaca (1).............	1813 (1)	1 F	1
Chaguino.............	1779 (1)	1 F	1
"Chanháhe de la Tular"........	1813 (1)	1 F	1
Chano (23)............ Chanu (3) "Chano, sita cerca de la rancheria de Scahuayo," 1792	1774 (2); 1775 (3); 1776 (5); 1777 (1); 1778 (1); 1779 (1); 1780 (9); 1781 (2); 1783 (1); 1791 (2); 1802 (1); 1803 (2); 1792 (2); 1799 (3)	12 M, 14 F, 10 C	36
Checate.............	1787 (1)	1 C	1
Chegue............. Chehu Tschehue Tschehua	1779 (2); 1803 (2)	1 M, 1 F, 2 C	4
Chenna (2)............ Tchena (2) Tene (2) Tena (1)	1773 (2); 1791 (4); 1775 (1); 1778 (1); 1802 (1)	3 M, 3 F, 3 C	9
Chesquio (3)............ Chetskio Tceshó	1794 (2); 1798 (1); 1802 (1); 1803 (1)	5	5
Chiguegua............. Chiquiagua Chiquiega Chiquieuga Chechehua Chchegua	1773 (1); 1794 (1); 1800 (2); 1803 (4)	2 M, 6 F	8
Chilimacstusú............. Chilimaxtùsu Chilimustusu Silimastus	1782 (1); 1788 (2); 1802 (1)	1 M, 2 F, 1 C	4
Chiongsun.............	1775 (1)	1 F	1
Chixiel.............	1794 (1)	1 F	1

NOTE.—Pad., "Padron" or register. Figures in parentheses following rancheria names in first column indicate number of occurrences of that variant; figures in parentheses following dates in second column indicate number of baptisms.—Ed.

* M, male(s); F, female(s); C, child(ren).—Ed.

SAN LUIS OBISPO MISSION—*Continued*

Rancheria	Year of baptism	Baptisms	Total number of baptisms
Chliquin (6)................ Chliquini Chiliquin Chligini Cligin "Sclegin, junto al Arroyo Grande" Siliquin Sligin Sliguini Esliquini Tsliquin Tslegini Tiliquin	1776 (1); 1780 (2); 1779 (1); 1791 (2); 1792 (1); 1793 (2); 1794 (1); 1796 (2); 1798 (3); 1799 (1); 1800 (3); 1803 (3)	10 M, 10 F, 2 C	22
Chmimu (15)............... Chmimo Cmimu Gmimu (3) Exmimu Estmimo (2) Smimu (5) Texmimu (2) Tsmimu (3) Tchmimu (2) Tgmimu	1773 (1); 1779 (1); 1791 (1); 1792 (4); 1794 (2); 1795 (1); 1796 (1); 1798 (1); 1799 (1); 1800 (1); 1802 (1); 1803 (22); 1804 (1)	12 M, 18 F, 8 C	38
"parage llamado Chmitu".......	1798 (1)	1 C	1
Chmoli (7)................. Chismole (3) Chismoli Cismòli (2) Cixmoli Ctsmoli Gismolg Hismoli Esmole Esmoly Echmolgi Ssmoli Tchmòli Tsmoli (3) Timol	1774 (1); 1778 (3); 1779 (1); 1780 (1); 1788 (1); 1791 (4); 1792 (2); 1793 (1); 1794 (3); 1798 (2); 1801 (1); 1803 (4); 1804 (1)	7 M, 10 F, 8 C	25
Chmonimo (9)............... Chmonimu Esmonimo (3) Exmonimo Smonimo (4) Smomimo Chusmonim	1777 (1); 1790 (2); 1791 (1); 1792 (1); 1794 (5); 1796 (1); 1798 (4); 1802 (1); 1803 (3)	8 M, 8 F, 3 C	19
Chocta......................	1790 (1)	1 C	1
Chocxiolo..................	1802 (1)	1 C	1

SAN LUIS OBISPO MISSION—*Continued*

Rancheria	Year of baptism	Baptisms	Total number of baptisms
Chogoy.	1813 (1)	1 M	1
Chojuale (11).	1775 (3); 1776 (2); 1778 (2); 1779 (3);	10M , 8 F, 9 C	27
Chojoale	1788 (2); 1791 (1); 1795 (1); 1798		
Chojale	(1); 1803 (12)		
Chocuale			
Chujuale			
Xojuale			
Choquala			
Chaquale (3)			
Choquale			
Chot Coula			
Choinoc (2)			
Chóinoc (4)			
Nacion de Chóinoc (70)			
Rancheria de Chóinoc			
Tsoynoc en el Tular			
Chonexle.	1794 (1)	1 F	1
Chotcagua (6).	1774 (1); 1775 (1); 1776 (3); 1777 (2);	5 M, 9 F, 6 C	20
Chotcague (2)	1778 (1); 1783 (1); 1785 (1); 1791		
Chotcaua (5)	(2); 1792 (1); 1793 (1); 1799 (1);		
Chotcahua	1802 (1); 1803 (5)		
Chotcaghua (2)			
Chotgaghue			
Chodcauha			
Chetcague			
Chotnegle alias Santa Margarita. .	1791 (1); 1792 (2); 1801 (3)	3 M, 3 F	6
Chotpnelc (2)			
Chotmnelj			
Chotmnelge			
Chotosilul (2).	1792 (1); 1800 (2)	1 M, 1 F, 1 C	3
Chotquacilul			
Chul.	1785 (1)	1 F	1
Chulucucunách (2).	1791 (1); 1803 (6)	2 M, 4 F, 1 C	7
Chulucucunas (2)			
Chunucucuna (2)			
Chulucucunaxa			
Nacion Chunut (12).	1834 (5); 1835 (6)	4 M, 4 F, 3 C	11
Cheuneut (Pad., 3)			
Chuspil.	1778 (1); 1779 (1)	1 M, 2 C	3
Chicpil (2)			
Couho.	1792 (2)	1 M, 1 F	2
Chouho			
Electec (2).	1782 (2)	1 M, 1 F	2
Elmismey.	1803 (2)	2 F	2
Elmismeye			
Emerenciana (2).	1776 (2)	1 M, 1 F	2
Epcheùa.	1796 (1)	1 C	1
Espejatpono.	1802 (1)	1 M	1
Extatjoto.	1796 (1); 1799 (1)	1 F, 1 M	2
Estacotocol			
Extimuxa.	1794 (1)	1 M	1

SAN LUIS OBISPO MISSION—*Continued*

Rancheria	Year of baptism	Baptisms	Total number of baptisms
Gebetpu.....................	1788 (1)	1 M	1
Gelecto (3)................... Ljelecto (3) Ljualacto Lquelecto	1791 (1); 1796 (1); 1813 (6)	4 M, 3 F, 1 C	8
Gmimu (2)................... Chmimu Essmimu Squimimu	1778 (1); 1779 (1); 1789 (1); 1790 (1); 1796 (1)	1 M, 2 F, 2 C	5
Gmosmu (8).................. Cmosmu (8) Comosmu (1) Lgmosmu Lmosmu (4) Moxmu (4) Mocmu Tecomosmu (2) Tzmozmu Tmozmu	1774 (1); 1775 (2); 1776 (2); 1777 (1); 1778 (1); 1780 (1); 1784 (1); 1791 (3); 1792 (3); 1794 (6); 1798 (1); 1799 (2); 1803 (5)	9 M, 12 F, 8 C	29
Guaslague (2)................ Tuaslague Tuaslaqui	1803 (6)	3 M, 3 F	6
Guasna (5)................... Ljuasna (6) Lguasna (9) Elguasna Lhuasna Uazna	1779 (2); 1788 (1); 1791 (2); 1792 (3); 1794 (1); 1796 (1); 1803 (12)	8 M, 14 F	22
Guegetmimu (3)............. Guejetmimu Guajatmimu Gajatmimu	1774 (3); 1777 (1); 1790 (1); 1791 (1)	1 F, 5 C	6
Guenegelc...................	1802 (1)	1 F	1
Guiguamic (2)...............	1813 (2)	1 M, 1 F	2
Guiyequamne...............	1813 (1)	1 F	1
"Hinahú junto a Tulame".......	1813 (1)	1 F	1
"Nacion Huoulasi"*...........	1834 (1)	1 M	1
Huohual.................... Guogual	1813 (1); 1835 (1)	2 M	2
Jahuamhemha................	1803 (1)	1 F	1
Jalàma..................... Sjlàlama Ljalama Xalama	1788 (2); 1782 (1); 1791 (1)	1 M, 3 F, 1 C	5
Kagua.....................	1776 (1)	1 F	1
Lachictó (10)................ Lassigto Laxictó (7) Lassictò Lacito (7)	1778 (1); 1781 (5); 1782 (3); 1787 (1); 1788 (3); 1790 (1); 1791 (9); 1792 (3); 1799 (1)	6 M, 13 F, 8 C	27

* Spelled Gualasi, Huoulasi, Huoulacsi in Pad., 1835.

SAN LUIS OBISPO MISSION—*Continued*

Rancheria	Year of baptism	Baptisms	Total number of baptisms
Lauto...................	1782 (1)	1 C	1
Llecmoni (6)............... Lejmoni (2) Lgecmoni (2) Lecmoni G'licmoni Lijmoni	1791 (1); 1792 (3); 1793 (2); 1796 (1); 1800 (6)	4 M, 5 F, 4 C	13
Lipespa................... Llipepsa	1772 (1); 1776 (1)	1 M, 1 F	2
Lhueque (2)............... Lhueqüe Lhuehqué Luegue Lluegque L, luegge Ljuegue (3) Elgueje (4)	1791 (4); 1792 (1); 1796 (1); 1799 (3); 1803 (6)	6 M, 6 F, 3 C	15
Ljauamesm................	1778 (1)	1 M	1
Lluoncho................	1804 (1)	1 M	1
Ltexmu (4)...............	1792 (2); 1793 (2)	1 M, 2 F, 1 C	4
Ltue (3)................ Ltùe Thue	1773 (1); 1791 (1); 1799 (1)	1 M, 1 F, 1 C	3
"Luasa, junto a Buenavista en los Tulares"...............	1816 (1)	1 M	1
Lucucuxaxla...............	1803 (1)	1 F	1
Lumpòc................	1788 (1)	1 M	1
"Paraje del Micoco"...........	1795 (1)	1 C	1
Migunu................	1775 (1)	1 C	1
Mismci................	1794 (1)	1 M	1
Naccùc................ Lnacuc (4) Lnauc Anacuca Nacuco Nauco Nahuca	1781 (1); 1788 (1); 1791 (4); 1792 (1); 1794 (1); 1796 (1); 1802 (1); 1813 (2)	4 M, 7 F, 1 C	12
Noctó (2)............... Nocto (2) Noto	1782 (1); 1785 (1); 1787 (2); 1790 (1); 1792 (1)	3 F, 3 C	6
Nogio................	1788 (1)	1 F	1
Necsuni................ Nucsuni	1780 (1); 1782 (1)	1 M, 1 C	2
Pismú (7)............... Pitsmu (6) Pismó Tpizmu	1774 (5); 1775 (5); 1776 (3); 1777 (5)	4 M, 7 F, 7 C	18
Psocia................	1796 (2)	1 M, 1 F	2

SAN LUIS OBISPO MISSION—*Continued*

Rancheria	Year of baptism	Baptisms	Total number of baptisms
Petpatsu (4).................. Patpatzo (2) Puetpacho (3) Pacpacsu Lpatpatsu	1774 (1); 1775 (2); 1779 (2); 1780 (1); 1792 (1); 1793 (1); 1794 (1); 1796 (1); 1798 (1)	3 M, 2 F, 6 C	11
Quichechs.................. Lquichecxe	1791 (1); 1803 (1)	2 F	2
Saccaya.....................	1802 (1)	1 M	1
Sajalmat....................	1791 (1)	1 M	1
Saljuaya (6)................ Saluaya	1791 (1); 1792 (1); 1794 (1); 1796 (1); 1799 (2); 1803 (1)	3 M, 3 F, 1 C	7
Sasinege....................	1774 (1)	1 C	1
Satajas.....................	1801 (1)	1 C	1
Satanilac...................	1813 (1)	1 M	1
Satohuc....................	1794 (1)	1 M	1
Sataóyo (6)................ Satayoho Satagoyo (2) Satahuoyo Satagoio (2) Satahoyo (2) Satooyo Sathahuoyo (4) Sathaoyo (2) Sathahoyo (5) Tsataoýo (2) Zatahoio Zatahui	1774 (1); 1776 (1); 1777 (1); 1779 (1); 1780 (1); 1783 (1); 1789 (1); 1791 (2); 1792 (2); 1795 (1); 1796 (1); 1800 (1); 1802 (3); 1803 (10); 1804 (1)	12 M, 10 F, 6 C	28
Scceele (4).................. Scceel (2) Scscecl (2) Scseelc Tciele Siele	1791 (7); 1793 (1); 1780 (1); 1798 (1); 1799 (1)	5 M, 1 F, 5 C	11
Scscitce (3)................ Scsitce (2) Scsotcitcha	1790 (1); 1791 (4); 1792 (1)	5 M, 1 C	6
Sespil (5).................. Secspill Sexpil Sexpill Sechpil Tsxpili Sispili Chixpili (2)	1788 (5); 1791 (3); 1792 (4); 1798 (1); 1799 (2), 1803 (2); 1782 (1)	7 M, 8 F, 3 C	18
Setpú (10).................. Chetpú (11) Seppu Seppo (2) Sedpu Ssetpú (2) Zeppo (2)	1774 (1); 1775 (1); 1776 (1); 1777 (3); 1778 (2); 1779 (3); 1780 (3); 1782 (1); 1784 (1); 1785 (1); 1792 (3); 1794 (1); 1798 (1); 1802 (3); 1803 (2)	10 M, 7 F, 13 C	30

SAN LUIS OBISPO MISSION—*Continued*

Rancheria	Year of baptism	Baptisms	Total number of baptisms
Setjala (4).................. Sepjala Setpjàla (2) Sapjàla Setjayya (2) Setjaya Zetcaya Zepcagua Chet-cala (2) Ssetcala Chatjala "Setjaya en la playa inmediate a la larga" Septcato (2)	1773 (1); 1774 (1); 1776 (2), 1777 (1); 1779 (1); 1791 (1); 1793 (1); 1796 (2); 1803 (8), 1804 (4)	9 M, 10 F, 4 C	23
Sepjato (18).................. Sepkato Sepcato (3) Sepjátu Sypjato Setjata Zepjato Zapjato Chepjato (7) Chaptjato Chetjato Cepjato (4) Xepjato	1773 (1); 1774 (2); 1775 (9); 1776 (4); 1777 (4); 1778 (1); 1779 (4); 1780 (3); 1783 (1); 1791 (3); 1792 (1); 1793 (1); 1794 (2); 1796 (3); 1798 (1); 1799 (2); 1802 (1); 1803 (4)	16 M, 20 F, 10 C	46
Sisui........................	1796 (1)	1 F	1
Sgelètspe.................... Squeletspè Tsquele-tspi Lquelechpe Lqueletspe Quelechpe Elexpe	1782 (1); 1788 (2); 1791 (2); 1792 (1); 1799 (1)	3 M, 3 F, 1 C	7
Scaluilimu.................. Sjalihuilimu Sjaluhilimu	1791 (1); 1803 (2)	1 M, 1 F, 1 C	3
Slepin.......................	1774 (1)	1 C	1
So.......................... Tzo Zo	1790 (5); 1791 (2)	2 M, 5 C	7
Solnecge....................	1802 (1)	1 F	1
Sososquiquia................ Sossosquique "Lsoskiquihe, junto a la Asumpcion" "Csosquiquie, llamada la Asumpcion" "Ksosquiquie ó Santa Ysabel" Sosquiquie Choisquiquie	1802 (6); 1803 (1); 1812 (1)	4 F, 4 C	8

SAN LUIS OBISPO MISSION—*Continued*

Rancheria	Year of baptism	Baptisms	Total number of baptisms
Sotsito	1781 (1)	1 M	1
Spaxche	1794 (1)	1 C	1
Spile (5) Ejpil (2) Expili Chpili	1781 (8); 1782 (1); 1785 (2); 1788 (1); 1791 (1)	2 M, 7 F, 4 C	13
Stacalocloc	1800 (1)	1 M	1
Stacamo (3) Stajamo Stajam Stajamu Estacamo (4) Extajamu Estacamu Tstjamu (4) Tstjamo	1778 (4); 1783 (3); 1786 (1); 1787 (1); 1788 (2); 1791 (1); 1794 (1); 1782 (2)	3 M, 8 F, 4 C	15
Stjahuayo acia el Pinar Extajuayo Tcaghuayo Tscauaio Tscauayo Tscahuayo Scauiaio	1778 (1); 1791 (2); 1792 (1); 1794 (1); 1796 (1); 1803 (1)	4 M, 3 F	7
Stamajuni	1800 (1)	1 C	1
Stamimu Tamitmu	1778 (1); 1779 (1)	1 M, 1 C	2
Stemectatimi (29) Stemetatimi (8) Steme-ctatimi Stemectani Stemeltatchimi Estemactatimi (3) Temetatimi (2) Tstemectatimi	1775 (1); 1776 (3); 1778 (2); 1779 (2); 1780 (1); 1785 (1); 1790 (1); 1791 (7); 1792 (4); 1793 (2); 1794 (7); 1795 (5); 1796 (4); 1797 (1); 1798 (2); 1799 (3); 1800–1803 (13)	22 M, 22 F, 15 C	59
Tachi (2)	1834 (1)	1 M	1
Tachuthamin	1813 (1)	1 F	1
Tamajso Tamaxso	1801 (1); 1802 (1)	1 M, 1 F	2
Tajuseja	1776 (1)	1 C	1
Taslipu Taslib	1794 (1); 1813 (1)	2 M	2
"Taxpalala en la playa"	1804 (1)	1 F	1
Tchouich	1791 (1)	1 F	1
Tecocco Tejucu	1773 (1); 1803 (1)	1 M, 1 C	2
Tejani (2)	1776 (2)	2 F	2
Télamne (7) Tulamne Tulame (4)	1813 (4); 1834 (4); 1835 (5)	10 M, 3 F	13

SAN LUIS OBISPO MISSION—*Continued*

Rancheria	Year of baptism	Baptisms	Total number of baptisms
Temequimi (2)................ Tomiquimi Lmiquime Elmequime	1775 (1); 1780 (2); 1791 (1); 1797 (1)	1 F, 4 C	5
Tez (8).................... Teichz Techez ⌐ Tech Techa (2) Ts Texa	1780 (1); 1785 (1); 1790 (2); 1792 (3); 1793 (3); 1794 (2); 1796 (2); 1798 (2); 1803 (4)	4 M, 8 F, 8 C	20
Thaaj (2)..................	1782 (1); 1783 (1)	1 M, 1 F	2
Tmaps (15)................ Tgmaps (7) "vulgo la Laguna Larga" (1) Tamaps (2) "Tamapse (2), alias Laguna Larga" (1) Smaps (2) "Kmapse junta a la Laguna Larga" Gmapse Cmapse Atmaps	1781 (1); 1788 (2); 1790 (2); 1791 (15); 1792 (6); 1794 (2); 1799 (1); 1800 (1); 1803 (3); 1778 (1); 1779 (1)	8 M, 16 F, 11 C	35
Tichimachu (2)..............	1804 (2)	1 M, 1 F	2
Tipexpa................... Tipaxpa Tipajpa Ltipexpa	1773 (1); 1779 (1); 1796 (1); 1803 (2)	1 M, 3 F, 1 C	5
Tipu (10).................. Ltipu (4) Spstipu	1774 (1); 1794 (5); 1798 (3); 1799 (2); 1802 (1); 1803 (4)	5 M, 7 F, 4 C	16
Tmimual...................	1783 (1)	1 C	1
Tmipu....................	1792 (1)	1 M	1
Toachlaqui.................	1798 (1)	1 F	1
Toipo.....................	1788 (1)	1 C	1
Topomó alias Santa Margarita...	1775 (2)	2 C	2
Tpelipe................... Lpelipe	1794 (2); 1798 (1)	3 F	3
Tpiteccoco.................	1803 (1)	1 M	1
Tpocolo...................	1792 (1)	1 C	1

SAN LUIS OBISPO MISSION—*Concluded*

Rancheria	Year of baptism	Baptisms	Total number of baptisms
Tsquieu (11).................	1777 (4); 1778 (2); 1779 (1); 1780 (6);	15 M, 18 F, 7 C	40
Tsliquiu (2)	1781 (1); 1783 (1); 1791 (1); 1792		
Squieu (2)	(2); 1800 (3); 1802 (6); 1803 (13)		
Squugue			
Esligiui			
Esquiegue (6)			
Etsquieu			
Esquiegu			
Chiquieu			
Chquieuqua			
Tthequie			
Ttequie (2)			
Tequia			
Tequie			
Ltequie			
Tsnocsum....................	1775 (1)	1 C	1
Tsquele....................	1780 (2)	1 M, 1 F	2
"Tuaya, sita en el rio de rio de Nacimiento".............	1792 (1); 1796 (3)	1 M, 3 F	4
Tuaya			
Tuchip....................	1782 (1); 1783 (1)	2 M	2
Tuchipi			
Tomajmo....................	1778 (1), 1779 (1), 1780 (1)	3 F	3
Tumojmo			
Tomojmu			
Xoltalhe....................	1813 (1)	1 C	1
Xoxtepax....................	1794 (1)	1 C	1
"Nacion ó tribu Yóucol (4)......	1834 (4)	4 M	4

Indians also recorded from rancherias at: Del Espada (1 C, 1786); Las Gallinas (1 F, 1804); Laguna Larga (1 M, 1 F, 1788, 1794); El Morro (1 M, 1777); Del Pleyto (1 M, 1804); Del Puppu (1 M, 1 C, 1786); Los Pedernales (1 M, 1786).

SAN MIGUEL MISSION

The following list of rancherias was compiled from material obtained in 1919 from the Book of Baptisms of San Miguel Mission, corrected from information in the Book of Deaths of the same mission. In these two books, rancheria names for recorded Indians are given in both text and margin. The title page of the Book of Marriages says that the mission was founded in the place called by the natives Vahcá.

The San Miguel records are deposited as follows: at San Miguel Mission, "Libro de Bautismos de San Miguel" (1792–1862) and "Libro de Difuntos de San Miguel" (1797–1861); at San Luis Obispo Mission, "Libro de Casamientos de San Miguel."—Ed.

SAN MIGUEL MISSION

Rancheria	Year of baptism	Baptisms*	Total number of baptisms
Ajole (6)...................	1803 (5)	2 M, 1 F, 2 C	5
Acutznija (1)................	1797 (1)	1 M	1
Auyamné (21)............... Auiamne (14) Auyamé (1)	1813 (46); 1814 (3); 1816 (5)	19 M, 28 F, 7 C	54
Azzil (12)..................	1779 (3); 1798 (4)	3 M, 1 F, 2 C	6
Bubal (92).................. Bubal del Tular Vuval (2) Ubal (2)	1806 (1); 1810 (1); 1812 (4); 1814 (27); 1816 (4); 1820–35 (124)	46 M, 85 F, 30 C	161
Camate (2)................. CCamaate Camate (Dif.)	1802 (1); 1803 (1)	1 M, 1 F	2
Casjantel.................. Casjamtel (2)	1802 (2)	1 M, 1 F	2
Cazz (11).................. Catz (2) Case (2)	1798 (4); 1799 (3); 1801 (1); 1803 (5); 1806 (1)	6 M, 5 F, 3 C	14
"Chal, como 3 leguas distante de esta Mision".............. Chaál Cha,al Chahal Chajal	1797 (1); 1798 (5)	6 C	6
Checax (2)................. Chájas (1) χecax† χecac† χecas†	1798 (3); 1797 (1)	2 M, 2 C	4

NOTE.—Figures in parentheses following rancheria names in first column indicate number of occurrences of that variant; figures in parentheses following dates in second column indicate number of baptisms. Names in brackets are written in the margin.—Ed.
* M, male(s); F, female(s); C, child(ren).—Ed.
† The symbol represented here by the Greek Chi is illegible in the copy.—Ed.

SAN MIGUEL MISSION—*Continued*

Rancheria	Year of baptism	Baptisms	Total number of baptisms
Chelacosaoné (3)............. Solocosaoné (2) Selecochoané ʒilecochaune [ʒilecocague-né]*	1778 (1); 1804 (2); 1806 (1); 1810 (4)	2 M, 2 F, 4 C	8
Chemama (3)................ Cheman	1803 (1); 1804 (3)	2 M, 2 F	4
Chenén (34)................ Chenem	1803 (1); 1804 (18); 1805 (14); 1807 (1); 1810 (5)	14 M, 16 F, 9 C	39
Cheyne (10)................ Cheine (6) Chenez (7) Tcheyne Tchanes (2) Theneze (2) Tchayne (3) Zthenez	1801 (7) (7); 1802 (6); 1803 (7); 1804 (1); 1805 (8)	10 M, 14 F, 5 C	29
Chetacol (1)................	1803 (2)	1 M, 1 F	2
Chócsa..................... Thoxco (Dif.)	1801 (1)	1 F	1
Cholaam (16)................ Choolam (7) Cholam (110) Cho,lam (15) Chola (5) Cho,la (4) Cholan (10) Chölam (3) Cholom (1) Choolam or Del Recodo Del Recodo (13) Chulam (5) Chuláme	1797 (2); 1798 (41); 1799 (32); 1800 (28); 1801 (49); 1802 (32); 1803 (45); 1804 (11); 1806 (1)	71 M, 92 F, 78 C	251
Chonague................... Chonahue (3)	1803 (2); 1804 (1)	3 M	3
Chopésso (1)................ Chohuesso (2)	1802 (1); 1803 (1)	2 M	2
Chtataquel (2)...............	1803 (2)	1 M, 1 F	2
Chuclac.................... Suc-lac (2) Zthulac	1797 (1); 1799 (1), 1802 (1)	1 M, 2 C	3
Echetama [Lamaca]...........			
Esjeleymú..................			
Esnetiltiya.................	1810 (1)	1 F	1
Etay [parage Tay]............ Tay (2)	1803 (4)	2 F, 2 M	4
Etsmál (37)................ Etzmal (9) Chmal (11) Chsmal (10) Esmal (2)	1797 (4); 1798 (28); 1800 (18); 1801 (10); 1802 (13); 1803 (14); 1805 (1)	27 M, 30 F, 31 C	88

* The symbol represented here by the Greek Zeta is illegible in the copy.—Ed.

SAN MIGUEL MISSION—*Continued*

Rancheria	Year of baptism	Baptisms	Total number of baptisms
Gechegetisja (2)...............	1802 (1)	1 F	1
Guenejel (2)...................	1813 (1)	1 M	1
Guetcheyne...................	1798 (1)	1 F	1
Pachap (Dif., for same person)			
Haguachao (2)................	1813 (1)	1 F	1
Haasaltaanel.................	1798 (1)	1 F	1
Hahasaltaanel			
Hasaltanel (Dif., 1801)			
Hugual (6)...................	1803 (2); 1811 (1); 1812 (1); 1813 (10);	20 M, 19 F,	
Hugual en el tular	1814 (4); 1815 (8); 1816 (11); 1834	13 C	52
Huohual (15)	(15)		
Huohal			
Guogal			
Gugual (8)			
Gugual en el tular			
Ugual (8)			
Jejacochum..................	1797 (1)	1 C	1
Joyuclac (29)................	1799 (1); 1800 (8); 1801 (22); 1802 (4);	15 M, 11 F	
Joyac-lac (3)	1803 (3); 1805 (1); 1814 (1)	14 C	40
Joyclak (3)			
Joyclac (2)			
Joyuklak (2)			
Kemel......................	1803 (2)	2 F	2
Kmel			
Kepexäu or Quepexäu (Dif., 1801)	1801	1 M	1
Lacome (2)...................	1805 (1)	1 C	1
Leccatam (4).................	1801 (4); 1803 (4)	2 M, 4 F, 2 C	8
Lacatam (6)			
Lapá al oriente de Joyaclak (2)...	1802 (1); 1804 (1)	1 F, 1 C	2
Löyam (7)...................	1802 (11)	2 M, 4 F, 5 C	11
Loyam (2)			
Lööyam			
"Leujge rumbo de las Gallinas"..	1799 (1); 1802 (3); 1803 (13)	6 M, 7 F	13
Luege (2)			
Lúege [Luége]			
Lueje (3)			
Luexe			
Lehuexe [Luexe]			
Lehueje (4)			
Lexuejes			
Lejuexes			
Leguexes			
Leüege			
Leguexe			
Macüla.....................	1801 (1); 1802 (1)	1 M, 1 C	2
Macaulat			
Menegue (2)..................	1803 (1)	1 F	1
Monet......................	1811 (1)	1 F	1
Namsuk (1)..................	1802 (1)	1 M	1
Na-na (6)...................	1798 (5)	3 M, 1 F, 1 C	5

SAN MIGUEL MISSION—*Continued*

Rancheria	Year of baptism	Baptisms	Total number of baptisms
Natcete Nacit	1810 (2)	1 M, 1 F	2
Notonto (2)	1834 (1); 1835 (1)	1 M, 1 F	2
Onetsala [Onet.] Honet	1797 (1); 1802 (1)	1 F, 1 C	2
Oquethilac (2)	1798 (2)	2	2
Pachac (8) Pazac (2) Pat-χiac (12)* Pat-χac (6) Pachaque (6) Paχac* [del Nacimiento] de las ymediaciones de Patχac* [de la Playa] del Nacimiento (53) Rio del Nacimiento (3) Parage del Nacimiento (1)	1797 (5); 1798 (11); 1799 (5); 1800 (5); 1801 (12); 1802 (1); 1803 (41); 1804 (2)	27 M, 27 F 28 C	82
Palet (1)	1797 (1)	1 C	1
Panau (2) Panao (2)	1804 (1); 1818 (3)	3 M, 1 F	4
Pel (19) Pil (6) Piil (3)	1800 (1); 1801 (7); 1803 (18); 1804 (3)	11 M, 14 F, 4 C	29
Pôn (2)	1798 (1)	1 F	1
Quechál	1798 (1)	1 F	1
Quiuamne (2) Quiyamne [Quiamne] Quiyamne (1)	1812 (1); 1813 (3)	....	4
Satawoyo (1)	1803 (1)	1 M	1
Scanam (2) Scanam [Escanam] Zcäanam Ezzanam (2)	1798 (1); 1799 (1); 1800 (1); 1802 (1)	2 M, 1 F, 1 C	4
Selecocsmcoy (2) Zilecoezmicoye (2)	1798 (1); 1810 (2)	2 M, 1 F	3
"Sic, pats del rumbo del Oriente de mas alla de la ra. lla. Pel." Sic,pats (4) Sicpath Sicpazth Sipcats Zcizpac Sipcass for same Indian (Dif., 1805)	1800 (6); 1801 (2); 1802 (2); 1803 (1)	4 M, 3 F, 4 C	11
Smomonel (2)	1803 (1)	1 F	1

* The symbol represented here by the Greek Chi is illegible in the copy.—Ed.

SAN MIGUEL MISSION—*Continued*

Rancheria	Year of baptism	Baptisms	Total number of baptisms
Sulaltap (10)................ Suleltap (1) Suleltep (2) Xulaltap Solaltag (2) Solatap [Sulatap] Solalta Tsolaltap Conquena ó Sulaltap	1801 (2); 1802 (3); 1805 (1); 1810 (3); 1811 (7)	8 M, 8 F	16
Sumtache (22)............... Tsumtache en el tular Tsumtache (39)	1812 (3); 1834 (9); 1835 (55)	2 M, 11 F, 54 C	67
Sta (1).....................	1803 (1)	1 M	1
Stajahuayo (2)................ CSta-jauayo	1801 (1); 1805 (2)	3 M	3
Staquel (6)................... Staquil (2) Stachil (1) Estaquel "Natural del oriente, llamada su rancheria Staquel"	1801 (1); 1803 (5); 1804 (4); 1808 (1); 1811 (3)	3 M, 9 F, 2 C	14
Suajal (2)...................	1800 (2)	1 F, 1 C	2
Szajuc (3)................... taaáuj (6)	1803 (3); 1800 (3)	1 M, 5 C	6
Tache (14).................	1810 (4); 1815 (2); 1824 (1); 1833 (1); 1834 (14); 1835 (1)	10 M, 5 F, 8 C	23
Tásslipu (1).................	1813 (1)	1 M	1
Telesmecoyo................ Chelesmecoyo	1806 (4)	1 M, 1 F, 2 C	4
Tegquic (1).................	1803 (1)	1 M	1
Tejacochumaal (2)........... (Same spelling, Dif., 1801)	1797 (1)	1 C	1
Telecotech.................	1797 (1)	1 C	1
Tepaseyat (2)...............	1804 (4)	3 M, 1 F, 1 C	5
Tetaxo (2)..................	1797 (2)	2 C	2
Tisagues (18).............. Tisahuex (5) Tixauex (4) Tisauex (1) Tisahuess (2) Tixauic (6) Tisahues (3) Tesagues (4) Tesaguess (1) Texagues (6) Thexagues Thexauex (4) Thexahex Thexahuex Thisahuex Tichaues (2) Tichagues (2)	1800 (2); 1801 (6); 1802 (5); 1803 (26); 1804 (6); 1805 (3); 1808 (7); 1811 (4); 1813 (3); 1816 (2); 1821 (1)	19 M, 35 F, 11 C	65

SAN MIGUEL MISSION—*Concluded*

Rancheria	Year of baptism	Baptisms	Total number of baptisms
Tisja (4)................... Tisxa Tixsjà Tisxat Tixat Texjá Texat (3) Teycha Thexja	1797 (2); 1800 (2); 1801 (2); 1802 (2); 1803 (7)	8 M, 4 F, 3 C	15
Tissimassu, o de la playa........ Tissimasu (4) Tichimachu Chissimasu (2) Chisimaso (4)	1803 (3); 1804 (3); 1805 (2); 1816 (1)	4 M, 5 F	9
Togyo (2).....................	1801 (1)	1 C	1
Tilecojopnel (1)...............	1798 (1)	1 M	1
Tójolojom................. Zojolojom (2)	1798 (2)	1 M, 1 F	2
Tseneychis (2)...............	1813 (1)	1 F	1
Tsican (2)................... ZZical (2)	1798 (2); 1813 (2)	4 F	4
Tuc-chuate (2)...............	1806 (1)	1 M	1
Tuchajale (2)................	1813 (2)	2 M	2
Tucsussu, or Tache [Tucsussu]....	1835 (1)	1 M	1
Tulamne (5)................... Telame (4)	1813 (5); 1814 (2); 1815 (5); 1816 (1)	3 M, 9 F, 1 C	13
Ugal (2).................... Ual Uual Uál (6)	1803 (1); 1805 (1); 1810 (1); 1813 (3)	3 M, 3 F	6
Uchamné (2)................	1813 (1)	1 M	1
Yaulemne, "adta. de la Sierra Nevada"................ Yaulamne Yúlamne Yulamné en el tular Yulamne del Tular	1811 (1); 1812 (2); 1816 (1)	2 M, 2 F	4
ZZavezz....................	1798 (1)	1 M	1
Zelacocol.................. Tilecocol	1798 (2)	1 M, 1 F	2
Zilecotitx...................	1797 (1)	1 M	1
Zimochoinaz [Zimoʒoyneess]*....	1799 (1)	1 F	1
Zimoque (2).................	1798 (1)	1 C	1
Ztacay (2)................... Chacay for same Indian (Dif.)	1798 (1)	1 C	1
Zojoy (2)...................	1813 (1)	1 M	1
Ztheneclac (4)...............	1803 (7)	3 M, 3 F, 1 C	7

* The symbol represented here by the Greek Zeta is illegible in the copy.—Ed.

Indians are also recorded from rancherias at La Asuncion (1 M, 3 F); Atascadero, camino de San Luis; Buenavista en el tular (1 F, 1 C); El Pleyto (2 M, 2 F, 1 C); Las Gallinas (22 M, 15 F, 9 C); Santa Ysabel (1 M, 2 F).

SANTA CLARA MISSION

The following list of rancherias is compiled from records obtained in 1919 from the Books of Baptisms of Santa Clara Mission, corrected from information in the Book of Marriages and the Book of Deaths of the same mission. From 1777–1804 only Spanish names are given for the rancherias; from 1805 on, Indian names are given in text and margin. For only one rancheria (Arsoy, called San Antonio and Del Coyote by the Spaniards) can the corresponding Spanish and Indian names be identified.

All of the Santa Clara records are at Santa Clara College, Santa Clara. They include the following: "Libros de Bautismos de Santa Clara" (3 vols., 1771–1860); "Libro de Casamientos de Santa Clara" (1777–1863); "Libros de Entieros de Santa Clara" (2 vols., 1774–1866).—Ed.

SANTA CLARA MISSION

Rancheria	Year of baptism	Baptisms*	Total number of baptisms
Achachina (6)................. Los Achachinas (6) Achachines	1820 (32); 1821 (4); 1822 (1); 1824 (7)	17 M, 15 F, 12 C	44
Agualimbre...................	1837 (1)	1 F	1
Apelamenes (9)............... Apelames (9)	1818 (8); 1819 (28); 1820 (6); 1821 (2); 1822 (4)	18 M, 16 F, 14 C	48
Arsoy, "llamada San Antonio, alias del Coyote"............	......	......	....
Atsnil (9)...................	1821 (10); 1822 (63); 1823 (1); 1826 (3)	43 M, 28 F, 6 C	77
Los Bolbones.................	1813 (3)	3 F	3
Caujil (2)...................	1821 (2); 1824 (3)	5 F	5
Chacahuinime.................	1836 (1)	1 F	1
Chapaisemé (del tular) (16)...... Chapaisme (11)	1836 (28)	1 M, 8 F, 19 C	28
Chauchiles (del Sierra Nevada)...	1834 (1)	1 C	1
Chauculumbre (1).............	1837 (1)	1 F	1
Chipeyquis (17)............... Chipoyquis (3) Chipegis Chipoyquina (2) Chipeyquinas	1815 (2); 1817 (1); 1818 (2); 1820 (12); 1821 (6); 1822 (4); 1823 (6); 1824 (1)	15 M, 15 F, 4 C	34
Chonolumno (del tular).........	1836 (1)	1 M	1
Chuguea (18)................. Chugeas (5) Chugueas (9)	1823 (40); 1824 (19); 1825 (12); 1826 (27), 1827 (4)	30 F, 45 F, 27 C	102
Cochomache (del tular).........	1836 (1)	1 M	1
Colomugre...................	1837 (1)	1 F	1
Copolimbre..................	1836 (1)	1 M	1

NOTE.—Figures in parentheses following rancheria names in first column indicate number of occurrences of that variant figures in parentheses following dates in second column indicate number of baptisms.—Ed.
* M, male(s); F, female(s); C, child(ren).—Ed.

SANTA CLARA MISSION—*Continued*

Rancheria	Year of baptism	Baptisms	Total number of baptisms
Cotuplanime................ Cutuclanime	1837 (2)	2 F	2
Cuyens (14)................	1811 (17); 1812 (50); 1813 (21)	38 M, 37 F, 13 C	88
Cuyomuunos................	1837	1 F	1
Etelombro.................	1837	1 F	1
Guacalotumbre............. Guacalochumbre	1837 (2)	2 F	2
Gualansemne (9)............ Gualansemnes (4) los Gualancemnes (2) Gualamcemnes (tulares) Galancemnes Gulansemne	1821 (1); 1825 (16); 1825 (44), 1827 (35), 1830 (5)	26 M, 53 F, 22 C	101
Gualapalamnes..............	1826 (1)	1 F	1
Guechileme................. Guechilimbre	1836 (2); 1837 (1)	1 M, 2 F	3
Gomcomna (3)............. Goncomna (2) Guomcomne Guoncomna	1822 (1); 1824 (6); 1825 (4)	2 M, 5 F, 4 C	11
Huyustemo (2).............	1822 (2)	1 M, 1 F	2
Jalanames................. Jalamnes	1821 (2); 1822 (1)	1 M, 2 F	3
Joyimas (2)................	1835 (1)	1 C	1
Los Junas "de la familia de los Junas"..................	1809 (9); 1813 (1); 1815 (1)	5 M, 5 F, 1 C	11
Lamames (6)............... Los Lamamas	1813 (9); 1814 (1); 1815 (15); 1816 (2)	10 M, 13 F, 4 C	27
Laquisimas (15)............ Lacquissimis	1816 (3); 1818 (3); 1819 (1); 1820 (8); 1821 (1); 1823 (1)	6 M, 9 F, 2 C	17
Los Luechas (7)............	1805 (69; 1806 (8); 1808 (2); 1809 (2)	34 M, 37 F, 10 C	81
Mayemas (7)............... Mayemes (4) Mayeme	1813 (1); 1816 (52); 1817 (1); 1818 (1); 1819 (29); 1820 (2); 1821 (3); 1822 (1); 1823 (1)	35 M, 44 F, 12 C	91
Olonochombre..............	1837 (1)	1 F	1
Pacachi (2)................	1826 (1)	1 F	1
Pitemes (8)................ Pitemas (18)	1814 (8); 1815 (39); 1816 (12); 1831 (1)	28 M, 21 F, 11 C	60
Sacayaquimis..............	1839 (1)	1 M	1
Sineminne.................	1821 (2)	1 M, 1 F	2
Sunomna (9)............... Sunomno (8) Sonomna (4)	1823 (10); 1824 (3); 1826 (1); 1827 (94); 1829 (8)	36 M, 50 F, 30 C	116
Sutunuyes (tulares)...........	1831 (2)	2 F	2
Suyumno..................	1822 (1)	1 C	1
"Rancheria de los Tahuanos" (2).	1839 (1)	1 C	1

SANTA CLARA MISSION—*Concluded*

Rancheria	Year of baptism	Baptisms	Total number of baptisms
Tauhalames (30)............ Tauhalemes (3) Taualames (14) Tahualame (4) Tagualemes Tagualame (9) Thahualame Tahualemes (14)	1817 (82); 1818 (39); 1819 (1); 1820 (24); 1821 (34); 1822 (16); 1823 (11); 1824 (18); 1825 (26); 1826 (4); 1827 (8)	113 M, 110 F, 40 C	263
Tayssenes (13)............ Taysenes (3) Taijsenes (5)	1806 (91); 1807 (2); 1808 (34); 1809 (3); 1811 (12); 1805 (91)	114 M, 109 F, 20 C	243
Tinelames (3)............ Tinelame (11)	1824 (7); 1825 (3); 1826 (5); 1827 (6)	7 M, 10 F, 4 C	21
Tonul (20)............ Los Tonules (2)	1820 (1); 1821 (3); 1822 (24); 1824 (7); 1826 (1); 1827 (3)	15 M, 16 F, 8 C	39
Totote (2)............ Totoche (2) Los Tototes (5) Trotrochi (1)	1826 (7); 1827 (25); 1836 (1)	2 M, 29 F, 2 C	33
Toynumbre (del Tular)........ Toynombres	1836 (1); 1837 (1)	1 M, 1 F	2
Tucusuyum............ Tucusuyumnis (4) Tucusuyumni Tucuyumnis (2) Tucasoyumno Tucosuyumno (3) Tucusomnis	1821 (1); 1823 (6); 1824 (1); 1825 (2); 1827 (8)	3 M, 10 F, 5 C	18
"de la rancheria de los Tugites"... Los Tugites (8)	1811 (88); 1814 (3), 1815 (16), 1816 (4); 1820 (2); 1813 (12)	52 M, 59 F, 14 C	125
Utomno............ Hutomno	1821 (2); 1823 (1)	1 M, 2 F	3
Ylamcomno............	1836 (1)	1 F	1
Youmalimne............	1821 (1)	1 F	1
San Antonio............	....	....	500 (approx.)
San Bernardino............	....	....	500
San Carlos............	....	....	500+
San Francisco Solano............	....	....	135
San Francisco............	....	....	71
San José Cupertino............	....	....	12
San Joseph............	....	....	55
San Juan Bautista............	....	....	90
Santa Agueda............	....	....	385
Santa Clara............	....	....	37
Santa Ysabel............	....	....	16

SAN JOSE MISSION

The following list of rancherias is compiled from records obtained in 1919 from the two Books of Baptisms of San Jose Mission (1797–1830; 1830–1859). The introduction to the first Book of Baptisms states that this mission was founded in the place called by the natives Oryson. No rancherias are given in the Book of Deaths or the Book of Marriages of this mission. These four manuscripts are in the office of the Archbishop of San Francisco, 1100 Franklin Street, San Francisco.—Ed.

SAN JOSE MISSION

Rancheria	Year of baptism	Baptisms*	Total number of baptisms
Alaguali.................... Aleguali	1816 (55); 1817 (2)	24 M, 20 F, 13 C	57
Anizumne..................	1812 (199); 1816 (20); 1817 (1); 1818 (20); 1820 (1); 1822 (1); 1825 (2)	92 M, 91 F, 61 C	244
Asirin (6)................. Assirin (2)	1803 (5); 1804 (15); 1805 (1)	8 M, 5 F, 8 C	21
Aunan.....................	1803 (4)	2 M, 2 F	4
Canapa....................	1817 (1)	1 F	1
Canicaymo................. Caymus ó Canicay	1818 (2); 1820 (6)	1 M, 6 F, 1 C	8
Causen....................	1803 (1); 1804 (8); 1807 (1)	5 M, 3 F, 2 C	10
Cavurun (4)............... Caburun	1803 (1); 1804 (20)	6 M, 11 F, 4 C	21
Chaminimne...............	1824 (1)	1 F	1
Chapaes (2)............... Chapay (2) Chapae Chapasin	1827 (3); 1834 (4)	1 M, 6 F	7
Chemoco..................	1822 (1)	1 F	1
Chilamne..................	1818 (1); 1819 (1); 1820 (2); 1821 (9); 1822 (5); 1826 (14); 1827 (29); 1828 (14); 1832 (1); 1833 (1); 1834 (3); 1835 (1)	25 M, 46 F, 10 C	81
Chocouai.................. Chocauai	1817 (1); 1818 (1)	1 M, 1 F	2
Cholbon (24).............. Cholvon (13)	1806 (13); 1808 (53); 1809 (21); 1811 (47); 1812 (3); 1813 (7); 1820 (3); 1821 (2); 1824 (1)	47 M, 68 F, 35 C	150
Choquoime (75)............ Chocoime (10) Chocoyme (3)	1815 (84); 1816 (11); 1821 (1)........	37 M, 36 F, 23 C	96
Chucumne.................	1816 (6); 1817 (10); 1818 (20); 1819 (2); 1821 (1); 1822 (5); 1823 (166); 1824 (156); 1825 (3)	146 M, 148 F, 75 C	369
Chupcan.................. Chupan	1804 (1); 1811 (63); 1812 (1)	22 M, 25 F, 18 C	65

NOTE.—Figures in parentheses following rancheria names in first column indicate number of occurrences of that variant; figures in parentheses following dates in second column indicate number of baptisms.—Ed.
* M, male(s); F, female(s); C, child(ren).—Ed.

SAN JOSE MISSION—*Continued*

Rancheria	Year of baptism	Baptisms	Total number of baptisms
Chupumne................. Chupumney	1828 (7); 1836 (1)	3 M, 4 F, 1 C	8
Ciemne................... Siemne	1811 (2); 1821 (1)	1 M, 2 F	3
Cosome (3)............. Cosomne (2) Cossomne (2) Cossum Cossom Josomne Osomne (2)	1826 (14); 1827 (3); 1828 (9); 1834 (41); 1835 (5); 1836 (12)	33 M, 39 F, 12 C	84
Coybos (2).............. Joybos	1808 (2); 1809 (1); 1811 (11); 1812 (56); 1813 (5); 1815 (4); 1817–1826 (15)	31 M, 50 F, 13 C	94
Culumu..................	1836 (1)	1 M	1
Cusscun..................	1804 (2)	1 M, 1 F	2
Elpamne..................	1826 (1)	1 F	1
Guaypem (5)............ Guaypen Guaypemne Guaipeyne Guaipemne	1821 (1); 1824 (1); 1825 (3); 1826 (1); 1827 (10); 1828 (24); 1834 (1)	10 M, 24 F, 7 C	41
Gualacomne (33) Guacalamne Gualacumne (2) Güalacames (2) Ualacomne (5) Ualacaye Ualaquimne Ualacácaye	1825 (4); 1826 (3); 1827 (9); 1828 (1); 1834 (38); 1835 (1); 1836 (1)	22 M, 31 F, 4 C	57
Güelecme (4)............. Guelacme (3) Gualacme Guelamne	1834 (9)	5 M, 4 F	9
Ilüasiüeneüa................	1816 (1)	1 M	1
Jalalon...................	1811 (6); 1812 (2); 1817 (1); 1818 (9); 1819 (8); 1824 (2); 1825 (2)	11 M, 14 F, 5 C	30
Jomchom.................	1826 (1)	1 C	1
Jossmit (29)............. Josmite (7) Josmit	1811 (43); 1812 (13); 1814 (13); 1815 (9); 1816 (3); 1821 (5)	24 M, 48 F, 14 C	86
Junizumne (7)............. Junisumne (7) Junisomne (5) Punizumne Unisumne (2) Unizumne Unisuyne Unsùmne	1813 (1); 1816 (7); 1821 (3); 1824 (1); 1827 (9); 1828 (58); 1829 (4); 1831 (6); 1833 (15); 1834 (11); 1836 (4)	54 M, 57 F, 8 C	119

SAN JOSE MISSION—*Continued*

Rancheria	Year of baptism	Baptisms	Total number of baptisms
Lacquisemne................. 　Laquisùm (2) 　Laguisomne	1811 (1); 1812 (1); 1815 (2); 1817 (1); 1820 (77); 1821 (30); 1822 (12); 1825 (3); 1834 (7)	52 M, 56 F, 26 C	134
Lamamne..................	1811 (1); 1820 (1)	2 M	2
Lelamne (4).................	1821 (1); 1834 (18); 1835 (2); 1836 (1)	7 M, 15 F	22
Liuayto (2)................ 　Libayto 　Liguaitu	1826 (3); 1833 (2)	2 M, 3 F	5
Locolomne.................	1826 (15); 1827 (18); 1828 (1); 1829 (5); 1831 (10); 1833 (2); 1834 (1)	17 M, 19 F, 16 C	52
Lopotstimne...............	1824 (1)	1 F	1
Loyume...................	1824 (1); 1828 (1)	2 F	2
Luecha...................	1805 (13); 1806 (10); 1809 (1); 1812 (2)	10 F, 8 M, 8 C	26
Lupay....................	1825 (3)	2 F, 1 C	3
Machemne (2)............ 　Machén 　Maché 　Omuchamne 　Omochomne 　Amuchamne 　Amuchomne	1834 (12); 1835 (1)	4 M, 8 F, 1 C	13
Malacaye.................	1826 (6); 1827 (1)	3 M, 2 F, 2 C	7
Muqueleme (6)........... 　Mugelemna (5) 　Muguelemne	1817 (1); 1818 (1); 1820 (3); 1821 (1); 1823 (5); 1824 (3); 1826 (3); 1827 (2); 1828 (6); 1833 (1); 1834 (111); 1835 (6)	48 M, 84 F, 11 C	143
Musupum (2).............. 　Musupumne (2) 　Musuppu	1818 (4); 1819 (3); 1824 (21); 1825 (6); 1827 (4); 1828 (8)	16 M, 22 F, 8 C	46
Napian (2)................	1814 (27); 1815 (116); 1816 (3); 1817 (2); 1818 (7)	59 M, 71 F, 25 C	155
Nemesia..................	1817 (1)	1 F	1
Nochochomne (3).......... 　Nototomne	1814 (3); 1815 (32); 1816 (32); 1818 (29); 1821 (1)	36 M, 45 F, 16 C	97
Noipune................. 　Noypum 　Noypumne	1827 (2); 1828 (3); 1834 (1)	2 M, 4 F	6
Ochejamne............... 　Oocheganes (2)	1829 (2); 1830 (115); 1831 (268); 1833 (13); 1834 (26); 1836 (4)	173 M, 192 F, 63 C	428
Olombali.................	1816 (6); 1817 (217); 1818 (3)	42 M, 166 F, 18 C	226
Olonàpatme (12)..........	1834 (13); 1835 (1)	7 M, 7 F	14
Ompin...................	1811 (91); 1812 (17)	44 M, 44 F, 20 C	108
Pasasime (1 up to 1820)...... 　Pasassimne	1812 (1); 1813 (2); 1814 (5); 1815 (7); 1816 (2); 1817 (17); 1818 (43); 1820 (30); 1821 (24); 1823 (3); 1824 (6); 1826 (1); 1828 (4)	49 M, 65 F, 31 C	145
Patlan..................	1803 (3); 1804 (2); 1805 (1)	1 M, 5 F	6

SAN JOSE MISSION—*Continued*

Rancheria	Year of baptism	Baptisms	Total number of baptisms
Pelnen......................	1803 (15); 1804 (30); 1805 (3); 1808 (2)	20 M, 23 F, 7 C	50
Petaluma...................	1815 (2); 1816 (44); 1817 (11); 1818 (5)	20 M, 28 F, 14 C	62
ra. Polayum (2)............... Pulaye	1829 (3)	3 F	3
Posscon (3).................. Poscon	1807 (3); 1811 (1)	2 F, 2 C	4
ra. Pujetsemne (2).............	1822 (1)	1 F	1
Puscuy......................	1816 (1)	1 M	1
Puttá.......................	1816 (1); 1826 (3)	1 M, 3 F	4
Quenemsia (6)............... Quenensia (3) Jenensia (5) Jenemsia (3)	1811 (2); 1816 (1); 1818 (5); 1819 (2); 1821 (1); 1824 (2); 1825 (92); 1826 (75); 1828 (5)	69 M, 80 F, 36 C	185
Quicoma.....................	1825 (1)	1 F	1
Quisapquela.................	1821 (1)	1 F	1
Saoam (5)................... Ssaoan	1803 (10); 1804 (47); 1805 (43); 1811 (1)	31 M, 45 F, 25 C	101
Seunen...................... Sseunem Seunem Sseauné	1803 (14); 1804 (9); 1805 (1); 1806 (1); 1808 (1); 1834 (1)	8 M, 15 F, 4 C	27
Seuamne (4).................. Seyuadme (8) Següamne (4) Seyuabme Seoagme Seguoame Ssaguamne Zeuamne (2)	1821 (2); 1826 (1); 1827 (1); 1829 (33); 1834 (8); 1835 (2)	21 M, 20 F, 6 C	47
ra. Silepum..................	1829 (1)	1 F	1
Siusumne (5)................. Ssibusumne (2) Ssiusomne Ssiuzumne Ssigusóme, ra. o rumbo lla Sigusumné (2) Seusumne	1827 (4); 1828 (2); 1834 (7); 1836 (1)	4 M, 4 F, 6 C	14
Souyen (3)................... SSouyen	1803 (20); 1804 (18); 1805 (40); 1807 (2)	26 M, 29 F, 25 C	80
Sonolomne (2)................ Ssonolomne	1828 (9); 1834 (3)	1 M, 6 F, 5 C	12
Ssulmiyamne.................	1834 (1)	1 F	1
ra. lla. por los naturales Suchui y por los Nuestros de la Asumpcion................ Sstchui o de las Pulgas Súchui	1781 (5)	5 M	5

SAN JOSE MISSION—*Continued*

Rancheria	Year of baptism	Baptisms	Total number of baptisms
Tamalcolo (17)............ Tamalcolu (6) Tamalculo	1816 (7); 1817 (17)	8 M, 12 F, 4 C	24
Tamcan.................	1806 (1); 1808 (7); 1809 (6); 1810 (2); 1811 (88); 1812 (1); 1813 (10); 1814 (1); 1815 (2); 1816 (4); 1817 (4); 1818 (9); 1824 (1)	39 M, 71 F, 26 C	136
Tauilemne (2).............	1829 (1)	1 F	1
Taunan.................	1803 (19); 1804 (15); 1805 (2)	17 M, 17 F, 2 C	36
Tauquimne............... Tahquime Tauquiyne	1815 (1); 1818 (5); 1819 (8); 1824 (51); 1825 (5); 1828 (3)	24 M, 24 F, 25 C	73
Tihuechemne (15)........... Tigüechimne (3) Tiuechemne (3) Tiguechime Tiguichime Toguicomne	1820 (1); 1821 (4); 1822 (2); 1823 (2); 1824 (4); 1827 (3); 1828 (1); 1829 (10); 1834 (6); 1835 (1); 1836 (1)	10 M, 22 F, 3 C	35
Tolema................. Tolenas	1815 (6); 1816 (34); 1817 (15); 1818 (1); 1819 (15); 1820 (62)	42 M, 59 F, 32 C	133
Tuguits.................	1808 (1); 1811 (6)	5 M, 2 F	7
Tuibun.................	1803 (20); 1804 (1)	10 M, 10 F, 1 C	21
Tuleomi.................	1816 (1); 1817 (9)	4 M, 5 F, 1 C	10
Tuseale................. Tuzeale	1825 (7); 1827 (1); 1835 (2)	1 M, 6 F, 3 C	10
Tzotolomne (3)........... Tzololamne Sotolomne (2)	1820 (1); 1821 (3); 1825 (1); 1828 (1)	1 M, 5 F	6
Ulpun (4)............... Julpun	1807 (1); 1808 (3); 1811 (103); 1812 (2); 1813 (4); 1818 (18); 1819 (5); 1821 (2); 1824 (6); 1825 (1); 1827 (3)	45 M, 66 F, 37 C	148
Ululatu (2)............. Ululato	1825 (6); 1826 (26); 1827 (28); 1833 (2)	25 M, 28 F, 9 C	62
Uoscomne.................	1818 (3)	1 F, 2 C	3
Volvon................. Borbon (4) Volvon del Sur	1803 (1); 1805 (44); 1808 (1); 1811 (1)	16 M, 6 F, 25 C	47
Yacumusmo...............	1804 (3)	3 M	3
Yalacomno...............	1821 (1)	1 F	1
Yatchicumne (3)........... Yatsicumne	1814 (1); 1815 (5); 1816 (4); 1818 (42); 1819 (33); 1820 (1); 1821 (2); 1822 (3); 1823 (11); 1824 (13); 1827 (2); 1828 (1)	42 M, 52 F, 24 C	118
Ylamné (6)............... Ylamnes	1818 (3); 1819 (3); 1820 (1); 1822 (1); 1823 (1); 1824 (4); 1825 (1); 1826 (1); 1834 (48); 1835 (2); 1836 (9)	32 M, 41 F, 1 C	74
Yrgin.................	1803 (50); 1804 (15); 1805 (5)	24 M, 41 F, 5 C	70
Yulien.................	1803 (1); 1804 (14); 1805 (5); 1807 (1)	9 M, 7 F, 5 C	21
Zicatme.................	1834 (1)	1 M	1

SAN JOSE MISSION—*Concluded*

Rancheria	Year of baptism	Baptisms	Total number of baptisms
Zicomne (2)................ Sicamne Ssicomne (2)	1834 (4); 1836 (4)	4 M, 4 F	8
Zoneto (11)................ Zonetto (2) Soneto Ssonoto (3)	1820 (1); 1821 (2); 1822 (4); 1824 (6); 1825 (1); 1826 (4); 1827 (1)	4 M, 10 F, 5 C	19
Zoneyomi (2)................ Zuniomi	1819 (1); 1820 (2)	1 M, 1 F, 1 C	3
Zuicun.................... Suycun (2) Zuisumne Zuizume	1803 (1); 1804 (7); 1807 (4); 1834 (3)	2 M, 6 F, 7 C	15
Corte de la Madera...........	1790 (1)	1 M	1

BIBLIOGRAPHY

ANTHROPOLOGICAL PUBLICATIONS

1903
"Some Little-known Basket Materials," *Science*, n.s., 17:826.

1904
"Distribution of Indian tribes in the Southern Sierra and Adjacent Parts of the San Joaquin Valley, California," *Science*, n.s., 19:912–917.

1905
"The Indian Population of California," *American Anthropologist*, n.s., 7:594–606.

1907
"Distribution and Classification of the Mewan Stock of California," *American Anthropologist*, n.s., 9:338–357.

1908
"Corrections concerning California Indians," *American Anthropologist*, n.s., 10:356–357.
"Totemism in California," *American Anthropologist*, n.s., 10:558–562.

1909
"Ethnological Evidence that the California Cave Specimens Are not Recent," *Science*, n.s., 29:805–806.
"Transmigration in California," *Journal of American Folk-Lore*, 22:433–434.

1910
The Dawn of the World: Myths and Weird Tales Told by the Mewan Indians of California. The Arthur H. Clark Co., Cleveland. 273 pp.

1916
"Indian Names in the Tamalpais Region," *California Out-of-Doors* (April), p. 118.
"A Defense of the Indian." Review of *The Fighting Cheyenne*, by G. B. Grinnell. *Yale Review*, n.s., 6:199–201.

1917
"Indian Village and Camp Sites in Yosemite Valley," *Sierra Club Bulletin*, 10:202–209.

"How Mah'-tah, the Turkey Buzzard, Lost His Speech," *American Museum Journal*, 17:557.

1918

"The Acorn, a Possibly Neglected Source of Food," *National Geographic Magazine*, 34:129–137.

1921

"A California Elk Drive," *Science Monthly*, 13:465–475.

1922

"The Unforeseen in Indian Vocabulary Work," *Natural History*, 22:82.

1923

"Application of the Athapaskan Term Nung-kahhl," *American Anthropologist*, n.s., 25:276–277.

"Erroneous Identification of 'Copper Effigies' from the Mound City Group," *American Anthropologist*, n.s., 25:424–425.

1924

"Forced Allotments," *in* "A Cycle on the American Indian," *The Forum*, 72:712–713.

1926

"Source of the Name Shasta," *Journal of the Washington Academy of Science*, 16: 522–525.

"Indian Tribes of California." [Testimony.] Hearings, U. S. Congress, House Committee on Indian Affairs, 69th Cong., 1st sess., on H.R. 8036 and H.R. 9497. Washington.

"Reservation Courts of Indian Offenses." [Testimony.] Hearings, U. S. Congress, House Committee on Indian Affairs, 69th Cong., 1st sess., on H.R. 7826. Washington.

"The Classification and Distribution of the Pit River Indian Tribes of California." Smithsonian Misc. Coll. No. 2874, 78:1–52. Washington.

1927

"Care and Relief of Indians . . ." [Testimony.] Hearing, U. S. Congress, Senate . . . Committee on Indian Affairs, 69th Cong., 2d sess., on S. 3020. Washington.

1928

"Why not More Care in Identifying Animal Remains?" *American Anthropologist*, n.s., 30:731–732.

An-nik-a-del: the History of the Universe as told by the Mo-des'-se Indians of California. The Stratford Co., Boston. 166 pp.

1929

"The Cop-éh of Gibbs," *American Anthropologist*, n.s., 31:136–137.

1930

"Little-known Tribes of the Salmon, New, and Trinity Rivers in Northwestern California," *Journal of the Washington Academy of Science*, 20:148–149.

"The New River Indians Tló-hōm-tah-hoi," *American Anthropologist*, n.s., 32: 280–293.

"Concentrations of Remnants of Indian Tribes in Northwestern California," *Science*, 71:546.

"A Remarkable Case of Word Borrowing among California Indians," *Science*, 71:546.

"The Em'-tim'-bitch, a Shoshonean Tribe," *American Anthropologist*, n.s., 32: 496–499.

Index